CAMBRIDGE SOUTH ASIAN STUDIES

BENGAL AGRICULTURE
1920–1946

A quantitative study

CAMBRIDGE SOUTH ASIAN STUDIES

These monographs are published by the Syndics of Cambridge University Press in association with the Cambridge University Centre for South Asian Studies. The following books have been published in this series:

BENGAL AGRICULTURE
1920–1946

A quantitative study

M. MUFAKHARUL ISLAM

Associate Professor of History
University of Dacca

With a foreword by K. N. Chaudhuri

CAMBRIDGE UNIVERSITY PRESS
CAMBRIDGE
LONDON · NEW YORK · MELBOURNE

Published by the Syndics of the Cambridge University Press
The Pitt Building, Trumpington Street, Cambridge CB2 1 RP
Bentley House, 200 Euston Road, London NW1 2DB
32 East 57th Street, New York, NY 10022, USA
296 Beaconsfield Parade, Middle Park, Melbourne 3206, Australia

First published 1978

Photoset and printed in Malta by Interprint (Malta) Ltd

Library of Congress Cataloguing in Publication Data
Islam, M. Mufakharul
Bengal Agriculture 1920–1946: A Quantitative Study
(Cambridge South Asian Studies; 22)
Bibliography: p.
Includes index
1. Agriculture—India—Bengal—Statistics—History.
2. Agriculture—Economic aspects—India—Bengal—History. I. Title
HD2075.B4175   333.1′095′14   76-57098
ISBN 0 521 21579 X

TO MY PARENTS
LATE ABDUR RAHMAN
NURUNNAHAR BEGUM

CONTENTS

LIST OF TABLES AND FIGURES

List of tables

FIGURES

FOREWORD

BY K. N. CHAUDHURI

This book marks a new approach to the study of Indian economic history. The great issues in the debates among historians so far have been the effects of colonial rule in the subcontinent during the nineteenth and twentieth centuries. Economic institutions were investigated in depth mainly from the point of view of policy-makers. The actual performance of the economy, the rate of its integration, and the decomposition of the causal forces at work were questions to which only insufficient attention was paid. Dr Islam takes as his central theme of inquiry the measurement of agricultural output in Bengal during the period from 1920 to 1946. The extension of the market for agricultural crops, which was a notable feature of the agrarian economy of India in the nineteenth century, failed to produce any significant concomitant industrial–urban development. Furthermore, agriculture itself stagnated after the initial effects of market expansion had worked itself out. The absence of major industrialising efforts not only limited the produce and labour markets but also prevented innovation in crop techniques and possible changes in the institution of landholding. Dr Islam has taken these questions as his point of departure and tried to quantify the precise direction of Bengal's economy for a critical period of this century. His book is the first serious attempt on the part of a historian from South Asia to use advanced statistical methods and techniques of computer analysis to provide answers to historical problems. Dr Islam has made an exhaustive analysis of the available crop statistics for all the districts of Bengal and computed the trend rates for output, yield, and acreage. He has also thrown new light on the accuracy and reliability of the basic data. His work supplements the pioneer study undertaken by George Blyn many years ago in the pre-computer age and it adds a new insight into the subject. When Dr Islam began his research as a post-graduate student his training was that of a historian. It is a considerable achievement on his part to have ventured out into a new methodological area and successfully mastered its technical details.

K. N. CHAUDHURI

The School of Oriental and African
Studies, University of London

PREFACE

The present work attempts a detailed study of the historical experience in the agricultural sector in undivided Bengal during the period 1920/21 to 1945/46. The book is divided into two parts. The first part is devoted to an examination of the quality of the officially published crop statistics and the analysis of the trends in crop output, acreage under cultivation and yield per acre. The second part deals with the most important factors which directly or indirectly influenced the trends in agricultural production, viz. impact of price, physical capital assets, credit and the role of the landlords.

The research which finally led to this study was begun in 1968 and an earlier version of this book was presented for the degree of PhD in the University of London in 1972. During these years of work on this book I have incurred a long list of obligations. None are greater than those I owe to Dr K. N. Chaudhuri who supervised my research and the writing of the dissertation. I am most grateful to him for the many hours of careful attention he gave, for the unrestrained development of thought which he encouraged and for his useful criticisms and advice. I am also grateful to him for writing the 'Foreword'. The preparation of the revised manuscript was started when I was working with Prof. Dietmar Rothermund at the South Asia Institute of Heidelberg University. I am grateful to him for his valuable suggestions. I am also indebted to Mr B. H. Farmer, Director, Centre of South Asian Studies, University of Cambridge, who took keen interest in the publication of this book.

I benefitted from the stimulating discussions I had with Dr John Hurd II (University of Oakland, USA), Dr M. D. Morris (University of Washington), Dr Biplab Das Gupta (University of Sussex), Michael Hodd and T. J. Byres (School of Oriental and African Studies, University of London) and Prof. A. Razzzaque (University of Dacca). Miss J. Skegg and Mrs J. A. Lallor helped me in processing the huge volume of statistical data. I would like to record my gratitude to all of them. Others who helped me in different ways include Dr A. M. Chaudhury, Dr Sirajul Islam, P. N. Chaudhuri, Akhter Hussain, Dr S. Ghatak, Dr S. K. Dey, B. R. Khan, Ahmed Kamal, Sushil Ranjan Howlader, Fariduddin Ahmed, Mizanur Rahman, A. Salam, Hedayet Hussain and Tajul Islam Hashmi. I offer my sincere thanks to all of them.

Preface

My thanks are also due to Faruk Chaudhuri and Nurul Islam for their secretarial assistance, and to Muntasir Mamun and Hossain Shahid Faroqui for their help in proof-reading.

I must also extend my thanks to the Syndics of the Cambridge University Press for undertaking the publication of this book. My thanks are also due to all the members of the staff who worked on the design and production of this book, and especially to Mr Francis Brooke who saved me from numerous errors by his persistent questioning and patient sub-editing of the manuscript.

I am grateful to the authorities of the University of Chittagong for granting me study leave for the period of research. I also gratefully acknowledge the financial assistance I received from the School of Oriental and African Studies and the Central Research Fund, University of London. The financial help from the Central Research Fund enabled me to obtain some essential research materials from Calcutta.

For my research materials I depended on the following libraries: The British Museum Library, the India House Library, the India Office Library and Records, the Library of the London School of Economics, the National Library of India (Calcutta), the Library of the School of Oriental and African Studies, the Senate House Library, Dacca University Library and the Library of the Bangladesh Institute of Development Studies. I am grateful to the Librarians and other members of the staff of these Libraries. My thanks are also due to the members of staff of the University of London Computer Centre and the Computer Department of the University College, London.

Finally my thanks are due to Nahar, my wife, for all her encouragement and assistance. All erros of logic and facts are, however, entirely my own.

M.M.I.

INTRODUCTION

The establishment of British rule in India led to a great expansion of the external demand for her agricultural raw materials. Whereas in the preceding centuries production for domestic consumption and transactions in kind had been the dominant pattern, under the changed circumstances in the nineteenth century agriculture became much more market oriented. In other words, growing emphasis began to be put on the production and marketing of certain crops which were needed for export on the world market. Working in the same direction was the influence of the growth of commercial centres and the development of certain industries. The net result was that the surplus productive capacity in agriculture, which had for so long been locked up as a result of the small size of market, now came to be increasingly utilised.

Among the regions of India where the impact of the widening of the market was felt, Bengal occupied an important position. The effect of the widening market was naturally concentrated most in the agricultural sector. In particular, foreign demand for raw jute and the development of the jute industry in and around Calcutta stimulated the production of this crop.[1] The impetus which was thus given by the establishment of wider commercial contact with the outside world led to a remarkable expansion of agriculture but it seems that by 1920 the possibilities for the further expansion of cultivation had become limited. An important development which accompanied the process of widening of the market was the gradual increase of the pressure on land along with the growth of population.[2] As the expansion of agriculture was not accompanied by industrial—urban development on a sufficiently large scale the man—land ratio gradually deteriorated. Thus, according to the Census of 1921 the percentage of total population directly dependent on agriculture was as high as 77.3 and cultivated land per worker was only 2.3 acres.[3]

[1] For details see, B. B. Chaudhuri, 'Growth of Commercial Agriculture in Bengal 1859–1885', *Indian Economic and Social History Review*, Vol. 7 (1970), pp. 25–60; 'Growth of Commercial Agriculture and its Impact on Peasant Economy', *ibid.*, pp. 211–52.

[2] For a discussion on the trends in the growth of population in India and their explanation see, K. Davis, *The Population of India and Pakistan* (New York, 1968), Chs. 2, 5.

[3] *Census of India, 1921, Bengal* (Calcutta, 1923), p. 377. If it is believed that there was substantial 'de-industrialisation' in India during the British rule, this would mean that the increase in the number of people engaged in agriculture was not only in absolute but also in

The present study is an attempt to examine the performance of the agricultural sector in such an environment. We are directly concerned with a period which is much later than the time when market forces began penetrating rural areas. However, in order to place the present study in its proper perspective it is necessary that an attempt be made to review the process by which this environment was created, the theoretical justifications which were put forward by the classical economists and the policy implications which the British imperial government derived from such reasonings. This will show that the assumptions of the nineteenth-century economists and administrators, which were generally very different from the thinking of present-day economists who advocate growth, were largely responsible for the creation of conditions of stagnation rather than self-sustained economic development.

CLASSICAL AND CONTEMPORARY VIEWS OF DEVELOPMENT

On the basis of their strategy for the economic development of the under-developed countries the present day advocates of growth may be broadly divided into two groups. One group believes that the economic life of the under-developed countries could be transformed by giving industrialisation top priority. The second group recommend that the development of the two sectors of the economy – agriculture and industry – should proceed simultaneously.[1]

The thinking of the classical economists was in sharp contrast to the opinions of contemporary development economists, particularly those belonging to the first group. They advocated economic development through the international division of labour, and recommended that the underdeveloped countries should specialise in the production of primary products for which they were suitable, and the exports from which could finance the imports of manufactured goods from abroad. It was believed that this strategy would transmit economic growth to all parts of the world. Thus, Adam Smith, the most prominent advocate of such a model of economic develop-

proportional terms. For a discussion of this problem on the basis of Census data see, Daniel and Alice Thorner, *Land and Labour in India*, (Bombay, 1962).

[1] The various assumptions of the economists in the first group are discussed by R. M. Hartwell, *The Industrial Revolution and Economic Growth* (London, 1971), Ch. x; H. Myint, *The Economics of the Developing Countries* (London, 1964), Ch. vii; Concurrent Growth of agriculture and industry is advocated by, among others, W. A. Lewis, *The Theory of Economic Growth* (London, 1955), pp. 276–83; R. Nurkse, 'The Conflict between "Balanced Growth" and International Specialisation' in *Lectures on Economic Development* (Istanbul, 1958); H. Gaitskell, 'Importance of Agriculture in Economic Development' in W. W. Mcpherson (ed.), *Economic Development of Tropical Agriculture* (University of Florida Press, 1968).

ment, contended that international trade would overcome the small size of the domestic market and create an effective demand for primary products. This has been called the 'vent for surplus' theory. Another feature of this school of thought is its belief that, by widening the extent of the market, international trade would lead to the division of labour and raise general productivity. This would improve human skill, encourage technical innovations and thereby would provide a satisfactory basis for continuous economic development.[1]

Although the dynamic aspect of international trade did not occupy a central place in the writings of other classical or neoclassical economists there was nonetheless some recognition of the growth-transmitting aspect of trade above and beyond the static gains from comparative advantage. In this interpretation gains from trade were entirely consistent with the gains from growth. Indeed, the latter could be expected to increase *pari passu* with the extension of foreign trade. J. S. Mill was exceptionally clear on this point. Trade, according to comparative advantage, results in a 'more efficient employment of the productive resources of the world', and this may be considered the 'direct economical advantage of foreign trade. But', he emphasises, 'there are, besides, indirect effects which must be counted as benefits of a high order.' One of the most significant of these 'indirect' benefits is 'the tendency of every extension of the market to improve the process of production. A country which produces for a larger market than its own, can introduce a more extended division of labour, can make greater use of machinery and is more likely to make inventions and improvement in the process of production.'[2]

THE INFLUENCE OF POLITICAL ECONOMY

Further, once such a dynamic role was assigned to international specialisation it did not remain confined to political economists but became the 'confirmed conviction'[3] of the rising class of merchants, traders, manufacturers and their representatives in the British Parliament. It was contended that since international specialisation was so beneficial in raising productivity and transmitting economic growth the government should go beyond the negative policy of removing all obstacles to commercial intercourse and

---

[1] This part of the discussion is based on the article by H. Myint, 'The "Classical Theory" of International Trade and Underdeveloped Countries', *Economic Journal*, Vol. 68 (1958), reprinted in I. Livingstone (ed.), *Economic Policy for Development* (London, 1971), pp. 85–112.

[2] Cited by G. M. Meier, *The International Economics of Development: Theory and Policy* (Tokyo, 1968), pp. 217–18. The names of other classical economists who shared this view are mentioned in this book.

[3] F. F. Clairmonte, *Economic Liberalism and Underdevelopment* (Bombay, 1960), p. 16.

3

initiate a positive policy of facilitating increased production and export of primary goods. Under such an impulse the foreign rulers of India pursued what may be called a policy of selective intervention. In other words, while the government maintained a policy of non-intervention in some areas, for example denial of tariff protection to indigenous industries, non-interference in foodgrain movements under conditions of recurring famines, unwillingness to play a positive role in industrial development, in some other areas it went far beyond strict *laissez-faire* policy, for example in subsidising or guaranteeing private investments, altering land regulations to aid investment in plantations and providing incentives for the production of agricultural raw materials through irrigation and investment in infrastructure, including transport facilities[1] for raw materials export.

Thus, the notion of complementary development within the empire and the stress on India's comparative advantage in the production of agricultural raw materials (as against England's advantage in the production of industrial goods) led the new generations of administrators, merchants and manufacturers to argue that the government should do all in its power to help India perform her special role as the supplier of raw materials. The conventional wisdom came to be that to stimulate the production and export of raw materials 'was the best means of improving [India's] internal resources' (Wilson), 'agriculture must be her staple industry' (Trevelyan). The exchange of manufacturers from Europe 'for those raw staples in the production of which this country has special advantage' (Bengal chamber of commerce) was the ideal division of labour between the colony and the metropolitan country.[2]

ECONOMIC DEVELOPMENT

There have always been dissenters from this optimistic view of economic development by backward countries through specialisation in the production of agricultural raw materials. With the present concern for the under-

[1] Route mileage of railways increased from 288 in 1857 to 7322 in 1877. That the expectation of raw material supply was an important consideration behind railway investment has been shown by W. J. Macpherson, 'Investment in Indian Railways 1845–75', *Economic History Review*, Vol. VIII (New Series), 1955; and Daniel Thorner, *Investment in Empire: British Railway and Steam Shipping Enterprise in India 1825–49* (Philadelphia, 1950). The impact of railways on the relative production of the different groups of crops is examined by M. B. McAlpine, 'Railroads, Cultivation Patterns and Foodgrains availability: India 1860–1900', *The Indian Economic and Social History Review*, Vol. XII, No. 1. Out of a total acreage of 197.25 millions under cultivation in 1880 the irrigated area in the country was 29.2 million acres; see, *Report on Moral and Material progress 1882–83*, p. 182.

[2] Cited by S. Bhattacharya, *Financial Foundations of the British Raj* (Simla, 1971), p. liv. This author has shown that State action in increasing the production and exports of agricultural raw materials was advocated by the classical economists. See pp. 17–18.

developed countries the critics of the optimistic school are more numerous and their arguments more challenging. Several points of view have been strongly put forward. Firstly, the thesis which has been most widely discussed is the secular deterioration in the commodity terms of trade for the countries producing raw materials and the consequent transfer of income. This deterioration is attributed to the relative decrease in the demand for primary products and the relative increase in the demand for manufactured goods, diverse movements of primary product prices and industrial prices over successive business cycles, the greater number of monopoly elements in industrial markets and differences in the distribution of gains from increased productivity. With regard to the diverse movements of prices over successive business cycles it has been argued that the prices of agricultural raw materials have increased sharply during periods of boom but have subsequently lost their gains in the downswing of the trade cycle. On the other hand, though the prices of manufactured goods have risen less in prosperous years they have not fallen as far in depressions as they have risen in booms. Thus, over successive cycles the gap between the prices of the two groups of commodities has widened. The differences in the gains from increased productivity achieved though technical progress are attributed to the fact that whereas in the industrialised countries the gains from increased productivity in manufactured goods have been distributed in the form of higher wages and profits rather than lower prices, in the case of food and raw material production in the underdeveloped countries the gains in productivity, although smaller, have been distributed in the form of price reductions. Secondly, a transfer of income away from the countries specialising in the production of agricultural raw materials comes about not only through the deterioration in the terms of trade but also from the official transfer of funds ('Home charges' in the case of India), private remittances by foreign officials, dividends and interest payments by shipping and banking interests, plantations and other investors. Thirdly, there is the familiar view that since agriculture is subject to diminishing returns the expansion of primary exports will come to a stop sooner or later when suitable natural resources have been fully brought into use or are exhausted. Fourthly, outlook and institutions in the agricultural sector are generally conservative. It is rightly argued that such conservatism becomes an obstacle to rapid technical progress in the production process.[1]

---

[1] There are, of course, differences of emphasis in the various arguments. For detailed discussion on the views of the different authors critical of the classical model see Myint, *op. cit.*, Ch. 9; Szentes, *The Political Economy of Underdevelopment* (Budapest, 1971), Ch. VI; Meier, *op. cit.*, particularly Chs. 3 and 7; W. Baer, 'The Economics of Prebisch and the ECLA', *Economic Development and Cultural Change*, Vol. 10, No. 2. Some estimates of economic drain from British India are presented by Angus Maddison, *Class Structure and Economic Growth* (London, 1971), pp. 63–70.

For all these reasons it is now generally believed that self-sustained economic development cannot be built on the expansion of primary products alone.

Industrial–urban development. A closer scrutiny, however, would suggest that far from maintaining self-sustained growth under the classical scheme, even the opportunity for the realisation of the full potential of agricultural development remains limited in a long-settled country like India. According to T. W. Schultz economic development takes place in a specific locational matrix which is primarily industrial–urban in composition. With particular reference to agriculture Schultz hypothesised that those parts of agriculture located favourably relative to the industrial–urban centre are more developed than those situated at the periphery.[1] In other words, the structural diversification of the economy through industrialisation creates a favourable environment for the transformation of the agricultural sector through its impact on the product market, as well as labour and capital markets. Industrialisation creates an expanding domestic market for the increased and diversified products of the agricultural sector. The availability of such a market is necessary in order to ensure a more remunerative price level both in the short and the long-run and thus to induce cultivators of food to make use of new technology. Then, the emerging industrial sector absorbs an increasing proportion of the available labour force. This contributes to the reorganisation of agriculture by preventing an aggravated pressure on land. Moreover, as there is a rise in the level of wages (imputed or paid) in the rural areas those who remain in agriculture are induced to find ways of raising their productivity so that they are worth these high wages. This makes it possible to increase the scale of farming and raise the capital–labour ratio. Thirdly, the increase in the capital–labour ratio is facilitated by the increase in the aggregate financial resources in the rural and urban areas. New financial institutions come into being and these cater for the needs of both the industrial and agricultural sectors.

From such an elaboration of the contributions of industrial–urban development to the transformation of the agricultural sector it should not, however, be concluded that the basic relationship between the two sectors is one of

[1] T. W. Schultz, 'Reflections on Poverty Within Agriculture', *Journal of Farm Economics*, Vol. LVIII, No. 1 (1950), pp. 1–15; *The Economic Organisation of Agriculture* (New York, 1953). This hypothesis has been substantiated by the findings of different authors. See, W. H. Nicholls, 'Industrialisation, Factor Markets, and Agricultural Development', *Journal of Political Economy*, Vol. LXIX, No. 4 (1961), pp. 319–40; A. M. Tang, *Economic Development in the Southern Piedmont, 1860–1950: Its Impact on Agriculture* (Chapel Hill, 1958); W. H. Nicholls, 'The Transformation of Agriculture in a Semi-Industrialised Country: The Case of Brazil' in Eric Thorbecke (ed.), *The Role of Agriculture in Economic Development* (New York, 1969), pp. 311–85.

unidirectional causation from the former to the latter. In a number of ways agriculture makes a decisive contribution to industrialisation. Firstly, in the earlier periods, when industrial capital has not been accumulated, an agricultural surplus may be mobilised for the financing of industrialisation. This is suggested both by economic and historical reasoning and experience.[1] Secondly, agricultural development contributes to industrialisation by expanding the market for new products. Finally, agriculture helps industrialisation by releasing labour and providing food supplies for the expanding labour force. The problem of providing food supplies for the growing labour force has received special attention in several views of the development process.[2] Lewis emphasises the supply of subsistence food to industrial labour as an important capital contribution from the agricultural sector.[3]

From the foregoing discussion it can be argued that the basic relationship between agriculture and industry is one of mutual rather than unidirectional causation. The historical experience of the economic development of Japan clearly points to such a relationship.[4] Similarly with regard to the place of agriculture in British economic growth it is now being argued that the relationship between the agricultural and industrial sector is not one of unidirectional causation from industry to agriculture or vice versa, but one of mutual interrelatedness. Thus, after a careful examination of the timing and progress of the two related features of agricultural development – the enclosure movement and adoption of new farm technology – Deane comes to the conclusion that the Agricultural Revolution did not precede the changes in the methods and levels of industrial production. Nor did the Industrial Revolution cause the transformation in agriculture.[5] Changes in industry and agriculture were ultimately related in a process in which the main relationship was one of simultaneous interdependence or mutual causation.[6] Thus, to

---

[1] B. F. Johnston, "Agricultural Productivity and Economic Development in Japan', *Journal of Political Economy*, Vol. LIX (December, 1951).

[2] J. C. H. Fei and G. Ranis, *Development of the Labour Surplus Economy: Theory and Policy* (Homewood, Irwin, 1964); W. H. Nicholls, 'An "Agricultural Surplus" as a Factor in Economic Development', *Journal of Political Economy*, Vol LXXI (February, 1963); D. W. Jorgenson, 'The Development of a Dual Economy', *Economic Journal*, Vol. LXXI (June, 1961).

[3] W. A. Lewis, *The Theory of Economic Growth* (London, 1955).

[4] The sectoral interdependence in Japan is shown by Kazushi Ohkawa, 'Concurrent Growth of Agriculture and Industry: A Study of the Japanese Case' in R. N. Dixey (ed.), *International Explorations of Agricultural Economics* (Ames, Iowa, 1964). See, also by the same author, 'Phases of Agricultural Development and Economic Growth' in K. Ohkawa, B. F. Johnston and H. Kaneda (eds.), *Agriculture and Economic Growth: Japan's Experience*, (Tokyo, 1969), Ch. 1.

[5] P. Deane, *The First Industrial Revolution* (Cambridge, 1967), p. 43.

[6] R. M. Hartwell, *The Causes of the Industrial Revolution in England* (London, 1967), pp. 16–17. There are two other views about the nature of the relationship between agricultural and industrial growth in England which might be mentioned. At one extreme

conclude this part of the discussion, it would appear that,

In general, the process of economic growth contains, as one of its major characteristics, the interdependence between various sectors of the economy: the growth (or retardation) of a particular sector influences, and in turn is influenced by, the growth (or retardation) of the other sectors.... Economic growth usually leads to an increasingly close sectoral interdependence of the economy. Agriculture and industry would follow this general trend, but with a variety of patterns from one country to another and from one phase to another within a single country.[1]

In the case of a long-settled country like India the importance of the concurrent growth of the industrial and agricultural sectors assumes particular significance. Since the pressure on land was increasing, what was most needed for the transformation of agriculture was the structural diversification of the economy through industrial–urban development. But the classical scheme of economic development through specialisation in the production of agricultural raw materials hardly left any scope for large-scale industrialisation in India. Thus, the implementation of the classical scheme implied that whereas the absolute size of the labour force engaged in the agricultural sectors of countries undergoing industrial–urban development would decline or remain constant, in India the pressure of population on land would become more acute with the passage of time. This, in turn, would be crucial for agricultural development in India. This is so because emphasis on agriculture would mean that even allowing for an improvement in per capita income as a result of the initial expansion of the agricultural output, increasing population would lead to shrinking agricultural surplus and consequent lower levels of reinvestment.

In this connection another important feature of industrial–urban development may be pointed out. Economic development involves the transformation of the wider cultural matrix against which economic activities take place. Industrialisation helps achieve such a transformation to the extent that it creates an intellectual environment which is more secular in outlook and less tradition-bound.[2] In this respect also we see the particular importance of industrial development for a country like India. But specialisation in the production of agricultural raw materials would mean that the desired transformation of the traditional value system would not take place.

there is the view of Arthur Young and his associates that the Agricultural Revolution arose out of the needs of the Industrial Revolution. The other extreme is that increase in agricultural productivity was a 'precondition' for the Industrial Revolution. For details see, W. W. Rostow, *Stages of Economic Growth* (Cambridge, 1971).

[1] Ohkawa, *op. cit.*, p. 205. For a discussion on how lack of industrialisation can have adverse effects an agriculture see, C. Geertz, *Agricultural Involution: The Process of Ecological Change in Indonesia* (Berkeley, 1963).

[2] W. H. Nicholls, 'The Place of Agriculture in Economic Development', in C. K. Eicher and L. W. Witt (eds.), *Agriculture in Economic Development* (New York, 1964), pp. 7–44.

Technological development. The importance of concurrent development of the two sectors of the economy can, therefore, hardly be exaggerated in the case of a country like India. However, before we proceed it must be pointed out that though a simultaneous development of the industrial sector fulfils a necessary condition for agricultural development, this, in itself, is not sufficient. In a long-settled country the scope for the extension of cultivation to new areas is obviously more limited than in a newly-settled country. In such a situation what is needed, particularly once cultivation has extended as far as is possible, is improvement in the productivity of land already under cultivation. Up to a point this can perhaps be done by increasing the use of such traditional inputs as labour, animal power and implements for tillage and the improvement of the methods of irrigation or the pattern of crop rotation. But sooner or later a stage is reached when the gains from the increase of these inputs, with which the cultivators have long been acquainted, will be severely limited.[1] In other words, better resource allocation, more savings and investment restricted to the traditional factors of production will not be remunerative. At such a stage the necessity of obtaining additional output will require the introduction of a technology which will lead to an upward shift of the aggregate production function. Again, it is not the introduction of a once-for-all change. If agricultural development is to be sustained the techniques of production must be constantly changing. When they stop changing agriculture once more becomes stagnant.

Technological progress as defined here may be viewed as the combined effect of two processes: (*a*) research and experimentation and (*b*) diffusion. The first process includes the search for new methods and materials from other countries, testing them for their usefulness locally and perhaps modifying them. Among these methods may be mentioned experimentation to develop new strains of crops, soil treatment, disease control measures, livestock medicine and machinery, all of which make agriculture more productive. Once the new techniques are developed at the research station there arises the further necessity of popularising them among the cultivators through agricultural extension services and ensuring their regular supply in the market. For two overriding factors such research and experimentation and the popularisation of new techniques must usually be undertaken by the State. Firstly, private agencies cannot take advantage of all the benefits from increased production made possible by the development and distribution of new techniques. Secondly, there are known indivisibilities in the methods and staff of scientists required for the production of new factors. One or two

---

[1] The discussion on the importance of the introduction of new technology and the necessity of its development and supply by the government is based on the work by T. W. Schultz, *Transforming Traditional Agriculture* (Yale University Press, 1965).

scientists with a simple laboratory can hardly be expected to produce new agricultural factors of production suited to the conditions in a particular region. This task usually requires a large number of scientists and expensive facilities for experimental works. Similarly, in the case of agricultural extension services there are important size considerations. For these and other reasons it is clear that it is the government which should take up responsibility for research into it and the popularisation of new techniques of production.[1]

Thus, given that the cultivators respond favourably to new opportunities, sustained growth in the agricultural sector depends on (*a*) an environment characterised by favourable product, labour and capital markets through industrial development; and (*b*) the availability of constantly changing technology which will require some element of state action.

The conditions for development, and the case of India. How far were these two conditions fulfilled in India or Bengal? With regard to the creation of a favourable economic environment through industrialisation it is needless to mention that by any standard India remained backward in the field of industrial development.[2] As mentioned earlier, this backwardness cannot wholly be attributed to the classical scheme of economic development and the policy implications drawn from it by the foreign rulers.[3] However, it must be pointed out that the policy of the government with regard to industrial development in India was unfavourable, and this was of crucial significance.[4]

[1] A. M. Tang has tried to explain measured technological progress in Japanese agriculture in terms of government expenditure on agricultural research, extension and rural education by forming a regression of the former on the latter. On the basis of the goodness of fit he has claimed that more than 70% of the variation in outputs is explained. For details see his 'Research and Education in Japanese Agricultural Development, 1880-1938', *Economic Studies Quarterly*, Vol. 13 (1969), pp. 27–41 and 91–9.

[2] Between 1901 and 1931 the proportion of industrial workers in the total labour force hardly changed and although there was no detailed computation in 1941 the evidence available from other sources indicates that there was hardly any change over 1931. For details see Thorner, *op. cit.* For a discussion on the record of industrialisation in British India see, D. H. Buchanan, *The Development of Capitalistic Enterprise in India* (London, 1966), Chs. VII, X, XI and XII.

[3] Many authors have attributed the industrial backwardness of India to the following factors: scarcity of capital, absence of entrepreneurial talent, and social traditions and institutions. For details see V. Anstey, *Economic Development of India* (London, 1957); P. P. Pillai, *Economic Conditions in India* (London, 1925), Ch. X; P. S. Lokanathan, *Industrial Organisation in India* (London, 1938), Chs. I and VIII; G. C. Allen, 'The Industrialisation of the Far East', in *Cambridge Economic History of Europe* (Cambridge, 1965), Vol. V, Part II.

[4] The *laissez-faire* policy of the government was criticised by the nationalist leaders and since then it has been criticised by many authors. For details of these criticisms see A. K. Bagchi, *Private Investment in India, 1900–1939* (Cambridge, 1972), Chs. 2 and 14; S. K. Sen, *Studies in Industrial Policy and Development* (Calcutta, 1964). For the views of the nationalist leaders and newspapers see B. Chandra, *The Rise and Growth of Economic Nationalism in India, 1880–1905* (New Delhi, 1966), pp. 112–22 and pp. 716–32.

Its policy of *laissez-faire* and free trade deprived India's industries of the kind of state patronage which they deserved at that particular stage of development and which was being enjoyed by industries in other countries, including the two sister colonies of Canada and Australia.[1] It is true that the influence of the scheme of economic development through international specialisation did not last all through the period of foreign rule. But the change of policy was slow to come and when it came it did not mean an abandonment of the general policy of *laissez-faire* in favour of a positive plan for industrialisation. As a result of the tariff protection which was granted in the 1920s a number of industries benefited.[2] But the scale of industrial–urban development remained low,[3] so that its dynamic impact on the agricultural sector remained insignificant.

As to the research and experimentation with new methods and techniques of agricultural production, the role of the government was in one respect more positive. Public support of agricultural research was available from the turn of the present century when the Imperial Agricultural Research Institute was established. There were also experimental centres under the supervision of the Provincial Department of Agriculture. Successful experiments were made to evolve new varieties of seeds of such crops as jute, cotton, rice, wheat, sugarcane and tobacco. But efforts in the field of demonstration and propaganda remained inadequate. This was due to the fact that from the very beginning the Agricultural Department remained badly understaffed. Though there was normally a trained Agricultural Officer in every district, the number of demonstrators was very small (there were only 130 demonstrators and 23 government farms in the whole province of Bengal). This meant that it was impossible for the District Agricultural Officer to contact a substantial section of the cultivators. As a result the majority of the peasantry remained ignorant of the advances that were being made in the techniques of production.[4] It was rightly pointed out that by 'far the most important and difficult task before the agricultural officers in India is to bridge the great gulf separating the agricultural experimental stations and

---

[1] H. G. J. Aitken (ed.). *The State and Economic Growth* (New York, 1959). The economic development of Australia and Canada is discussed in Chs. 2 and 3.

[2] These are discussed by Bagchi, *op. cit.*

[3] In its 'Survey of Indian Industries' made at the end of 1936 *The Economist* commented that 'although India has begun to modernise her industries it can hardly be said that she is as yet being industrialised'. Quoted by Clairmonte, *op. cit.*, p. 133.

[4] The Bengal Paddy and Rice Enquiry Committee remarked that 'witness after witness told us in course of our tours in the mofussil that the great majority of the paddy growers had never heard of improved seeds and did not know where they could get them from'. For details see, Government of Bengal, *Report of the Bengal Paddy and Rice Enquiry Committee* (Calcutta, 1939.), Vol. I. p. 72. See also, *Report of the Bengal Land Revenue Commission* (Calcutta, 1940), Vol. I, pp. 102–3.

the few large-scale farmers from the peasants who cultivate by far the largest portion of land. It is not new science so much as fuller use of existing science that is needed.'[1]

It is clear that since propaganda was so inadequate the new seed was demanded by only a small percentage of the cultivators. But even this limited demand could not be met by the Agricultural Department. The demand for new seed almost always exceeded the available supply.[2] There was one area of effort which remained completely untouched. This was the introduction of new artificial fertilizer to aid crop production. The experiments that were conducted with artificial fertilizer were often badly designed and were conducted in a very irregular fashion.[3]

Thus, the overall situation in Bengal was such that there was neither the availability of modern inputs which would significantly increase yields given the institutional set-up nor a sufficiently favourable economic environment to sustain the large-scale use of new techniques of production by the cultivators. While the first factor was due to the inadequate efforts of the government, the second was caused by the lack of industrial–urban or market development on a sufficient scale.

How would agriculture respond in such an environment? Was the type of specialisation visualised by the classical economists really possible when the growth of population was aggravating the pressure on the available land and the cultivators were virtually left to themselves to effect technological improvement in their production process? It is in any case likely that the foreign demand for raw materials would have led to an expansion of agricultural output. At the time of the establishment of wider commercial contact there must have been a considerable surplus of land and labour in India. The domestic market was too small to absorb the additional output which could be obtained even if there was no technological improvement. In such conditions the expansion of foreign trade, the development of the means of transport, communication and irrigation by the state, the introduction of new crops and the establishment of more stable conditions would be expected to make the agricultural sector much more market oriented than before. Up to this point the propulsive effects of international trade cannot be denied, as it is very likely that the growth of exports would mean an increase in per capita national income shared in different proportion by the different sections of the community.

[1] Sir John Russell, *Report on the Work of the I.C.A.R. in Applying Science to Crop Production in India* (Simla, 1937), pp. 221–2.
[2] This was admitted in the *Annual Report of the Bengal Department of Agriculture*.
[3] See the evidence of C. M. Hutchinson in the *Report of the Royal Commission on Agriculture in India: Evidence, Vol. IV, Evidence taken in the Bengal Presidency* (Bombay, 1927), pp. 296–301.

But the more important question that has to be asked is whether the expansion of output would be achieved merely by the extension of cultivation or a new combination of the factors of production. Would specialisation mean merely a movement along the given 'production possibility' curve or would there be technological innovations which would lead to an upward shift in the aggregate production function? Since the cultivators were virtually left to themselves it would seem that increased output would be achieved more by the extension of cultivation than through improvement in yield per acre. Under such circumstances could it not be predicted that after an initial spurt the agricultural sector would again begin to stagnate once the extension of cultivation had reached its natural limits? Further, since the expansion of the agricultural sector would not be accompanied by industrial development on a sufficient scale, would not this stagnation in agriculture given the increasing population create 'disguised unemployment' with its adverse effects on per capita income, the level of investment (even in the traditional factors of production) and on the availability of marketable surplus? In sum, would not the particular conditions in India provide a classic example of 'expansion without growth'?

THE STUDY OF INDIAN AGRICULTURE

There has been a considerable number of secondary works on Indian agriculture. But the attention of scholars has so far remained confined to the estimation of the trends in crop output as 'representative of change in agriculture as a whole',[1] and the main controversy has centred on whether production increased or decreased or remained constant. There is no denying the fact that these trends are the main indicators of the agrarian economy as a whole. But in order to have a better understanding of the underlying trends it is necessary that these should be discussed within a framework comprehensive enough to include, apart from the wider background we have outlined, all the variables which directly or indirectly determine such trends, viz. labour, capital, credit, the price level and the land system. However, even within this narrow scope there are several other limitations in the existing literature. Firstly, in most of these works no attempt has been made to check the officially published data against the data available from independent sources and much less to revise them. Those revisions which have been attempted are mostly elementary or based on guess work. Secondly, most of the works fail to estimate trends in all the major individual crops. The

---

[1] G. Blyn, *Agricultural Trends in India, 1891–1947, Output, Availability and Productivity* (University of Pennsylvania Press, 1966), p. 19. The findings of the other works are summarised by this author.

obvious result of such an omission is that we lack a detailed picture of the changes in the yields of particular crops which may have taken place in changing circumstances. Lastly, all these works are at the all-India level. Since agriculture is dependent on location and conditions over the sub-continent are not uniform such studies have obvious limitations. The only exception to this pattern (as in the case of trends in individual crops) seems to be the work by George Blyn.[1] He not only estimates the trends in pro-duction and their relationship with land and labour but also presents his estimates at the regional level. But here again we do not get an independent picture of Bengal as such since Blyn treats Bengal along with Bihar and Orissa. It is likely that the inclusion of these two other provinces considerably depresses the agricultural trends of Bengal proper.

In the present work an attempt is made to examine the agricultural trends in Bengal proper (i.e. Bengal without the two native states of Cooch Bihar and Tippera) for the period from 1920/21 to 1945/46. As against the limited scope of the existing literature the purpose here is to examine both the trends in crop output and the problems connected with these trends, positive or negative, slow or fast. This approach will focus attention not only on the quantity and the quality of the factors which have direct impact on output, viz. land, labour and capital and the mutual relationships among them, but also on those factors which have indirect influence on growth such as availability of credit, the pattern of institutional control of land and the shifts in the price level. In this way the scope of the present work is con-siderably more comprehensive.

The present concern for the economic development of the underdeveloped countries has led to a renewed interest among economists in history and this, in turn, has given rise to the 'New economic history'[2] based on the application of economic theory and statistical techniques of measurement. Paucity of relevant data permits of only a limited application of these techniques in the present study. But as far as possible attempts have been made to use economic theory to explain specific problems or to examine the assumptions made about them at various levels. The need for such an approach has been particularly felt in the examination of such issues as the role of landlords in agricultural development and agricultural indebtedness with all its attendant evils and the attempts made at its solution.

[1] *Op. cit.*

[2] For discussion on the 'New economic history' see M. Desai, 'Some Issues in Econometric History', *Economic History Review*, Second Series, Vol. XXI (1968), pp. 1–16; R. W. Fogel, 'The New Economic History: Its Findings and Methods', *Economic History Review*, 2nd Series, Vol. XIX (1966), pp. 642–56; L. Davis, 'Professor Fogel and the New Economic History', *ibid.* pp. 657–63.

We have also tried to present a more detailed and systematic analysis of the trends in the different variables and to test some hypotheses about the production behaviour of the peasantry. For obvious reasons the main focus of attention has been the trend of production and its two determinants – acreage and yield. We have included 13 crops which accounted for more than 90 per cent of the total acreage under cultivation. In order to obtain more reliable estimates of these trends we have revised the officially published data in the light of evidence available from independent sources. The two sets of trends estimated from the revised and unrevised series have been presented both for all-Bengal and the regional units. The method of revision is the most rigorous yet attempted. The problems of capital formation and credit have similarly been examined at the aggregate and regional level. It is believed that such a comprehensive approach and the use of the new research techniques, even in their limited form, will enable us to have a better understanding of the performance of the agriculture of Bengal and its underlying implications during the period under review.

PART ONE

I

NATURE OF CROP
STATISTICS AND REVISION

The quality of the basic core of statistics is of primary significance in any quantitative study. But it is in this respect that students of Indian agriculture have been faced with their greatest problem. Statistics had been collected in India in the pre-British period,[1] but it was only in the second half of the nineteenth century that government interest in famine control and in the commercial needs of India led to the creation of a Department of Agriculture, which addressed itself, at least in its early years, primarily to the task of compiling reliable statistics, as this was recognised to be the first step in the direction of agricultural development.[2] But it is generally believed that, in spite of this long history, agricultural statistics for all parts of India in general and those of Bengal in particular are unreliable. Thus, according to the Royal Commission on Agriculture 'these are merely guesses, not infrequently manifestly absurd guesses'.[3] Similar views have been expressed by various other official bodies and individual authors.[4] Most of them have not, however, referred much to quantitative evidence and their opinions are based on considerations of the defects of the primary agency which collected these data and the methods it used.

In this chapter it is proposed to examine the basis of these beliefs and discuss some of the methodological problems. Could it be argued that the estimation of the different components of crop-output was influenced by the subjective judgement of the reporting agencies even more than usually supposed and, therefore, the officially published data are likely to be more unreliable? This question calls for a re-examination of the official estimating formula and the agencies responsible for making the estimates.

---

[1] See Lord Meston, 'Statistics in India', *Journal of the Royal Statistical Society*, XCVI (1933), pp. 1–20.
[2] *Report of the Royal Commission on Agriculture in India* (London, 1928), p. 20.
[3] *Ibid.*, p. 605.
[4] See for example: Govt. of India, *Report of the Indian Economic Enquiry Committee* (Calcutta, 1925), Vol. 1, pp. 16–19; Govt. of Bengal, *Report of the Bengal Jute Enquiry Committee* (Calcutta, 1934), p. 82; *Report of the Bengal Paddy and Rice Enquiry Committee* (Calcutta, 1939), Vol. 1, pp. 82–9; *Report of the Bengal Land Revenue Commission* (Calcutta, 1940), Vol. 1, pp. 76–9; *Report of the Bengal Jute Enquiry Committee* (Calcutta, 1939), pp. 89–91. Opinions of some of the individual authors are referred to later.

1.1 THE ESTIMATING FORMULA

The estimating formula used by the Agricultural Department was as follows:

$$O_t = A_t \frac{(S \times C_t)}{100} \tag{1}$$

where O_t = crop output at time t, A_t = area under cultivation, S = standard yield and C_t = condition factor of the same year expressed as a percentage of the standard. For example, if the area under cultivation of a crop was 200 acres, standard yield per acre 1200 lbs and the condition of the current yield 75 per cent of the standard, the output was

$$180\,000 = 200 \frac{1200 \times 75}{100} \tag{2}$$

1.2 ACREAGE STATISTICS

In the temporarily settled areas where the primary source of crop data was the village accountant or Patwari 'it is generally agreed that the annual figures on areas sown with various crops are on the whole accurate and they compare in this respect very favourably with those published for any other country in the world'.[1] But as revenue demand was permanently fixed in Bengal, the government did not maintain any such staff at the village level and it is believed that the estimates submitted, in the absence of such a staff, by the village watchmen or Chowkidar are 'almost worthless'.[2]

Did the Chowkidars really constitute the primary agency in the collection of crop statistics? There is no reference either in the *Chowkidari Manual*[3] or the *Manual for the Preparation of Crop Reports and Agricultural Statistics* to any such duty assigned to the Chowkidars.[4] On the other hand, according to the Bengal Paddy and Rice Enquiry Committee the agency responsible for the submission of acreage statistics was to be:

(a) Preferably a Khash Mahal Tahsildar, if he had duties in the thana which gave him opportunities of judging the area and quality of the crop.

(b) Next a Circle Officer 'who has been appointed to a circle as a per-

[1] *Royal Commission, op. cit.*, p. 605.

[2] For such references see, for example, *Report of the Indian Economic Enquiry Committee, op. cit.*, p. 17; R. C. Desai, *Standard of Living in India and Pakistan, 1931–1941*, (Bombay, 1953) p. 7. See also the categorical assertion to this effect by R. S. Finlow and Mclean in the *Report of the Royal Commission, op. cit.*, Vol. IV (Evidence Taken in Bengal), p. 14.

[3] *Bengal Chawkidari Manual* (Calcutta, 1916).

[4] *Manual of Rules for the Preparation of Crop Report and Agricultural Statistics*, (Calcutta, (1922), Third Edition. (Henceforth referred to as *Manual*).

manent measure' provided he must not be asked to submit an estimate for
more than a normal Circle of 20 to 40 unions.

(c) Failing the above the Thana Officer.

(d) In addition, either a Kanungo or a District Agricultural Officer might
be employed to make an estimate without restriction as to permanency or
knowledge of the crop area covered by the estimate.[1]

Thus, there is no reference to the fact that the Chowkidars were the
primary agency for the estimation of crop statistics. The area for which
estimates were made by the Khas Mahal Tahsilders must have been very small
as the land revenue of nine tenths of the total area of Bengal was permanently
fixed. Therefore, it is reasonable to assume that forecasts were submitted by
the Thana and Circle Officers. But it is also obvious that the units (comprising
roughly 200 to 400 villages in the case of a Circle Officer) for which such estimates were submitted by the primary agency were too large to enable him to
make any objective judgement about the acreage under the cultivation of
different crops (and their yield per acre). In this connection it has to be
mentioned that neither the Thana nor the Circle Officers belonged to the
Department of Agriculture and it seems that compilation of crop statistics
was but an additional duty discharged by them. Under the same Rule of the
Manual the district officers were allowed to 'reject or amend' any estimate
'received from the interior' in the light of their 'knowledge or experience'.[2]
But it is difficult to see how such estimates could have been improved by
district officers who had far less knowledge of agricultural conditions as they
were in charge of still larger areas.

The defects of the primary agencies were compounded by the rather
complicated method laid down by the *Manual* for the compilation of data.
Thus, under Rule 7 it was provided that a crop report was to contain an

---

[1] *Report of the Bengal Paddy and Rice Enquiry Committee*, p. 83. According to this report these
were laid down under Rule 5. But Rule 5 of the *Manual* already referred to provides that the
'initial reporting agency should be the same throughout the districts, and the practice under
which, in the same district a Kanungo submits estimation for the whole of the sadar sub-
division, while elsewhere the police submits estimates for each thana should be abandoned.
In most districts the thana should be the reporting unit throughout.' Thus, it is clear that
there is considerable difference between this Rule 5 and the one referred to by the above
committee. It is, however, possible that the committee was referring to a later edition of the
Manual which could not be consulted for the present work. The Chowkidars worked under
the direct supervision of the Presidents of the village Panchayets. A former President informed me that he had never had any knowledge of the Chowkidars compiling the crop
statistics.

[2] *Manual*, p. 5. It was pointed out to the *Paddy and Rice Enquiry Committee* that the net effect
of this provision 'was to reduce the calculation of the crop area to an entirely subjective
estimate – an estimate not of informed observers permanently resident in the locality, but of
casual visits of itinerant officers, who are required by the rules to sleep only a reasonable
number of nights out every month', *op. cit.*, Vol. II, p. 83.

estimate of the area sown with the crop in question in the current year and to compare it with the 'normal area' and the area sown in the previous year. The term 'normal area' was defined as 'the figure which, in the existing circumstances, might be expected to be attained in the year if the rainfall and season were of a character ordinary for the tract under consideration; that is neither very favourable, nor the reverse'. In other words it was defined to be the crop which past experience had shown to be the most generally recurring crop over a series of years. This was not, however, meant to 'imply a mechanically correct arithmetic average which would be misleading'.[1] Evidently the average intended here is the mode of a series, but this is hardly clear from the definition. On the other hand it was pointed out in the *Manual* that there was a tendency to confuse the normal for the maximum area available for the cultivation of the crop. It was found that 'in spite of weather and other conditions having been admittedly favourable to the cultivation of a crop, the area sown is estimated at a figure considerably short of the normal'.[2] Data presented in Table 1.1 seem to corroborate this view.[3]

Thus, except for tobacco and sugarcane, 'actual' area sown is less than the normal area and the discrepancy varies from 3 per cent in the case of summer rice to as high as 26 per cent for sesamum.

TABLE 1.1   *Comparison between normal and 'actual' area*

Crops (1)	Actual area under cultivation (2)	Normal area under cultivation (3)	(2) ÷ (3) % (4)
Winter rice	15 293.3	16 947.2	90
Autumn rice	5 446.0	5 743.0	95
Summer rice	406.7	418.3	97
Wheat	141.5	166.3	85
Barley	88.0	113.8	77
Gram	192.4	269.6	71
Mustard	752.3	911.6	83
Sesamum	168.9	229.7	74
Linseed	132.9	174.6	76
Tobacco	297.4	279.8	106
Sugarcane	298.0	202.0	148

Source: *Season and Crop Report of Bengal.*
All figures are in thousand acres.

[1]   *Manual*, p. 7.
[2]   *Manual*, p. 9.
[3]   This table has been prepared by averaging the acreage statistics for the period from 1920/21 to 1940/41. The latter data is selected in view of the upward trends in the acreage statistics after 1940/41. This will be shown in the appendix.

The *Manual* further provided that the normal figures were to be revised at the end of every five years in the light of the information obtained from Settlement Records, cadastral surveys and other sources. These were to be further supplemented by the district and other executive officers.[1] It is true that when the Settlement Reports of individual districts were published, the statistics were usually revised accordingly. But there are many instances when figures on 'normal' areas were revised without reference to any changes in their underlying determinants. This was frequently done even for districts where figures were available from the Settlement Reports.

The presumption that these weaknesses in the estimating formula and primary reporting agencies made the acreage statistics unreliable, and indeed more unreliable than usually supposed, is borne out by three sets of quantitative evidence – *District Survey and Settlement Reports, Agricultural Statistics by Plot to Plot Enumerations* and the *Sample Surveys* made by the Indian Statistical Institute. As already mentioned the defects of the crop statistics were pointed out from time to time by official bodies and individual authors. But it was only in the 1940s that steps were being taken by the provincial government to remedy the situation. The most important of these was the Plot to Plot Enumeration of 1944/45 conducted under the supervision of the then Development Commissioner, A. H. M. Ishaque.[2] The most immediate urge in this direction, however, came from the experience of the famine of 1943 and the necessity of obtaining, for the success of the Grow More Food Campaign, a clear picture about the pattern of land use in Bengal. Statistics available from this Report are the most reliable and detailed of their kind in the whole of the sub-continent. But, except for the case of autumn rice, sugarcane and sesamum, no direct comparison between the departmental estimates and the findings of this Report is possible, as the Agricultural Department, instead of submitting their own estimates for 1944/45, published the figures available from the Ishaque Report. Such a comparison would not, however, have been meaningful even if the official figures were available. This is due to the fact that there was considerable upward revision of the acreage data from 1941/42 (see Appendix). This makes it once again difficult to attempt any direct comparison.

Thus, it is clear that the findings of the Ishaque Report do not directly reflect the margin of error involved in the official acreage data. In order to obviate this difficulty, predicted values of the departmental estimates for

---

[1] *Manual*, p. 5.
[2] *Agricultural Statistics by Plot to Plot Enumeration in Bengal*, 1944/45, 3 Parts (Calcutta, 1946). (Henceforth referred to as Ishaque Report.)

1944/45 have been obtained by fitting the least square trend line and these are then compared with the figures available from the *Plot to Plot Enumeration*. In the case of sugarcane and sesamum the comparison is made directly between the official estimates and the figures available from the Ishaque Report. In the case of autumn rice the figures from this Report are compared both with the predicted values of the official estimates for 1944/45 and the actual estimates which were published. The comparative picture which emerges from this procedure is presented in Table 1.2. This shows that the official figures on the acreage under sesamum, sugarcane and tobacco are overestimated and in the case of other crops these are underestimated and that the error in total crop acreage is in the direction of underestimation. In the case of autumn rice comparison between predicted official estimates and the findings of the Ishaque Report shows that the official figures are underestimates. But the direction of error is just the opposite when comparison is made between the actual official estimates for 1944/45 and the figures

TABLE 1.2 *Predicted values expressed as a percentage of the figures from the Ishaque Report*

Crops (1)	All-Bengal (2)	Presidency (3)	Burdwan (4)	Rajshahi (5)	Dacca (6)	Chittagong (7)
Winter rice	74	72	64	65	88	87
Autumn rice	90	81	157	70	119	68
Summer rice	77	71	23	95	80	63
Gram	54	62	45	41	29	17
Wheat	89	110	37	92	79	–
Barley	47	79	83	27	70	–
Mustard	129	139	172	122	141	99
Sugarcane*	176	117	100	165	285	106
Tobacco	195	83	191	250	110	78
Autumn rice*	120	103	150	110	158	109
Sesamum*	156	25	192	368	42	114
Net cropped area	79	67	59	81	63	91
Double cropped area	66	84	58	35	91	57
Current fallow	428	581	570	629	61	167
Cultivable waste	127	186	186	114	34	100

* Official estimates expressed as a percentage of the figures from the Ishaque Report.

available from the Ishaque Report. For reasons to be discussed later on it is assumed that the official data on autumn rice up to 1940/41 are also under-estimates. It is significant that except in the case of sesamum the forecast figures are overestimates in those cases where the 'actual' area exceeds the normal acreage under such crops (Table 1.1). However, at the regional level the margin of error is not in the same direction in all the cases.

A second independent check in the case of winter rice, autumn rice and jute is provided by the findings of the sample surveys conducted by the Indian Statistical Institute. For reasons already referred to, here again direct comparison between these findings and the official forecast figures does not reflect the real margin of error in the latter. Secondly, acreage under the cultivation of jute was statutorily regulated from 1941/42 and it is, therefore, possible that the margin of error in these years was less than previously. What is, however, significant is that the direction of error remains the same, except in the case of autumn rice of 1945/46 (Table 1.3).

Another independent check is provided by the figures available from the Reports on the Survey and Settlement Operations in the districts. Here again, there is one important limitation. These operations were started in 1888 and by 1920 ten districts (comprising 46 per cent of the total area of Bengal) were surveyed. The survey operations for the remaining seventeen districts were completed by 1940. During this long period the acreages under the cultivation of different crops must have changed implying changes in the relative weights of particular crops in the total crop mix. Some idea of

TABLE 1.3   *Comparison between survey and official estimates of acreage*

Crops (1)	Years (2)	Survey estimate (3)	Official estimate (4)	(4) ÷ (3) % (5)
Jute	1943/44	2 755	2 146	77
	1944/45	2 106	1 694	80
	1945/46	2 520	2 018	80
	1946/47	2 273	1 493	66
Autumn rice	1944/45	7 873	8 084	103
	1945/46	6 884	6 671	97
	1946/47	6 262	6 699	107
Winter rice	1944/45	22 201	18 952	84
	1945/46	21 087	19 471	92

Source of the Survey estimate: Desai, *op. cit.*, p. 8.

In the case of Winter rice for 1944/45 the comparison is against the figures compiled by the Agricultural Department by the 'usual procedure'. See *Calcutta Gazette* , Vol. CLVIII, No. 2049, p. 532. All figures are in thousand acres.

such changes may be gained from Table 1.4 in which figures available from the Survey Reports are compared with the findings of the Ishaque Report.

These increases in the crop acreage, with the sole exception of sesamum, are once again reflected in the area designated as net cropped area, double cropped area, cultivable waste and current fallow. In view of this consideration it is not possible to make any estimate of the magnitude of error in the official acreage statistics by comparing these with the settlement figures. Strictly speaking, this is true even in the case of particular districts as it took several years (as many as 10 years in the case of Rajshahi district) to complete the survey operations. But even then the indications are unmistakeably clear. Table 1.5, in which the average of the official data for five years ending 1939/40 are compared with those available from the Settlement Reports, confirms the earlier finding that there is a considerable margin of error in the former. It is again significant that the direction of error in individual crops remains the same as in Table 1.2.

In the case of jute there are other independent sources which contain evidence to show that the official estimates on acreage are underestimates. For example, there is the 'actual' total of jute production as ascertained from trade statistics and village retention. The year-to-year discrepancies between the official estimates and such 'actuals' are presented in Table 1.6. This shows

TABLE 1.4   *Comparison between settlement figures and data in the Ishaque Report*

Crops (1)	Settlement figures (2)	Ishaque Report (3)	(2) ÷ (3) % (4)
Winter rice	19 093	20 864	91
Autumn rice	6 034	6 652	90
Summer rice	384	556	69
Gram	511	597	85
Wheat	166	199	83
Barley	171	213	80
Mustard	412	554	74
Sugarcane	153	174	87
Tobacco	143	165	86
Sesamum	134	82	163
Double cropped area	6 084	8 212	74
Cultivable waste	4 780	3 994	119
Current fallow	1 411	956	147
Net cropped area	28 841	30 435	108

Source: Agricultural Statistics of Bengal and *Ishaque Report* (*op. cit.*).
All figures are in thousands.

TABLE 1.5   *Comparison between settlement and official figures*

Crops (1)	Settlement figures (2)	Official figures (3)	(3) ÷ (2) % (4)
Winter rice	19 093	15 699	83
Autumn rice	6 034	5 788	97
Summer rice	383	418	110
Gram	511	256	50
Wheat	166	158	94
Barley	171	158	92
Mustard	412	745	180
Sugarcane	153	309	202
Tobacco	143	312	218
Sesamum	134	181	150
Net cropped area	28 841	24 303	84
Double cropped area	6 084	5 111	84
Cultivable waste	4 780	5 009	104
Current fallow	1 411	6 326	448

Note: All figures are in thousands.

that except for two years, 1929 and 1939, the departmental forecast figures on production are always underestimates.[1] It has already been shown (Table 1.3) that the error in the three years from 1943/44 to 1946/47 is due to the underestimation in acreage statistics. The same trend emerges from the findings of the Ishaque Report and another plotwise enumeration made in 1940/41. Compared with these findings the official data on acreage are found to be underestimated by 17 per cent in the case of the former and 52 per cent in the case of the latter. In a later section it will be shown that the yield per acre of jute was overestimated by the Agricultural Department. The fact that in spite of this overestimation official estimates of jute production remained lower than the 'actuals' would suggest that the officially published figures on jute acreage remained underestimates in the earlier period.[2] This unreliability in the acreage data on jute is of particular significance in view of the fact that, unlike other crops, these estimates are said to have been

[1] These figures also include production on jute in Bihar, Orissa, Assam and Cooch Bihar. But only a small quantity of jute was produced in these areas. It is reasonable to assume that the direction and margin of error here are representative of Bengal. The Department of Agriculture sometimes revised upward the final forecast figures on acreage and production. The margins of error indicated in this table would be bigger if comparison were made between final forecast figures on production and 'actuals'.

[2] It will further be argued that the margin of error was indeed bigger than indicated in this table.

27

TABLE 1.6   *Estimated jute production expressed as a percentage of 'actuals'*

Years	Official estimate (1)	Exports, mill purchases and local consumption in the year (2)	(1) ÷ (2) %
1920/21	5 915	7 881	76
1921/22	3 985	7 933	57
1922/23	5 408	6 436	84
1923/24	8 401	9 421	89
1924/25	8 062	9 165	88
1925/26	8 940	9 407	95
1926/27	12 132	12 407	98
1927/28	10 188	11 611	88
1928/29	9 906	11 097	89
1929/30	10 335	11 144	95
1930/31	11 205	10 320	109
1931/32	5 542	6 704	83
1932/33	7 072	8 874	80
1933/34	7 987	8 854	90
1934/35	8 500	9 966	86
1935/36	7 215	8 670	82
1936/37	9 611	10 932	88
1937/38	8 656	10 132	85
1938/39	6 819	9 920	69
1939/40	9 738	10 500	92
1940/41	13 172	9 714	135
1941/42	5 460	6 840	80
1942/43	9 047	9 180	98
1943/44	6 990	7 139	98
1944/45	6 189	7 650	89
1945/46	7 991	9 121	88

Source: Director General of Commercial Intelligence and Statistics, *Estimates of Area and Yields of Principal Crops in India* (Annual). Figures in thousand bales.

submitted by the presidents of the village panchayets and for this reason they have been regarded as reliable.[1] Secondly, from 1941/42 the acreage under jute cultivation was controlled under the Jute Regulating Act of 1941.

1.3 STANDARD YIELD

The two other elements in the estimating formula of the final output of a crop are the 'standard yield' and the 'condition factor'. Both of these elements

[1] *Manual*, p. 13.

have been strongly criticised from time to time, but it is only recently that attempts have been made to quantify the magnitude of error involved in them. Estimates of standard yields were worked out at the end of every fifth year on the basis of the crop-cutting experiments made during the preceding five years. Such estimates, once worked out, were taken to be the standard yield of the crops for the next 5 years. The definition of standard yield is the same as that of 'normal area' and as already mentioned was itself very confusing.[1] But there were other limitations to this procedure, as was pointed out by the National Income Committee. The experiments made by the district officials were not based on random sampling but on purposive sampling. Neither the size of the plot nor the number of experiments was adequate for the purpose of generalisation. The normal yield which was thus worked out was taken to be the normal yield of the entire district irrespective of variations within the district.[2] Some idea of the extent to which the subjective judgement of the officials was at work in the whole process of working out the standard yield may be gained from the fluctuations of the figures on standard yield at different quinquennial periods (Table 1.7). It seems that the explanation for these variations has to be sought more in the influence of the personal judgement of the officials than in any change in the underlying determinants of yield.

TABLE 1.7 *Standard yields in the quinquennia*

Crops	Standard yield of quinquennium beginning					
	1916–17	1922–23	1927–28	1932–33	1937–38	1942–43
Winter rice	1036	1029	1022	1111	1030	1020
Autumn rice	871	888	892	1023	914	865
Jute	1387	1387	1387	1387	1387	1387
Gram	867	826	811	935	833	738
Wheat	698	688	721	816	788	685
Mustard	480	485	483	624	571	535
Sesamum	404	503	495	610	580	529
Linseed	443	467	473	607	556	564
Sugarcane	2963	3004	3054	4643	4446	4388

Source: standard yield figures are available from *Estimates of Area and Yields of Principal Crops in India* (*op. cit.*) and the quinquennial reports on the crop-cutting experiments mentioned later in this chapter. The standard for jute is the simple average of the divisional averages which remained fixed from 1913. All yields are in lbs.

[1] *Ibid.*, p. 7.
[2] Govt. of India, *Final Report of the National Income Committee* (Delhi, 1954), p. 25.

This is further suggested by the comments made from time to time by different officials to justify these variations. Thus, while submitting the Report on the crop-cutting experiments in 1922 G. Evans, the Director of the Agricultural Department, pointed out that the standard yields were not more accurate than in the past except in the case of jute and that reliability could not be 'guaranteed' unless the whole work of the crop-cutting experiments was taken up by the Department of Agriculture from the Department of Revenue.[1] But in the next report submitted in 1927 it was argued that the 'present rates of yield may be regarded as fairly accurate' as yields in almost all the crops remained stationary.[2] The criterion of reliability again changed in 1932 when it was argued that as most of the experiments in the preceding quinquennium were made by the 'trained officers of the Agricultural Department with due care and accuracy greater reliance can be placed on the data on which the average yields have been based'.[3] The standard yields of all the crops showed a decline in the next quinquennium. This was ascribed to the deficient and very uneven distribution of rainfall during large parts of the previous five years.[4]

However, the usual assumption that the standard yield figures are unreliable is once again borne out by the findings of crop-cutting experiments made by the Indian Statistical Institute under the supervision of Professor P. C. Mahalanobis. A comparison with the figures on the yields of the three most important crops estimated by the Indian Statistical Institute shows that the standard yields worked out by the Agricultural Department are overestimates in all the quinquennial periods (Table 1.8).

The margin of error in the standard yield reaches the highest point in the figures worked out for the quinquennium beginning 1932/33. The explanation seems to lie in two changes introduced in this quinquennium. On an examination of the returns in 1911/12 it was admitted by the Government of India that the results were not reliable and accordingly the provincial governments were asked to transfer the crop-cutting experiments to the Department of Agriculture. But except for the case of jute this could not be

[1] Govt. of Bengal, *Report on the Crop-cutting Experiments During the Quinquennium from 1917/18 to 1921/22* (Calcutta, 1922), p. 1.

[2] Govt. of Bengal, *Quinquennial Report on the Crop-cutting Experiments for the Years 1922/23 to 1926/27* (Calcutta, 1927), p. 3.

[3] Govt. of Bengal, *Quinquennial Report on the Crop-Cutting Experiments for the Years 1927/28 to 1931/32* (Calcutta, 1932), p. 3.

[4] Govt. of India, Director General of Commercial Intelligence and Statistics, *Quinquennial Report on the Average Yield Per Acre of Principal Crops for the Period Ending 1936/37* (Calcutta, 1941). This argument is, however, contradicted by the evidence on seasonal conditions except for the cases of winter and autumn rice.

TABLE 1.8   *Standard yield expressed as a percentage of survey estimates*

Quinquennium beginning	Winter rice	Autumn rice	Jute
1916/17	145	133	121
1922/23	144	136	121
1927/28	143	136	121
1932/33	155	156	121
1937/38	144	140	121
1942/43	143	132	121

Note: Figures on the actual yields estimated by the Indian Statistical Institute are shown in Table 1.10. The standard yield of jute remained fixed from 1913.

done before quinquennium beginning 1927/28. As already pointed out, in the Report submitted in 1932 it was argued that as the majority of the experiments were made by 'trained' officers of the Agricultural Department the standard yield figures could be taken as reliable. It is not known if the procedure of crop-cutting experiments improved at all as a result of this transfer.[1] On the other hand, it is believed that in at least one respect the position deteriorated. The transfer of the crop-cutting experiments coincided with the increased endeavour on the part of the Department of Agriculture to popularise the improved varieties of seeds evolved at the experimental centres. It is possible that the increase which was known to have taken place from the records of the areas sown with selected seeds was very 'imperfectly shown in the figures. This may be the cause of the excess of the yield shown by the recent crop-cutting experiments over the standard'.[2] This increase in yield would have been much smaller if the former practice of averaging the standard yield estimated at the end of a quinquennium with the figures of the previous two quinquennia had been adhered to. But this was abandoned.[3] This practice was, however, revived in the next quinquennium when the average yield of all the crops estimated from the results of the crop-cutting experiments showed a decline.[4]

[1] The Royal Commission recommended that every provincial Department of Agriculture should have a Statistical Officer, see *Report*, p. 617. But this was not compiled with.

[2] Bowley, A. L. and Robertson, D. H., *A Scheme for and Economic Census of India*. (Delhi, 1934).

[3] *Quinquennial Report on the Crop-Cutting Experiments for the Years 1927/28 to 1931/32, op. cit.*, p. 1.

[4] *Quinquennial Report on the Average Yield Per Acre of Principal Crops for the Period 1936/37* (Calcutta, 1941), p. 4.

I.4   CONDITION FACTOR

The estimation of the condition factor was completely based on subjective judgement and is, therefore, likely to be even more unreliable. Under Rule 25 of the *Manual* the primary reporting agencies and the district officials were required to estimate the condition of current yields in terms of annas.[1] From this it seems that the same agencies (Circle and Thana Officer and Tahsilder) who submitted the acreage statistics also estimated the seasonal condition of the current yield, though here again, the usual assumption has been made that these were provided by the Chowkidars.[2] Yield per acre depends on far more numerous factors than does acreage under cultivation and these are more likely to escape the visual impression of the reporting agencies on the basis of which estimates were made. Therefore, the contention that the guesses made by the officials about acreage under cultivation could not but be unreliable applies to the forecast of the seasonal condition with greater force.[3] Again, as in the case of the acreage statistics this basic defect was compounded by the procedure which was laid down for quantifying the seasonal condition. Under the same Rule it was provided that 12 annas was to represent a normal crop and 16 annas a bumper one. This 'annawari' estimate was converted into a percentage estimate in the office of the Director of Agriculture.[4] But the significant feature that emerges from the figures

TABLE 1.9   *Index of Condition Factor*

Crops	1924–25	1929–30	1934–35	1939–40	1944–45
Winter rice	92	91	91	88	82
Autumn rice	80	77	87	75	80
Wheat	74	75	79	76	72
Gram	65	66	77	73	74
Linseed	70	68	75	73	71
Sesamum	71	74	80	77	75
Mustard	76	73	83	79	72
Sugarcane	81	82	89	83	76
Tobacco	90	93	90	83	80

Source: *Season and Crop Report*. Seasonal conditions of summer rice, barley and jute were not published.

[1] *Manual*, p. 11
[2] For example, see Desai, *op. cit.*, p. 12.
[3] But the *Royal Commission* argued that 'it is easy to take an exaggerated view of the consequent inaccuracy'. *op. cit.*, p. 608.
[4] *Manual, op. cit.*, p. 12.

presented in Table 1.9 is that in almost every year the yield per acre is below the normal or standard.

Attempts have been made to explain these lower 'annawari' estimates in different ways. The one reason which has been most widely referred to is the supposed pessimism of the village Chowkidars. Thus, it was pointed out by Meek that the Patwari or the Chowkidar 'being generally untrained and generally pessimistic by nature is hardly able to form a correct estimate of the outturn in terms of the normal crop. His idea of a normal crop is that which he longs to see but rarely sees and the result is that the standard with which he compares a crop is really something above the normal. Consequently his estimates generally fall below the mark'.[1] As already pointed out, it is doubtful if the Chowkidars really submitted any crop estimates. However, a comparison with the actual yields of three major crops estimated by the Indian Statistical Institute does not at all show that the primary reporting agencies were pessimistic (Table 1.10). Thus, except for jute in 1942/43 and 1943/44 when crop-cutting experiments were made respectively in 9 and 15

TABLE 1.10   *Official estimates of yield compared with survey estimates*

Crops (1)	Years (2)	Sample survey estimates (lbs) (3)	Official estimates (lbs) (4)	(4) ÷ (3) % (5)
Jute	1942/43	1522	1188	78
	1943/44	1251	1136	91
	1944/45	1267	1465	116
	1945/46	1254	1251	101
	1946/47	930	1210	130
Autumn rice	1944/45	773	732	95
	1945/46	617	691	112
	1946/47	576	658	114
Winter rice	1943/44	732	815	111
	1944/45	708	839	119
	1945/46	704	856	121

Source: Desai, *op. cit.*, p. 15.
Yield figures on winter rice for 1945/46 are taken from P. C. Mahalanobis, 'Recent Experiments in Statistical Sampling in the Indian Statistical Institute', *Journal of the Royal Statistical Society*, Part IV, 1946, p. 344.

[1] *Report of the Royal Commission, op. cit.*, Evidence, Vol. I, Part II, p. 358. The same view was taken by the Director of the Agricultural Department, Govt. of Bengal, Vol. IV, p. 14. See also, H. Sinha, 'Indian Agricultural Statistics', *The Journal of the Royal Statistical Society*, 1934, Part I, pp. 155–62.

districts, and for autumn rice in 1944/45, the official yield per acre is an overestimate.

Discrepancies between the findings of the Indian Statistical Institute and the 'actual' yield per acre estimated by the Agricultural Department in the quinquennial periods are presented in Table 1.11. The pattern remains the same as in the last quinquennial period – the official yield figures are over-estimates.

Thus, on the basis of these findings, it may be concluded that the primary reporting agencies overestimated the yield per acre. It is, how-ever, interesting that the range of error is smaller than in the case of the figures on standard yield. In many cases the range of overestimation would have been still lower if crop output were always estimated on the basis of reports submitted by the primary agencies. There are many inst-ances in which the condition factors on winter and autumn rice for the whole province as worked out from the 'annawari' estimates of the districts were revised upward by the Director of Agriculture, because he believed that the condition of the current yield was much better than that reported.[1] This suggests that the primary reporting agencies were aware of the fact that the standards were pitched high and, therefore, deliberately put the 'annawari' estimates below the normal.[2] Another pos-sible explanation for this practice is provided by the fear expressed by the Agricultural Department with regard to the acreage statistics – that there was a tendency on the part of the reporting agencies to confuse the normal with the maximum.[3]

Some authors believe that the primary reporting agencies tended to overestimate bad years and underestimate good ones.[4] In the absence of any positive evidence to indicate the true position regarding the yield per acre it is difficult to say anything about the merit of such an assumption. What is, however, important is that such a tendency, even if true, does not seem to create any problem so far as the measurement of the trend rate is

[1] So far as Bengal is concerned this evidence contradicts Desai's (*op. cit.*, p. 13) assumption that sometimes the Director of Agriculture tried to correct the overestimation in the results of selected crop-cutting experiments.

[2] W. C. Neale has suggested the possibility that the suppression of the increase in yield per acre was due to the nationalist politics of the 1920s and 1930s which wanted the foreign government discredited. See his *Economic Change in Rural India: Land Tenure and Reform in Utter Pradesh*, 1800–1955 (Yale University Press, 1962), p. 45. So far as Bengal is concerned the evidence presented here suggests an opposite possibility. For further evidence of how the standard yield figures for the quinquennium beginning 1937/38 were distorted by Finlaw, the Director of Agriculture, see *Paddy and Rice Enquiry Report*, Vol. II, p. 18.

[3] *Manual*, p. 9.

[4] *National Income Committee*, p. 27. The same view has been taken by V. G. Panse, 'Trends of Areas and Yields of Principal Crops in India', *Agricultural Situation in India*, Vol. VII, No. 3 (June 1952), p. 144.

concerned. For, if there were the same number of bad years and good years within the period under review it is possible that the overestimation and underestimation approximately cancelled each other out to leave the trend rates unaffected.[1]

Another aspect of the procedure of estimating the seasonal condition which has been given considerable importance is the fact that the condition could be expressed in the form of an integral number of 'annas'.[2] Because of this practice, it has been argued, when the 'annawari' estimates were first reported they were likely to be in excess of or below the true value by up to half an anna. The error could not have been a serious one in the case of a nearly normal crop, but for a crop much below the normal it could be large. If the errors were random, the ultimate margin of error would have been small. But it has been further argued that these were systematic and, there-fore, the condition factor as finally worked out is much smaller than the actual figure by a large percentage. In the case of Bengal, however, such an error seems to have been very small. Firstly, Rule 25 of the Manual required the primary reporting agencies to submit the estimates of the seasonal con-dition not only in terms of an integral number of annas but also in terms of fractions of annas. Fractions could be ignored only if smaller than one tenth. Secondly, under the same Rule a weighted average of the anna outturns of a crop in the different parts of the district was taken to represent the district estimate.[3]

The procedure of estimating the seasonal condition of yield was different in the case of jute. The average yield of jute for every district was estimated by the Director of Agriculture after consultation with the district officers. The basis was the results obtained from cropcutting experiments and infor-mation from cultivators who had harvested their crops.[4] The average yield

TABLE 1.11   *Range of error in the yield of rice and jute* (percentage overestimation (+) or underestimation (−) in the quinquennial yield per acre)

Crops	1920–24	1925–29	1930–34	1935–39	1940–44
Winter rice	+28	+26	+28	+30	+19
Autumn rice	+7	+3	+15	+9	+10
Jute	−7	+6	+12	+10	+3

Source: Computed from figures in the Appendix.

[1] This assumption will be elaborated later on.
[2] S. Subramaniam, 'Production and Prices', *Guide to Current Official Statistics*, Vol. 1, 3rd edi-tion, 1945, pp. 25–6. See also George Blyn, *Agricultural Trends in India, 1891–1947: Out-put, Availability and Productivity* (University of Pennsylvania Press, 1966), p. 48; K. M. Mukerji, *Levels of Economic Activity and Public Expenditure in India* (Poons, 1965), p. 16.
[3] *Manual*, p. 11.
[4] *Manual*, p. 13.

so obtained was then expressed as a percentage of the divisional normal fixed in 1913. The seasonal condition which was thus worked out considerably reduces, but does not fully offset, the high margin of error in the standard yield. It is only in the fourth quinquennium that the direction of error changes.

Discrepancies between the 'actual' and estimated production of jute have already been presented in Table 1.6. Now the evidence that the official data overestimate the yield per acre of jute largely substantiates the assumption already made: that the real magnitude of error in the acreage statistics is much larger than indicated in this table.[1]

1.5 DIFFICULTIES IN ASSUMING UNIFORM RANGE OF ERROR

From the preceding discussion it is clear that the official acreage statistics are in most cases underestimates and the yield figures overestimates. But as most of the existing works on Indian agriculture are at the aggregate level, no attempt has been made to quantify fully the range of error and much less to revise the official statistics in the light of the independent data available.[2] At the all-India level a problem which has been faced more squarely is the non-availability of crop statistics for certain areas.[3] So far as the error in the available statistics is concerned it has usually been argued, though on different assumption by different authors, that such errors would not introduce any significant bias into the trend rates.

Thus, according to Thomas and Shastry, for the purpose of comparison between the trends of population and food supply the deficiencies of the agricultural statistics are not serious, 'because the errors are more or less systematic'. They further argue that if the 'annawari estimates are more or less guesses, they have been so for the whole period under consideration. Therefore whatever error there is, is common for the whole period.' Thus, according to these authors the crop statistics, though inadequate for the estimation of total food supply are helpful for time comparisons.[4] Blyn proceeds on the same assumption and argues that 'neither the degree of error nor the likelihood of an error distribution making for maximum bias,

---

[1] *The Bengal Jute Enquiry Committee* of 1939, however, argued that the standard yield figures were not as unreliable as they were made out to be. The committee further erred in assuming that the crop-cutting experiments were made by the Presidents of the Union Boards. See Report, Vol. 1, *op. cit.*, p. 90.

[2] There seems to be only one such study, K. L. Datta, *Report on the Enquiry into the Rise of Prices in India* (Calcutta, 1914). Some adjustments are also made by Desai and Blyn, *op. cit.* These will be commented upon later on.

[3] For example see Blyn *op. cit.*, and Mukerji, *op. cit.*

[4] P. J. Thomas and N. S. R. Shastry, *Indian Agricultural Statistics* (University of Madras, 1939), p. 89.

was sufficiently large to significantly affect the British India trend rates for aggregates of crops over the whole period'.[1] Mukerji accepts the assumption made by Panse that there was a tendency among the crop reporters to over-estimate production in bad seasons and underestimate it in good ones – and argues that the tendency towards underestimation is of a comparatively recent origin: the late twenties. Therefore, he concludes that 'for the purpose of general comparison over a long period of fifty years or more this element of underestimation is not likely to be of great significance. On the whole, therefore, it would seem that working on the basis of agricultural output figures corrected for uniform coverage, subject to certain recognised short-comings that have already been noted, is justified.'[2] The same conclusion could be drawn on the basis of an opposite view put forward by Subramaniam. He argues that if the errors were random ones the successive averaging may be expected to make the error as small as possible. But these errors are systematic ones and are known to have strong downward bias.[3] In such a case the height of the trend line would be affected, but not the rate of change.

On *a priori* considerations it is difficult to accept any of these hypotheses to the complete rejection of the others. But in the light of the evidence already presented, Subramaniam's assumption seems to be the most relevant one for the acreage statistics up to the year 1940/41. From the point of view of individual crops, however, the position of Bengal seems to justify the as-sumptions of both Thomas and Shastry on the one hand and Subramaniam on the other in the sense that acreage statistics on certain crops are under-estimates and those on others overestimates and the margin of error re-mains uniform up to the year 1940/41. On inspection of the acreage data presented in the Appendices it seems that there are only four crops – sugarcane, jute, sesamum and gram – where this underlying assumption does not hold good. It seems that the volume of underestimation in gram is reduced from 1936/37 and that of overestimation is increased in the case of sesa-mum and sugarcane respectively from 1937/38 and 1931/32. For jute the range of error is more marked in the first quinquennium and the depression period. Then the general pattern changes, beginning from 1941/42 in the case of winter rice and autumn rice, and 1942/43 in the case of other crops, when the upward movements in the acreage statistics started. The only exceptions are seen in the case of sugarcane and tobacco. The series remains

---

[1] Blyn, *op. cit.*, pp. 55–6. He concedes that there could be some improvement in the accuracy of the estimates but argues 'some of the bias which would have resulted from this was removed, however, by the adjustment of the yield per acre series where changes in the parameters of estimation evidently occurred'.

[2] Mukerji, *op. cit.*, p. 21.

[3] Subramaniam, *op. cit.*, pp. 3–4.

stable in the case of the first and for the latter there is a drop in the acreage under cultivation.

In the official publications these increases were variously described as due to the 'Revision of Estimates', 'Success of the Grow More Food Campaign' and 'Favourable weather conditions'.[1] It is possible that there was an extension of cultivation as a result of the Grow More Food Campaign and a relative shift in the acreage under food crops in view of the famine. What, however, seems to be certain is that such increase was very marginal.[2] Under the conditions of an adverse man–land ratio and the inadequacy of food supply it is difficult to see why before 1941/42 the acreage under the cultivation of all crops, particularly of rice, should have decreased to such an extent as to be much lower than even the figures ascertained by the cadastral surveys. It is well known that the physical and climatic conditions of Bengal should have made the extension of cultivation to the possible limits relatively easy. Therefore, when the growth of population was pressing upon the available food supply it is reasonable to believe that the scope for the extension of cultivation in the 1940s was not as big as it was made out to be by the Agricultural Department. These considerations make it fairly clear that by showing the increase in the acreage data as due to the success of the Grow More Food Campaign and favourable weather conditions the Department was actually reducing the margin of underestimation in the acreage data. The only exceptions seem to have been sesamum and mustard where the margin was being increased. It is significant that the Agricultural Department did not ascribe all the increases to these factors either – as mentioned above, in a large number of cases these were accounted for by the revision of estimates. It is further significant that, in contrast with earlier years, these revisions were almost uniformly in the upward direction.

1.6 PROPOSED PLAN OF REVISION

From the preceding discussion it is quite clear that the assumption that the range of error (whether in the direction of overestimation or underestimation) was uniform over the entire period, leaving the percentage rate of change more or less unaffected, does not hold good in the case of Bengal. Therefore, it is proposed to revise the acreage statistics of all the crops by taking the

[1] Any increase or decrease of 10 per cent or upward in the acreage data of a year from those of the preceding year was accounted for in the *Agricultural Statistics of Bengal* (annual).

[2] This was also the belief of contemporaries. Thus Dr Rao commented that the campaign was 'being criticised all over the country both by economists as well as by laymen' and that the real increase under food crops brought about by this campaign was smaller than claimed by the Government. See his article, '"Grow More Food Policy" in India', *The Indian Journal of Agricultural Economics*, Vol. IV, No. 1 (March, 1949), p. 239.

findings of the Ishaque Report as point estimates. However, the trend rates of the official series on acreage and output are also measured and presented along with those of the revised data to facilitate comparison.

As already mentioned, Panse has argued that there was a tendency among the crop reporters to overestimate production in bad seasons and under-estimate it in good ones. Mukerji extends this thesis to the case of the acreage under cultivation and argues that 'the acreage of particular crops would have a tendency to be underreported when, for one reason or another, there is a tendency for acreage and production of that particular crop or particular group of crops to increase. Any measure of underestimation of crop acreage on the basis of the figures of a particular year is, therefore, not likely to provide one with a measure of under-reporting that can be used for correcting the officially published figures for crop output'.[1] It is not known how far this assumption is valid at the all-India level. But so far as Bengal is concerned the available evidence does not seem to substantiate the type of relationship suggested by Mukerji.[2] Thus, the difficulty seen by him in the way of the proposed revision does not seem to be genuine.

Such a difficulty may, however, be seen to arise from a different consideration. The acreage data show a good deal of fluctuations from year to year. This raises the question as to how far the predicted values of the departmental estimates for 1944/45 can be taken as a proxy for the actual estimates which would have been made had the Grow More Food Campaign not been launched and had the Plot to Plot Enumeration not been undertaken. If it is argued that such actual estimates would have been higher than the predicted values, it is clear that the discrepancies which are observed exaggerate the range of underestimation. The situation would be reversed if, on the other hand, it were argued that such values would have been lower than the predicted values. Obviously it is not possible to make any guess as to whether the actual estimates would have been lower or higher or fortuitously similar to the predicted values. But as a matter of fact these are, again, not genuine difficulties in the way of the proposed revision. The discrepancies observed between the findings of the Ishaque Report and the predicted values may exaggerate or underestimate the actual range of error in the official series, but under the proposed plan these are being uniformly distributed.

Technically, there are two problems which pose a real difficulty. Firstly, no allowance is being made for any seasonal fluctuations in the years for which different adjustment factors are being used, i.e. 1941/42 to 1943/44

[1] Mukerji, *op. cit.*, p. 21.
[2] See chapter 2, 3 and 4.

in the case of winter rice and 1942/43 and 1943/44 in the case of other crops excluding sugarcane and sesamum. Secondly, no account is being taken of any increase which may have been due to the Grow More Food Campaign and a run of favourable weather conditions. But it seems that the effect of these factors on the percentage rate of acreage change will be very marginal.

Before proceeding further to discuss the details of the planned revision, adjustments of the available data made by some authors will briefly be reviewed. It is convenient to start with the important work by Datta. He rejects the figures on acreage under cultivation, standard yield and condition factor as these had their origin in the guess work of the Chowkidars and revises the data in the light of the first-hand data which he and his assistants were able to obtain from their tours. Thus, Datta revises all three components of crop output. It seems that his assistants were neither the regular officials of the Agricultural Department nor residents of the locality for which they supplied the data. Therefore, it is reasonable to assume that they had much less familiarity with the agricultural conditions of the country than the usual crop reporters. Thus, it is difficult to see how statistics obtained by such enquiries could be any better than the ones submitted by the regular agencies. This is particularly so in view of the fact that the conditions of the great variety of crops, both with regard to acreage under cultivation and yield, differ so much between the different parts of the subcontinent.

Blyn's primary interest is in making adjustments for areas for which acreage or yield or both were not reported and in this respect his work is a significant contribution. But in doing so he also revises the yield figures of some crops for Madras, Bombay–Sind and United Province relating to certain years, as it appears to him that there is no real basis for the radical jump in the yield for those years. Therefore he assumes that the changes were due to differences in the government's crop estimation, and he raises (or lowers) the yield for all years up to the year of change by the percentage required to make the straight-line trend of that year equal to the straight-line trend in the following period projected back. There seems to be hardly any doubt about Blyn's basic assumption nor much objection against his method of correction as such. As already shown a more or less similar situation is noticed in Bengal in the early thirties when the crop-cutting experiments were transferred to the Department of Agriculture. It has also been argued that the quinquennial averages of yield which are expected to be free from the influence of seasonal fluctuations show considerable difference in many cases and that the explanation for this has to be sought mainly in the differences in the subjective judgement of the reporting agencies. But it seems that in building up a reliable estimate of crop output for the whole sub-continent it is not sufficient to correct the figures of one or two Provinces alone. For, apart from Madras and Bombay there are many other Provinces in which radical changes are noticed in the yield of particular quinquennia (Table 1.12). Obviously these changes are as much the result of changes in the government's crop estimation as observed by Blyn in Bombay-Sind, Madras and United Province. But he does not attempt any correction in such cases. Thus, his estimates of all-India crop output are only partially corrected.

Finally, the important work by Desai may be referred to. His method of correction of the available statistics is more straightforward and the coverage is once again very incomplete. For example, so far as Bengal is concerned, he finds that the three independent sources already referred to indicate, on average, an underestimation of 10 per cent in the acreage under the cultivation of rice and he, therefore, revises the data accordingly. It has already been pointed out that any direct comparison against the figures available from these three sources cannot be expected to reflect the real volume of error in the official data. On the other hand according to the procedure followed in this work it is quite clear that the margin of error is much bigger. Again, the underestimation in the acreage under the other crop of Bengal corrected by him – gram – is much larger than the twenty-five thousand acres which he adds to the officially published data. Desai does not change the yield per acre and the only adjustment in the official estimates of output is caused by the correction of the corresponding acreage data. But in the light

TABLE 1.12   *Fluctuations in the yield of certain crops in other provinces*

Crop (1)	Province (2)	Years (3)	Yield (lbs) (4)	Yield in next 5 years (lbs) (5)	(5) ÷ (4) %
Rice	Sind	1931–35	961	853	89
Rice	United Province	1936–40	628	556	88
Wheat	Central Province	1921–25	645	418	65
Jowar	Sind	1931–35	415	366	88
Barley	United Province	1931–35	919	785	85
Gram	United Province	1921–25	751	589	78
Gram	Central Province	1921–25	579	386	64
Sugarcane	Punjab	1936–40	1749	2425	139
Sugarcane	Bombay	1931–35	5906	4910	83
Sugarcane	Bombay	1936–40	4910	6960	142

Source: Blyn, *op. cit.*

of the evidence presented, to the effect that yield figures are generally over-estimated, it seems that this procedure is once again defective. The primary interest of Desai's work is in building up an estimate of consumer expenditure in the sub-continent. Therefore, in contrast with the present work, it is not the percentage rate of change but the estimation of the physical volume of crop output which is important. Considered in this context his method of correction and its coverage of only a few crops seems to be of considerable significance.

The details of the revision are as follows: acreage data on winter rice up to 1940/41, and those on net cropped area, double cropped area, current fallow, cultivable waste, summer rice, wheat, barley, gram, tobacco and mustard up to 1941/42 are revised according to the formula:

$$R_i = F_i\left(\frac{I}{P}\right) \tag{3}$$

where R = revised figures, F = official forecast figures, P = volume predicted by official estimates for 1944/45, I = figures from Ishaque Report and i = accounting year (1920/21 to 1940/41). The product of I/P is called the adjustment or revision factor. Thus, if the acreage under the cultivation of a crop for a particular year, say 1920, was 1800 acres, the predicted values for 1944/45 2000 acres and the corresponding figure from the Ishaque Report 2300 acres, the revised data would be:

$$2070 = 1800\left(\frac{2300}{2000}\right) \tag{4}$$

with an adjustment factor of 1.15.

The formula used for the period 1941/42 to 1943/44 is as follows:

$$R_i^\star = F_i^\star\left(\frac{P_i^\star \dfrac{I}{P}}{F_i^\star}\right) \tag{5}$$

where R_i^* = revised figure for the year i, F_i^* = forecast figure for the year i and P_i^* = predicted value for the year i. In other words this means that the forecast values are replaced by the product of the predicted values and the adjustment factor. Thus, if the predicted value of the acreage under the cultivation of a crop in 1941/42 is 1980 acres, the corresponding forecast figure 2100 acres and the other values remain the same as in the previous example the revised value is obtained as follows:

$$2277 = 2100\left(\frac{1980 \times \dfrac{2300}{2000}}{2100}\right) \tag{6}$$

The procedures followed in the case of autumn rice, jute, sugarcane and sesamum are slightly different. As already pointed out the Agricultural Department published their own estimates of the acreage under autumn rice for 1944/45 and when comparison is made with findings of the Ishaque Report the statistics of the Agricultural Department are found to be considerably overestimated. On the other hand the predicted values are considerably lower. That the departmental figures up to 1940/41 are underestimates has also been shown by comparing these with the figures available from the Settlement Reports. In view of these considerations the revision factors for the period up to 1940/41 are obtained, as in the case of other crops, by dividing the findings of the Ishaque Report by the predicted values, despite the fact that the actual official estimates for 1944/45 are available. No revision is attempted in the case of acreage data for 1941/42 and 1942/43 as these are more or less similar to the product of the predicted values and the revision factors. On the other hand, the departmental estimates for 1943/44 and 1944/45 are similar and these have been brought down to the level of the findings of the Ishaque Report.

For jute it has been shown that the official estimates of production are always underestimated but the range of underestimation is not uniform over all the quinquennial periods (Table 1.13). Thus, the range of error is largest in the third quinquennium and this may be due to the fact that the departmental propaganda for the voluntary restriction of jute cultivation during the depression years was not as successful as was supposed. On the other hand this volume is smallest during the last five years when the acreage under jute cultivation was statutorily regulated. In view of these, no single revision factor has been used for the entire period. Instead, the quinquennial averages of acreage have been marked up on the basis of the discrepancy found between the official estimates of jute production and the 'actual' production as ascertained from trade statistics. It is clear that this procedure does not take care of the entire range of error in the acreage data because there is considerable overestimation in the figures on the yield per acre.

TABLE 1.13 *Estimated jute production compared with 'actuals'*

Years	Estimated production as a percentage of 'actuals'
1920–24	79
1925–29	93
1931–35	75
1935–40	84
1941–45	91

In the case of sugarcane no significant upward movement is noticed in the acreage statistics from 1941/42 to 1944/45, for which departmental estimates are available. But there is one consideration which apparently makes it difficult to assume a uniform margin of error over the entire period. As the Great Depression set in, propaganda was launched for the extension of the acreage under sugarcane. This coincided with a sudden increase in the official estimate of sugarcane acreage beginning from 1931/32. This may raise doubt as to the reliability of the full increase thus shown. But there are at least two factors which make it reasonable to believe that there actually was some increase in the cultivation of this crop. These were the boosts given to the sugar industry by the grant of protection since 1928 and the distribution of an improved variety of seeds. For these reasons acreage under sugarcane has been uniformly deflated on the basis of the overestimation found by comparing the officially published data against the findings of the Ishaque Report.

A similar procedure is followed in the case of sesamum. This is due to the fact that the departmental estimates for 1944/45 are available. Secondly, in contrast with other crops, an upward movement in the acreage series is noticed from 1943/44. Acreage figures for sugarcane and sesamum for 1945/46 were not revised in the light of the data available from the Ishaque Report. These are, therefore, corrected on the assumption that the margin of error is the same as in 1944/45.

Data on the yield per acre of the different crops raise more complicated problems. This is because, as already pointed out, yield depends on a larger number of factors than does acreage under cultivation. The most important of these is rainfall. But yield does not depend only on the quantum of rainfall, but on its proper seasonal distribution. Secondly, the Department of Agriculture devoted most of its resources to the distribution of the improved variety of seeds evolved at the departmental experimental centres. It was claimed that these seeds could raise productivity by 25 per cent. By the late thirties almost the whole of the acreage under sugarcane and a considerable area under jute were being sown with these seeds. On the other hand, critics pointed out that the new seeds were tested only in the better soils and thus felt sceptical about the reliability of the yield differentials between the traditional and the new seeds as worked out by the Agricultural Department. These considerations make it very difficult to guess the variations in yield over the quinquennial periods. Ideally, a multiple regression with the known variables relating to yield might be attempted. But the volume of calculation which would be involved in working out the yield of thirteen crops grown in 27 districts over a period of 26 years is beyond the scope of the present work. Moreover, data are available only on rainfall and price and partly on the new seeds distributed. Further, independent estimates on yield are available for only three crops – winter rice, autumn rice and jute. In view of these difficulties no independent revision of the official data on yield has been attempted. Instead, output of the crops have been revised on the same basis as in acreage statistics.

1.7 SOURCES OF DATA AND MINOR ADJUSTMENTS

All the statistics on the acreage under the cultivation of different crops and the areas designated as net cropped area, double cropped area, current fallow and cultivable waste are obtained from the *Season and Crop Reports.* Issued annually by the Government of Bengal Department of Agriculture, this was the basic publication on all agricultural statistics. The *Season and Crop Reports* were published immediately after the final forecasts and included figures available from these forecasts. Acreage statistics are available also from the *Agricultural Statistics of Bengal,* another annual publication of the Department of Agriculture. This was a later publication and the idea was to make available the crop statistics in their final form, i.e. after any revision made to the final forecast figures. But on inspection it is found that the data available from these two publications are identical except in only a few cases. Therefore, no adjustment has been made in the data collected from the *Season and Crop Reports.* The *Agricultural Statistics* also contained crop data available from the cadastral surveys (whether completed or in progress) and explanation for any major variation in the crop statistics of the current year from those of the preceding year. Data on the seasonal condition of the current yield per acre of the different crops are available only from the *Season and Crop Reports.* Figures on standard yields are obtained from the *Reports on the Results of the Quinquennial Crop-cutting Experiments.* These are available also from the *Estimates of Area and Yields of Principal Crops in India.* Data on standard yields for the last quinquennium are taken from the *Calcutta Gazette.*

In some cases, however, figures on condition factors were not published for particular districts. In such cases data available for the district in the previous year has been expressed as a percentage of the provincial average and this relationship has been assumed to hold good in the year for which such data were not published. In the case of barley no data either on standard yield or condition factor was published. Total output figures are, therefore, obtained from the *Estimates* and the yield per acre is assumed to be the same in all the districts where barley was grown. This procedure is followed also in the case of summer rice as no data on the condition factor and only some data on the standard yield were published. In the case of tobacco no data on the standard yield was published before the quinquennium beginning 1927/28. Yield per acre for these years (i.e. from 1920/21 to 1926/27) has been assumed to be the same for all the districts. Regional variations in the trend rates of the output and yield per acre of tobacco have to be interpreted with reference to this limitation.

1.8 CLASSIFICATION OF CROPS

Crops could be classified in different ways. A division between food crops and non-food crops would place all the crops except tea, tobacco and jute in the former category. Therefore, such a classification does not seem to be meaningful. George Blyn divides crops between foodgrains and non-foodgrains. But this mode of classification is also defective as it describes crops such as sugarcane, tobacco, jute and tea as grains. A classification between commercial and non-commercial crops would show whether market forces had a favourable impact on the output of certain crops. But the problem in such a categorisation is that except for tea and jute no crops are fully commercial or non-commercial. This is clear from the following estimates of the 'gross village retention' of the major crops of India.[1] Rice, 59%; wheat, 49%; barley, 71%; gram, 55%; sugarcane, 13%; tobacco, 7%; linseed, 20%; rape, mustard and sesamum, 5 to 10%.

Thus, it is clear that since a substantial portion of their output is sold in the market, it will not be desirable to categorise rice (in our case the three varieties of winter, autumn and summer rice), wheat, barley and gram as non-commercial crops. Therefore, in the present study these crops are grouped as food crops. As pointed out earlier, linseed, sesamum, rape and mustard, and sugarcane should be categorised as food crops. But since only a small portion of the output of these crops was retained by the farmers, along with tea, tobacco and jute, these crops are classified as cash crops.

1.9 AGGREGATION OF CROP OUTPUT

For the purpose of aggregation, the physical volume of output of every crop is weighted by its price as these are the best indicators of the relative importance of particular crops. Prices are available both at the village and at the wholesale level. But for the present purpose, use is made of the harvest prices as these are supposed to be prices paid to the growers. The selection of base years, the prices of which would best reflect the relative importance of the different crops, does not seem to be very difficult. For obvious reasons the prices of the depression years and the famine years of 1940s cannot be used for the present purpose. Only the prices of the period from 1924 to 1929 may be regarded as normal.[2] Therefore, the averages of the prices of these years are used as weights.

---

[1] Blyn, *op. cit.*, p. 79.
[2] Bowley and Robertson, *op. cit.*, p. 44.

1.10 MEASUREMENT OF TREND RATES AND THEIR PRESENTATION

The trend rates of both the revised and unrevised series are derived by fitting exponential equations of the type $\log y = a + bt$ over the entire period. This, however, does not indicate variations within the shorter segments of time. In order to obviate this difficulty the data on output, acreage and yield per acre have been converted into index numbers. These are presented as five quinquennial averages to facilitate comparison. These quinquennial divisions broadly correspond to the five periods which in themselves are well demarcated from each other by certain special features. Thus, the post-war recovery may be said to have started in the first period (1920–24) and this reaches its peak in the second (1925–29). The third period from 1930 to 1934 roughly corresponds to the depression years and the fourth (1935–39) to the years of relative recovery. Finally, the last period, from 1940 to 1944, witnesses the Bengal famine and the consequent steep increase in the price level. This is also the period when the upward movements in the acreage statistics are noticed. So the proposed procedure may be said to have the added advantage of focusing attention on the response of different crops to the changed circumstances.

Data on the three components of crop output are available for the districts (27 in all) in which such crops were grown. Since the purpose in the present study is not only to examine the trend rates of output, yield per acre and acreage under cultivation at the all-Bengal level, but also to give an idea about the regional variations within Bengal, the districts should ideally be taken as the regional units. But in view of the complexity and bulk of work such a procedure would involve this is not attempted. Instead, output and acreage under the cultivation of individual crops for all the districts under a Division have been added up and trend rates measured.[1] The rates of change, however, have to be interpreted with reference to the percentage distribution of the output and acreage of the different Divisions or Regions. Therefore these are presented in the respective tables.

Growth of population provides a useful criterion on which to judge whether the trend rates are low or high. Therefore, the percentage rates of change in output and acreage of food-crops, cash crops and all-crops are compared with the growth of population. Variations over the successive quinquennial periods are indicated by the change in the index of the ratios between population and crop output. Such a comparison is not, however, an entirely satisfactory procedure in view of the fact that per capita availability

---

[1] There are some discrepancies in the all-Bengal output figures calculated in this work and those published in the *Estimates of Area and Yields of Principal Crops in India, op. cit.*

depends not only on net crop output (total output – seed requirements, livestock consumption, wastage, etc.), but also on net import (i.e. export – import). Therefore, an attempt has been made to estimate the per capita availability of foodgrains during the period under review.

2

TRENDS IN OUTPUT, ACREAGE AND YIELD: ALL-CROPS, FOOD CROPS AND CASH CROPS

In the preceding chapter it was shown that the officially published data on acreage under cultivation are mostly underestimates and those on yield per acre overestimates. Also discussed was how the revision of the official figures on acreage in the light of the data available from the Ishaque Report (1944/ 45) is likely to provide more reliable estimates of the agricultural trends in Bengal. The purpose of the present chapter is to analyse the percentage rates of change in crop output in the two series and their determinants – acreage and yield per acre. Trend rates of other provinces are also presented to indicate the comparative position of Bengal and, thus, to emphasise the greater rationality of the trends in the revised series. In order to bring out more clearly how the change in output, both at the provincial and regional level, was being influenced by the trends in acreage and yield, the three variables – output, acreage and yield – should be discussed simultaneously. But clearly such a mode of presentation would make the analysis more complicated than is desirable. Therefore, the percentage rates of change in the three items are presented separately. This is done first for all-Bengal and then individually for the five regions. The emphasis of the present chapter is on all the 13 crops taken together and then on the two groups of food crops and cash crops, though occasional references are made to some of the individual crops as well. In order to facilitate the interpretation of the differences in the percentage rates of change at the regional level the relative importance of these groups of crops in each region is also indicated. The analysis of the trends is followed by a discussion of the conceivable explanations for the contrast between the yields of food crops and cash crops.

2.1 ALL-BENGAL TRENDS IN ALL-CROP OUTPUT AND GROWTH OF POPULATION

Percentage rates of change in the production of all crops taken together are presented in Table 2.1 along with those of the other provinces of British India as estimated by Blyn.[1] During the period as a whole the provincial rate of

[1] George Blyn, *Agricultural Trends in India, 1891–1947: Output, Availability and Productivity* (University of Pennsylvania Press, 1966). Trend rates refer to the last four Reference Decades.

TABLE 2.1   *Trends in all-crop output*
1920–46

Regions	Annual rates of increase			
	Unrevised series	Revised series	Population	% of total output
All-Bengal	0.9	0.3	0.8	100
Presidency	2.0	1.1	1.2	15
Burdwan	0.0	−1.0	0.8	14
Rajshahi	1.4	0.5	0.3	29
Dacca	0.8	0.4	0.9	31
Chittagong	−0.2	−0.7	1.3	12
British India	0.4			
Madras	0.4			
Greater Bengal	−0.2			
Punjab	1.3			
United Province	0.3			
Central Province	−0.6			
Bombay–Sind	0.8			

Note: Blyn's estimates are presented in the lower half of the table: see Blyn, *op. cit.*, p. 119.

increase was not only much higher than in any other province (except the Punjab) but it also exceeded the growth of population. However, the picture that emerges in the revised series is completely different. Bengal is left with the lowest rate of expansion in the sub-continent and as a result the disparity between crop production and the growth of population becomes very marked. However, it may be mentioned here that even after this downward adjustment the growth rate remains much higher than in 'Greater Bengal' as estimated by Blyn. This shows that the inclusion of Bihar and Orissa has considerably affected the rate of increase for Bengal proper.

As to the trends in the quinquennial periods (Table 2.2) two main features may be pointed out. The rate of increase gradually slowed down during the first 20 years and this was followed by some acceleration in the last five years. The turning point in this respect, as already pointed out, came in 1941/42 when the acreage data started to be revised by the Agricultural Department. This increase in the volume of output does not, however, reflect the entire range of upward revision of the acreage data as there was a considerable drop in yield per acre during these years. Secondly, it seems that the Great Depression did not have any adverse impact on the level of crop production in Bengal. The volume of production continued to increase despite a sharp fall

TABLE 2.2 *Index of all-crop output in the quinquennia*
(1920/21 to 1922/23 = 100)

Regions	1920–24	1925–29	1930–34	1935–39	1940–44
All-Bengal	98(98)	104(100)	109(105)	113(109)	120(101)
Presidency	99(99)	104(101)	112(110)	115(114)	153(126)
Burdwan	92(92)	80(77)	88(84)	88(86)	85(69)
Rajshahi	100(100)	114(107)	123(116)	125(117)	136(108)
Dacca	101(101)	113(112)	115(111)	125(122)	122(108)
Chittagong	98(98)	96(93)	91(89)	92(91)	96(83)

Note: Figures in the brackets refer to the revised series. No adjustment has been made in the output or acreage figures for winter rice and autumn rice before 1939–40 for the revision of the corresponding figures on jute. This would not make any significant difference as the weight of this latter crop was too small compared to the combined weight of these two varieties of rice.

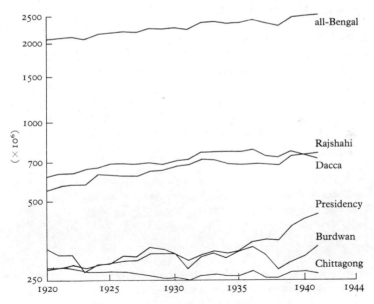

FIGURE 2.1 *All-crop output (official series), five years' moving average (log scale; output in arbitrary units, weighted by price)*

in the price level.[1] However, as shown later, this trend was not true to both of the two groups of crops. The revised series indicates a slight acceleration in the rate of expansion during the first 15 years and a slight drop in the fourth period. The trend is then reversed and as a result the volume of production during the last five years stands at about the level of the base period.

The trends of crop output per capita in the quinquennial periods reveal an important aspect of the agricultural economy of the province (Table 2.3). The volume of per capita crop production seems to have remained more or less constant, at the level of the base period, in all the successive quinquennia. Evidently this implies that the rate of growth in crop-production and population was the same for all the five periods. The same balance, though at a slightly lower level than in the base period, is noticed in the revised series up to the year 1939/40. Then, as expected, the balance is lost during the last five years when per capita all-crop output shows a decline of 15 per cent from the level of the base period.

2.2 REGIONAL ALL-CROP OUTPUT AND POPULATION GROWTH

The picture that emerges at the regional level is important as this shows that the provincial rate of expansion was representative of only one region – Dacca – which accounted for nearly one third of the all-crop production (Table 2.1). The four other regions belonged to two opposite extremes. Thus, in Rajshahi and Presidency Divisions the growth rate was considerably higher. But so far as the total picture is concerned these were almost wholly cancelled out by the stagnation in Burdwan and a slight decline in Chittagong. In the revised series the growth rate still remains higher in Presidency

TABLE 2.3 *Index of per capita all-crop output in the quinquennia*
(1920/21 to 1922/23 = 100)

Regions	1920–24	1925–29	1930–34	1935–39	1940–44
All-Bengal	98(98)	100(96)	100(96)	100(96)	101(85)
Presidency	99(99)	100(97)	103(101)	98(97)	121(100)
Burdwan	91(91)	77(74)	81(78)	79(77)	72(59)
Rajshahi	100(100)	112(105)	119(112)	119(112)	126(100)
Dacca	100(100)	108(107)	106(102)	110(107)	102(91)
Chittagong	97(97)	89(86)	79(77)	75(74)	74(64)

Note: Estimates based on the revised series are shown within brackets.

[1] This behaviour of the total volume of production during the depression years is explained in Chapter 4.

Division. But in Rajshahi and Dacca these rates are reduced respectively by one third and half. The most marked change, however, takes place in Chittagong and Burdwan, though in different directions. With regard to the relative growth of population and crop production it is clear that even in the revised series the position remains by far the best in Rajshahi and Presidency Divisions. An extreme case is presented by Burdwan which shows an annual decline of 1.0 per cent in crop production as against a growth of population at a rate of 0.8 per cent per year.

In Raishahi and Presidency Divisions the trends in all the successive quinquennia were the same as indicated by the provincial average. Dacca differed from this pattern only to the extent that there was a slight drop in output during the last five years. The two other regions had a negative trend in the second quinquennium. In Chittagong this drop continued up to the close of the depression period. This was followed by expansion at an increasingly higher rate during the last ten years. In the revised series the regional picture remains broadly the same as indicated by the provincial average. The only exceptions are noticed in the Presidency Division in the last quinquennium and Burdwan and Dacca in the third. Thus, to emphasise the trends of production during the depression years, at the regional level it is only in Dacca in the revised series and Chittagong in both series that output seems to have declined slightly.

As to the level of per capita crop production and its trend in the quinquennial periods the five regions fall under two groups. Thus, in Presidency and Rajshahi Divisions there was some improvement in food production during the first three and the last quinquennia. Dacca resembled Rajshahi in that crop production always exceeded the growth of population, though there was some drop in the third and the last quinquennia. The two other regions present a completely different picture. As already noted, fairly high rates of population growth were accompanied by stagnation and decline in crop production respectively in Burdwan and Chittagong and as a result the disparity became more and more marked. The position further deteriorates in the revised series, while in Rajshahi and Presidency Divisions crop output remained at the level of the base period.

2.3 ALL-BENGAL TRENDS IN FOOD CROP OUTPUT AND POPULATION GROWTH

Food crops accounted for 70 per cent of the total crop output and the average increase of 0.7 per cent per year (Table 2.4) considerably affected the trend in the latter. Changes effected by the revision of statistics are more marked when food crops are distinguished from cash crops. During the period as a whole

TABLE 2.4   *Trends in food crop output*
1920–46

Regions	Annual rates of increase			
	Unrevised series	Revised series	Population	Percentage distribution of output
All-Bengal	0.7	0.0	0.8	100
Presidency	1.8	1.0	1.2	17
Burdwan	−0.1	−1.0	0.8	18
Rajshahi	1.0	−0.1	0.3	23
Dacca	0.8	0.5	0.9	29
Chittagong	−0.3	−0.9	1.3	13
British India	0.03			
Greater Bengal	−0.6			
Punjab	0.9			
United Province	−0.2			
Central Province	−0.2			
Madras	−0.2			
Bombay–Sind	0.4			

Source: For Blyn's estimates presented in the lower half of the Table see Blyn, *op. cit.*, p. 99.

food production remained stagnant as against an annual growth of 0.8 per cent in population. But, as in the case of all-crop production, this seems to be more in line with the experience in most of the other provinces. This strengthens the belief that, subject to the limitations of the yield figures, the revised series presents a more reliable picture of the agricultural trends of Bengal.

As to the quinquennial trends in the official series, it is only in the second period that food crop output slightly declined (Table 2.5). In the other quin-

TABLE 2.5   *Index of food crop output in the quinquennia*
(1920/21 to 1922/23 = 100)

Regions	1920–24	1925–29	1930–34	1935–39	1940–44
All-Bengal	94	88	96	99	106(91)
Presidency	97	92	105	107	139(116)
Burdwan	92	79	86	88	83(68)
Rajshahi	94	92	106	105	111(88)
Dacca	94	93	99	107	110(103)
Chittagong	94	81	82	81	85(76)

Note: Revised estimates are shown in brackets.

quennial periods the volume of production increased. But there were considerable differences in the rates of increase. Thus, while the rate of expansion of the output of food crops during the fourth quinquennium was marginal, it was somewhat marked in the third and the fifth quinquennia. These trends in the production of food crops during the first 15 years seem to have been mainly due to the shifts in the production of cash crops caused by changes in market conditions. As shown in Section 2.6, the production of commercial crops registered a sharp increase during the first decade, but it declined slightly during the depression years. The substitution between the two groups of crops seems to have come to an end during the fourth quinquennium.

The volume of output during the last five years for the first time exceeded the level of the base period. Although there was, thus, a seemingly general increase in production according to official statistics, Bengal was in the grip of a severe famine during these years. This apparent contradiction seems to have escaped the attention of the official compilers of statistics. The picture that emerges in the revised series is completely different. For the province as a whole foodcrop output during these years stands at a level which is 9 per cent lower than in the base period. Almost the whole of this drop is due to the reduction in the output of winter and autumn rice caused by the revision of statistics.

The disparity between the growth of population and food production started at the outset of the period under review (Table 2.6) and the gap continued to widen later on except for a marginal improvement during the depression years. The rate of decline was the most marked during the last five years when per capita food production reached a level which was 25 per cent lower than in the base period.

At this stage it will be quite legitimate to ask whether the decline in per capita food production really meant a drop in per capita availability. Evidently this question calls for an attempt to estimate the net quantity of food crops available for consumption, i.e. total output − seed requirements − waste −

TABLE 2.6 *Index of per capita food production in the quinquennia*
(1920/21 to 1922/23 = 100)

Regions	1920−24	1925−29	1930−34	1935−39	1940−44
All-Bengal	93	84	89	87	89(76)
Presidency	96	89	97	91	110(92)
Burdwan	91	75	79	78	71(58)
Rajshahi	94	90	103	100	102(81)
Dacca	94	89	91	94	92(86)
Chittagong	93	75	71	66	65(58)

Note: Figures in brackets refer to the revised series.

livestock consumption + imports. The proportion of paddy required for seeds may be estimated on the basis of the acreage under food crops. However, since our purpose is to estimate the trends rather than the actual quantity available per capita and since there was no significant expansion of acreage under cultivation, it may be assumed that this proportion remained more or less constant over time. The proportion of food crops wasted in storage and required for livestock consumption has been estimated by different organisations.[1] But it is not known whether this proportion increased during the period under review and, if so, to what extent. Therefore, no deduction from the total output is possible on these grounds. Thus, the issue that needs to be resolved is whether trade with foreign countries and other provinces made any significant change in the gross quantity of food crops available for per capita consumption.

Statistics on the trade in rice (as also gram, wheat and barley) with foreign countries and other Indian ports are available for the entire period. But the data on the trade through land frontiers with Assam, Bihar, Orissa and United Province are available only from 1925/26. On the other hand, no data is available on the trade by river and train. On the basis of these data it seems that during the 15 years from 1927/28 imports exceeded exports, but the net import amounted to only four per cent of the total domestic supply in the official series and three per cent in the revised series. During the last four years (1942/43–1945/46) there was a sudden drop in net imports, which amounted to less than one per cent of the total output.

According to the calculations of the Famine Enquiry Commission,[2] during the five years from 1927/28 exports exceeded imports, but net exports accounted for only 2.1 per cent of total output in the official series and 1.6 per cent in the revised series. During the next ten years (i.e. up to 1941/42) there was a net import of 1.1 million tons per year which amounted to only 1.4 per cent of the domestic supply in the official series and 1.1 per cent in the revised series.

Thus, though there are discrepancies in the details of the statistics available from the two sources, two points clearly emerge from them. Firstly, Bengal became a net importer of rice, at least from the beginning of the 1930s. Secondly, the quantity of net imports did not, however, constitute a significant proportion of the total available food crops. Rice was the most important food crop. Therefore, on the basis of the available data it may be safely concluded that net external supply did not significantly contribute towards narrowing the gap between the supply of foodgrains and the growth of population.

---

[1] See, for example, Food and Agricultural Organisation, *Destruction of Food in Storage by Insects, Mites, Rodents and Mold Fungi: Report of Expert Committee, 1946*.

[2] Famine Enquiry Commission, *Report on Bengal* (Calcutta, 1944).

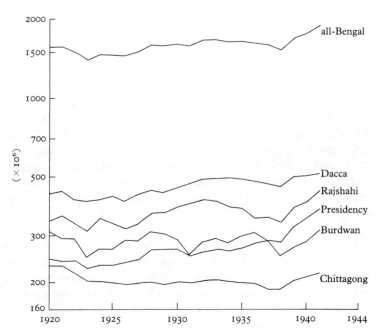

FIGURE 2.2   *Food crop output (official series), five years' moving average (log scale; output in arbitrary units, weighted by price).*

2.4 REGIONAL TRENDS IN FOOD CROP OUTPUT AND POPULATION GROWTH

At the regional level the provincial rate of increase of food crop output was representative of only Dacca Division (Table 2.4). Among the four other regions the rate was slightly higher in Rajshahi and much higher in Presidency Division. The annual rate of decline in Burdwan and Chittagong was not high, but as these two regions accounted for nearly one third of total food production this considerably depressed the provincial rate of expansion. The nature of change effected by the revision of statistics in the regional trend rates is more or less the same as in all-crop output and this is obviously due to the overwhelming importance of these crops in the total crop-mix. These variations in the trend rates of the different regions raise a number of important questions, but an attempt can best be made to explain them only after discussion of the two determinants of crop output – acreage and yield of individual crops. It may, however, be pointed out at this stage that these variations were not necessarily caused by the difference in the relative importance of these crops in each region.

In all the five regions the quinquennial trend up to 1934/35 was the same as indicated by the provincial average – a drop in the second period was followed by expansion in the third. It may, however, be pointed out that in Burdwan and Chittagong the drop was more marked than in the other regions. This similarity continued during the depression years when the index improved only marginally. During the post-depression years the five regions belonged to opposite extremes. In Chittagong and Dacca production declined slightly but in the other regions the improvement continued. This implies that the end of substitution between commercial and food crop output in this period indicated by the provincial average was representative of only three regions. In the revised series the drop in the index in Rajshahi and Burdwan is more marked than in the other regions.

At the regional level the unfavourable disparity between food production and population growth started, as indicated by the provincial average, at the beginning of the period under review (Table 2.6). But so far as the relative position in the subsequent quinquennia is concerned the three regions of Burdwan, Chittagong and Rajshahi merit particular attention as these belonged to opposite extremes. Thus in Rajshahi the disparity came to an end during the depression years. But, as expected from the high growth of population as against a decline in production, in Chittagong the disparity became more and more marked. The position in Burdwan was more or less the same except for the third quinquennium. To emphasise the level of per capita food production in the revised series it is clear that the all-Bengal picture during the last five years was not characteristic of any of the five regions.

A thorough investigation of the economic roots of the great famine of 1943 is outside the scope of this work.[1] However, some general comments may be made in the light of our findings on the trends in the per capita availability of food crops. On the basis of available data it has been shown that net imports constituted a small fraction of domestic output. Therefore, the stoppage of imports from other Indian ports and from Burma can not be said to have been an important factor behind the famine. At first sight this would suggest that the famine was caused by a decline in the level of domestic production. But a closer scrutiny suggests that this is not the whole truth. This is because even the decline in the per capita availability of food crops as indicated by the revised series does not fully explain the sharp rise in the price level during the last quinquennium. On the other hand, if we proceed on the basis of the

---

[1] The effects of the famine are examined by P. C. Mahalonobis, 'A Sample Survey of the After-Effects of the Bengal Famine of 1943', *Sankhya: Indian Journal of Statistics*, Vol. 7, Part 4 (1946); *Famine Commission Report*, op. cit., Part 2, chapters one and two.

picture that emerges in the official series it seems that there should not have been any significant increase in prices.

The investigation of the Famine Enquiry Commission proceeded on the basis of a different set of data. But the Commission came to a similar conclusion regarding the causes of the famine. According to the findings of the Commission the supply situation in 1943 was worse than in any of the preceding years. This was attributed to two main factors: (*a*) a poor harvest of winter rice and (*b*) a shortage of rice stocks (because of the poor harvest in 1940/41). It was estimated that as a result of all these factors the total supply in 1943 was sufficient for 49 weeks.[1] However, it was asserted by the Commission that supply was not so bad as to make starvation on a large scale inevitable[2] – only a moderate increase in the price level would have been justified.

Thus, as concluded by the Famine Enquiry Commission, it seems that the main cause of the famine of 1943 has to be sought in the factors which affected the level of the demand for and the supply of rice in 1943. In other words, we should also take into account the series of inter-connected events which occurred at the end of 1942 and the beginning of 1943 and the impact of those events on all classes of people in the province – merchants, traders, producers, sellers and buyers of food crops.

The danger of large-scale Japanese attack led the military authorities of India to put into operation in 1942 a 'denial' policy which involved two measures of far-reaching consequences. Firstly, it was decided to take from the coastal districts of Midnapore, Bakerganj and Khulna the rice which was estimated to be in excess of local requirements. Secondly, the government decided to remove all boats (carrying 10 passengers or more) from those parts of Bengal which were considered vulnerable to Japanese attack.[3] These measures brought home to the people the danger of invasion and created uncertainty and nervousness. This, in turn, produced an adverse impact on the level of the marketed surplus of rice and its demand. On the one hand, the prevailing fear and uncertainty probably encouraged the surplus producers to hold on to their grain as an insurance against worse days to come. Similarly, since the price was increasing the merchants and traders (as also many producers) are likely to have been encouraged to hold on to their stocks. On the other hand, it is very likely that the section of the people who depended on the market for

---

[1] *Famine Commission Report*, *op. cit.* p. 15. The Commission adjusted the figure by adding 20% to the figure given by the Director of Agriculture, See Appendix II, p. 215.

[2] One member of the Commission, Mr M. Afzal Hussain, believed that the shortage in total supply was the primary cause of the famine. He argued that for two thirds of the population 'so delicate was the balance between actual starvation and bare subsistence that the slightest tilting of the scale in the value and supply of food was enough to put it out of the reach of many and to bring large classes within the range of famine'. See *ibid.*, p. 16.

[3] *Ibid.*, pp. 25–7.

the whole or a part of their requirements tried to buy more than their immediate requirements. The pressure of demand on the available supply was also increasing due to the fact that larger and larger numbers were being employed in industry and construction, refugees were flowing in from Burma and there was the demand for food for the army.

Thus the situation in Bengal in 1942 and 1943 was such that there was a shortage in the supply for food crops at a time when demand was increasing. Since the level of production was a little lower there would have been a slight reduction in the volume of the marketed surplus of rice. But the problem was aggravated by the dislocation of the normal channels of distribution of available supplies and a tendency on the part of the producers, consumers and traders to hoard food crops. The course of events during 1942 led them to believe that an ever-increasing rise in prices was inevitable and could not be prevented. The effect of the prevailing fear and uncertainty as well as the profit motive was that a little drop in the level of production had disproportionate consequences.[1] In view of the non-availability of reliable data it is very difficult to draw firm conclusions regarding the roots of the famine of 1943. However, if we proceed on the basis of available evidence it seems that the famine was 'more man-made than an act of god'.[2]

Before concluding this section it may be asked how, if people were at subsistence level in the past they multiplied at a fast rate while the per capita availability of food crops was declining. This raises the wider and much discussed question about the interrelationship between population growth and food production. According to the well-known view of Malthus and his followers population growth is the dependent variable, determined by preceding changes in agricultural productivity which, in turn, is the result of extraneous factors. The other extreme view on this question is that the main line of causality is in the opposite direction. Population growth is the independent variable which, in turn, is a major factor determining agricultural developments. According to this view population explosion is a change in basic conditions which must be regarded as autonomous – in the sense that its explanation should not be sought in increases in food production, but in medical inventions and other factors.[3]

Evidently the picture that emerges in this study on the trends in the per

---

[1] This was also the view of Sir T. Rutherford. For details see his memorandum to the Marquees of Linlithgow in N. Mansergh (ed.), *The Transfer of Power 1942–7*, Vol. IV: *The Bengal Famine and the New Viceroyalty* (London, 1973), pp. 361–5.

[2] Opinion of the Bengal Congress Parliamentary Party cited by B. M. Bhatia, *Famines in India* (Bombay, 1963), p. 321.

[3] A strong advocate of this view is E. Boserup. For details see his *The Conditions of Agricultural Growth* (London, 1965). For a general discussion on population theories see, UNO, *The Determinants and Consequences of Population Trends* (New York, 1973), Vol. I, Chapter III.

capita availability of food crops in Bengal conforms to this second view on the interrelationship between food production and population growth. It is beyond the scope of this work to pass any judgement on the validity of either of these two views. However, it is significant that the experience in Bengal was similar to that in other provinces of British India and some underdeveloped countries.[1] Thus, it becomes very difficult to dismiss the view that population growth is independent of the improvement in food production.

2.5 ALL-BENGAL TREND IN CASH CROP OUTPUT AND POPULATION GROWTH

Trend rates in cash crop production present a very different picture (Table 2.7). For the period as a whole the rate of expansion was double the growth in population. However, as this group of crops accounted for only 30 per cent of

TABLE 2.7 *Trends in cash crop output*
1920–46

Regions	Average annual rate of increase			
	Unrevised series	Revised series	Population	Percentage distribution of the crops
All-Bengal	1.5	1.3	0.8	100
Presidency	3.0	2.7	1.2	8
Burdwan	0.6	0.7	0.8	3
Rajshahi	1.9	1.9	0.3	43
Dacca	0.8	0.5	0.9	37
Chittagong	0.5	−0.2	1.3	9
British India	1.1			
Greater Bengal	0.6			
Punjab	1.8			
United Province	1.4			
Central Province	−0.8			
Madras	1.3			
Bombay–Sind	1.8			

Source: For Blyn's estimates presented in the lower half of the table see Blyn, *op. cit.*, p. 112.

[1] During 1911–41 per capita food crop availability in British India declined by 26 or 0.83% per year. For details see Blyn, *op. cit.*, pp. 106–7. In Bangladesh per capita availability of food crops declined during the period from 1950/51 to 1962/63. For details see. M. Alamgir and L. J. J. B. Berlage, 'Foodgrain (Rice and Wheat) Demand, Import and Price Policy for Bangladesh', *The Bangladesh Economic Review*, Vol. 1, No. 1 (1973) Table 1. See also, UNO *op. cit.*, Chapter XII.

the all-crop output this higher rate did not much improve the overall growth in food production. Secondly, the change effected by the revision of statistics is much less marked and as a result the contrast between the trends in the two groups of crops becomes more marked in the revised series. It is also significant that this rate of increase still remains higher than in British India or 'Greater Bengal'.

Two main observations may be made with regard to trends in the quinquennial periods (Table 2.8). The rate of expansion was accelerating during

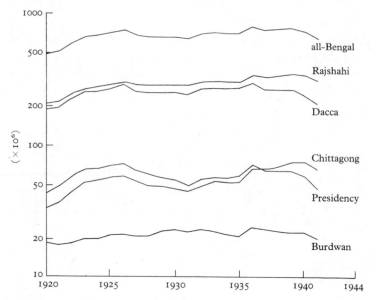

FIGURE 2.3   *Cash crop output (official series), five years' moving average (log scale; output in arbitrary units, weighted by price).*

TABLE 2.8   *Index of cash crop output in the quinquennia*
(1920/21 to 1922/23 = 100)

Regions	1920–24	1925–29	1930–34	1935–39	1940–44
All-Bengal	116(120)	168(166)	158(151)	167(164)	176(155)
Presidency	120(122)	209(198)	169(159)	192(186)	273(230)
Burdwan	92(91)	105(103)	116(113)	104(102)	111(105)
Rajshahi	112(115)	157(154)	155(147)	163(156)	184(173)
Dacca	121(125)	173(169)	163(153)	178(169)	158(125)
Chittagong	126(127)	205(190)	160(151)	173(171)	172(142)

Note: Revised estimates are shown in brackets.

the first 10 years and slowing down during the last ten. As already mentioned this drop in the rate of expansion was due to the end of substitution between food and cash crops. Secondly, as referred to earlier, changes in market conditions seem to have been the most important factor in determining the trends in the different quinquennia. Thus, it is clear that while there was a marked acceleration in production during the second period when prices were at their highest level before 1940, the depression years witnessed a considerable drop. Expansion started once again in the fourth period with the beginning of the post-depression recovery in prices. It may, however, be pointed out here that these shifts were mainly due to shifts in the production of jute, which was the most important crop in this category.

As anticipated from the preceding discussion, in sharp contrast to the change in per capita food crop output, per capita cash crop production

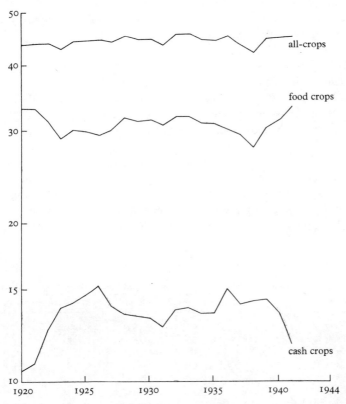

FIGURE 2.4 *Per capita crop production (official series, all-Bengal), five years' moving average (log scale; weighted by price).*

increased considerably during the period under review (Table 2.9). As to the rate of change, the five quinquennial periods fall into three unequal parts. During the first 10 years per capita output was improving at an increasing rate. This was followed by a marked drop during the third quinquennium. The fourth period witnessed some improvement, but the trend reversed again during the last five years.

2.6 REGIONAL TREND RATES IN CASH CROP OUTPUT AND POPULATION GROWTH

The rate of increase in the Presidency Division was double the provincial average. Conversely the growth rates in Dacca, Chittagong and Burdwan Divisions were much lower (Table 2.7). But it may be mentioned here that while in Burdwan and Dacca the rates were more or less the same as the growth of population, in Chittagong the disparity was marked. The picture that emerges in the revised series is more or less the same as indicated by the official series – the rates of expansion remain similar.

Except in Burdwan Division the quinquennial trends at the regional level were generally the same as indicated by the provincial average (Table 2.8). It is only in the last quinquennium that the trend was different in Dacca and Chittagong. On the other hand, in Burdwan Division the trend was the same as the provincial average only in the second and the last periods. In Dacca the drop in cash crop output during the last five years was caused by the fall in jute production. However, to emphasise the relative shift in production in response to changes in market conditions it is clear that the expansion of production in the second period was more marked in Presidency, Chittagong and Dacca Divisions than in the other regions. But the drop during the depression years was highest in Presidency and Chittagong Divisions.

The regional trends in per capita cash crop production in the quin-

TABLE 2.9 *Index of per capita cash crop output in the quinquennia* (1920/21 to 1922/23 = 100)

Regions	1920–24	1925–29	1930–34	1935–39	1940–44
All-Bengal	115(119)	161(159)	145(139)	148(144)	148(130)
Presidency	119(121)	200(190)	154(145)	164(158)	217(182)
Burdwan	91(90)	101(98)	106(104)	92(91)	95(89)
Rajshahi	111(114)	154(151)	150(143)	156(149)	171(161)
Dacca	119(124)	165(161)	150(140)	156(148)	132(105)
Chittagong	124(125)	190(176)	139(131)	142(140)	133(110)

Note: Estimates based on the revised series are shown in brackets.

quennial periods have two important features (Table 2.9). In sharp contrast to the change in per capita food production per capita cash crop output exceeded the growth of population in all the periods. The only exception was Burdwan. Secondly, the fact that for the province as a whole the rate of improvement was increasing during the first two quinquennia and declining during the last two was not true in all the regions: there was a drop in Dacca and Chittagong during the last five years.

2.7 PROVINCIAL TRENDS IN ALL-CROP ACREAGE AND THE SOURCES OF EXPANSION

The expansion of acreage under cultivation was the cause of almost the whole of the increase in all-crop output (Table 2.10). This is indicated by the almost identical growth for crop output (0.93) and crop acreage (0.87). Thus, during the period as a whole there was hardly any increase in yield per acre. In the revised series the annual rate of acreage expansion is reduced to nearly one fifth. However, it has to be pointed out here that this annual expansion of crop acreage at the rate of 0.2 per cent seems to be more in line with the experience in the other provinces. This, again, seems to strengthen

TABLE 2.10   *Trends in all-crop acreage*
1920–46

Regions	Average annual rate of increase			
	Unrevised series	Revised series	Population	Percentage distribution of acreage
All-Bengal	0.9	0.2	0.8	100
Presidency	1.7	0.9	1.2	17
Burdwan	0.2	−0.7	0.8	15
Rajshahi	1.0	0.1	0.3	26
Dacca	0.9	0.6	0.9	30
Chittagong	0.1	−0.6	1.3	12
British India	0.4			
Greater Bengal	0.3			
Punjab	0.4			
Madras	0.2			
United Province	0.3			
Central Province	0.1			
Bombay–Sind	0.4			

Note: For Blyn's estimates presented in the second half of the Table see Blyn, *op. cit.*, pp. 131–2.

the belief that the trend rates in the revised series provide a more accurate picture.

The trends in the quinquennial periods have two important features (Table 2.11). Firstly, they bring out an important point of difference between all-crop output and all-crop acreage. Thus, while during the first 20 years the rate of expansion was slightly slowing down in the former, it was increasing in the latter. The difference in the rate of increase (13 per cent in crop acreage and 6 per cent in crop output) during the last five years is of particular importance as this shows how a drop in yield per acre held down the volume of crop output during these years. Secondly, the fact that the depression did not have any positive impact on the level of crop output seems to be borne out by the expansion of acreage under cultivation during these years.

Expansion in crop acreage may be ascribed to three possible sources – transfer of land from other crops not included in this study, double cropping and finally cultivation of land classified in the official publications as 'cultivable waste', 'current fallow', 'forest' and 'not available for cultivation'. The percentage rates of change in these categories of land together with those on net cropped area and total crop acreage are presented in Table 2.12. From this it is clear that during the period as a whole double cropping was the most important source of acreage expansion in Bengal. The annual average double cropped area increased from 44.7 million acres in the first half of the period to 57.0 million acres in the second. In the revised series the corresponding figures are 67.5 and 72.7 million acres. The next important source was the reduction in the proportion of land left fallow by cultivators for a year or two to recover its productive power. The area of land transferred from other crops and the expansion of cultivable waste were insignificant. In the revised series fallow and waste land show some increase. This may be due to the different method of classification used in the Ishaque Report and the official publica-

TABLE 2.11 *Index of all-crop acreage in the quinquennia*
(1920/21 to 1922/23 = 100)

Regions	1920–24	1925–29	1930–34	1935–39	1940–44
All-Bengal	100(100)	101(98)	102(101)	105(105)	119(103)
Presidency	99(99)	100(98)	102(102)	115(115)	141(119)
Burdwan	98(98)	92(89)	94(92)	89(87)	101(84)
Rajshahi	98(98)	99(96)	100(98)	104(102)	120(97)
Dacca	102(102)	104(104)	108(107)	115(114)	123(114)
Chittagong	102(102)	101(99)	100(98)	98(96)	105(91)

Note: Figures in brackets refer to the revised series.

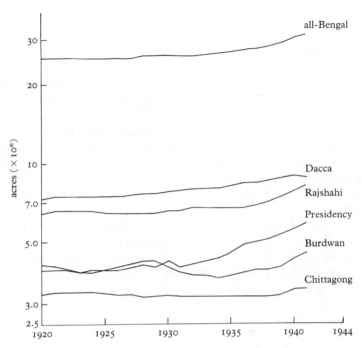

FIGURE 2.5   *All-crop acreage (official series), five years' moving average (log scale).*

TABLE 2.12   *Annual percentage rates of change in different categories of land 1920–46*

Land classified as	All-Bengal	Presidency	Burdwan	Rajshahi	Dacca	Chittagong
Net cropped area	0.7 (0.2)	1.8 (0.8)	0.2 (−0.9)	0.8 (0.2)	0.4 (0.5)	0.2 (0.0)
Double cropped area	1.9 (1.1)	2.1 (2.5)	0.2 (1.0)	2.5 (0.4)	2.4 (1.5)	0.4 (−0.4)
Cultivable waste	−0.2 (0.2)	−1.0 (−0.2)	−0.5 (0.4)	−0.6 (−0.3)	−2.8 (−3.9)	0.1 (0.1)
Current fallow	−1.4 (0.1)	−3.7 (−2.0)	1.4 (2.1)	−3.5 (−0.1)	−2.2 (−2.2)	2.6 (2.8)
Not available for cultivation	−1.0					
Forest	0.2					
Total crop acreage	(0.3)					

Note: Figures in brackets refer to the revised series.

tions. It is also possible that land transferred from the category of 'not available for cultivation' did not go directly into cultivation but was classified as cultivable waste and the land so transferred exceeded the area sown with crops. However, it is clear that the findings that double cropping and cultivation of fallow land were the two main sources of acreage expansion conform to what could be expected in a long-settled country with heavy pressure of population growth.

The areas of land classified under different categories in the quinquennial periods are presented in Table 2.13. These show how the changes in various classes of land influenced the trends in all-crop acreage in the different quinquennia. The rate of expansion in double cropped area was increasing during the first 15 years and slowing down during the last five. But in the case of fallow land it was only during the last 10 years that the extension of cultivation was taking place. This finding – the increase of fallow land during years of faster expansion in double cropping and slow decline when the rate of expansion in the latter was also small – may be of some significance. This may suggest that the cultivators were trying to make good at least a part of the loss in yield entailed by the increased double cropping by leaving more land fallow during the first three quinquennia. The decline in the area designated as 'not available for cultivation' may be regarded as more apparent than real.

TABLE 2.13 *Index of different classes of land in the quinquennia for all-Bengal* (1920/21 to 1922/23 = 100)

Classes of land	Land as % of total crop acreage	1920–24	1925–29	1930–34	1935–39	1940–44
Double cropped	17	99	103	112	119	149(125)
Current fallow	16	100	107	110	104	84(103)
Cultivable waste	21	102	101	104	106	98(102)
Forest		102	107	108	106	107
Not available for cultivation		97	90	83	85	79
Total crop acreage		99	99	101	104	118
Not cropped area	83	99	98	99	102	113(103)

Source: Computed from data presented in the Appendix.

For it is reasonable to assume that in a long-settled country with rapid growth of population the area not available for cultivation would increase. But this seems to have escaped the notice of the compilers of statistics.

2.8   REGIONAL TRENDS IN ALL-CROP ACREAGE AND THE SOURCES OF EXPANSION

Among the five regions the annual rate of expansion of all-crop acreage in Dacca and Rajshahi was almost identical with that of the province as a whole (Table 2.10). The other regions were at opposite extremes. Once again, as in the case of all-crop output, in the official series the rate of expansion of acreage was the highest in Presidency Division. Conversely in Burdwan and Chittagong the rate was rather marginal. In Burdwan, Chittagong and Dacca there was some decline in yield per acre of all-crops and, therefore, the changes in the rates of expansion of all-crop acreage are less marked than those of production.

What were the sources of these changes in the all-crop acreage at the regional level? In both series the increase in double cropping was mainly responsible for the expansion of acreage under cultivation in Presidency and Dacca Divisions. Conversely in Rajshahi this was the most important source only in the revised series. In the official series the reduction in fallow land led to most of the increase in all-crop acreage. The decline in Chittagong and Burdwan was mainly due to the increase in fallow land. There was some expansion in double cropping, but the proportion of land double cropped was so insignificant that it could not offset the decline in all-crop acreage.

2.9 ALL-BENGAL TRENDS IN FOOD CROP ACREAGE

The average annual rate of expansion in food crop acreage during the period as a whole (Table 2.14) was almost identical with that of all-crop acreage (0.9 per cent). This is not, however, surprising in view of the fact that acreage under this group of crops accounted for more than 80 per cent of the total crop acreage. However, in the revised series the rate of expansion is much lower – only 0.2 per cent per year. It is once again significant that this is more in line with the experience in the other provinces.

The trends in the quinquennial periods confirm the pattern noticed in the food crop output (Table 2.15). There was a drop in acreage during the years of rising prices (1924–29) and expansion during the depression years. Once again the substitution between food crop and cash crops seems to have come to an end during the fourth period, and the turning point in this process was

TABLE 2.14   *Trends in food crop acreage*
1920–46

Regions	Annual rates of increase			
	Unrevised series	Revised series	Popu-lation	Percentage distribution of acreage
All-Bengal	1.0	0.2	0.8	100
Presidency	1.7	0.9	1.2	18
Burdwan	0.3	−0.7	0.8	18
Rajshahi	1.1	−0.1	0.3	24
Dacca	1.2	0.9	0.9	28
Chittagong	0.2	−0.5	1.3	13
British India	0.4			
Madras	−0.03			
Greater Bengal	0.3			
Punjab	0.4			
United Province	0.3			
Central Province	0.6			
Bombay–Sind	0.6			

Source: For Blyn's estimates shown in the lower half of the Table see Blyn, *op. cit.*, pp. 131–2.

TABLE 2.15 *Index of food crop acreage in the quinquennia*
(1920/21 to 1922/23 = 100)

Regions	1920–24	1925–29	1930–34	1935–39	1940–44
All-Bengal	98	94	100	103	117(101)
Presidency	98	95	101	112	136(115)
Burdwan	97	92	95	89	101(84)
Rajshahi	96	92	97	99	115(92)
Dacca	100	97	106	113	125(116)
Chittagong	100	95	98	95	102(89)

Note: Figures in brackets refer to the revised series.

the year 1935/36.[1] As pointed out earlier, the marked expansion of acreage during the last quinquennium was due to the upward revision of area under winter rice.

[1] According to K. Mukerji, at the all-India level this came to an end in 1927/28. See his, *Levels of Economic Activity and Public Expenditure in India* (Poona, 1965), p. 31.

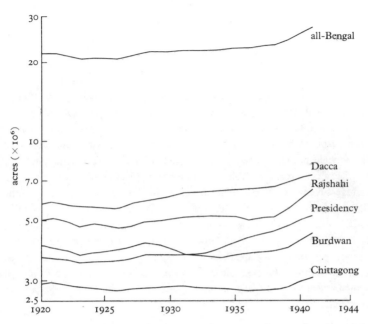

FIGURE 2.6   *Food crop acreage (official series), five years' moving average (log scale).*

2.10 REGIONAL TRENDS IN THE EXPANSION OF FOOD CROP ACREAGE

The picture presented by the trend rates at the regional level is more or less the same as indicated by the provincial average. In both the series the relative rates of acceleration or retardation in food crop acreage were similar (Table 2.14). The trends in the quinquennial periods also reveal the same pattern. It is only in Burdwan and Chittagong that there was a drop in the acreage under cultivation in the fourth period. This suggests that the substitution between food crops and cash crops was not yet over in these two regions. In the case of Chittagong this is particularly interesting in view of the fact that this region had the highest rate of population growth (1.3 per cent). Did the substitution come to an end during the last period? Nothing definite can be said about this, as the data on crop acreage was distorted by the upward revision. It may, however, be significant that, unlike in other regions, the revised series shows considerable expansion of acreage in these two regions.

71

2.11 ALL-BENGAL RATES OF EXPANSION IN CASH CROP ACREAGE

During the period as a whole cash crop acreage increased at the annual rate of only 0.2 per cent as against 1.0 per cent in food crop acreage (Table 2.16). In the revised series this comparative position considerably improves, though the rate of increase becomes very insignificant. It may be recalled here that the annual rate of increase in cash crop output was much higher than in food crop output. Obviously this has to be ascribed to the faster rate of increase in the yield per acre of this group of crops which will be noted later.

The same pattern which has been noted in cash crop output in response to changes in market forces is borne out, as in the case of food crops, by the quinquennial trends in the acreage under the cultivation of this group of crops – expansion during years of rising prices and contraction during years of falling prices (Table 2.17). However, it is clear that the drop in acreage in the depression period and the expansion in the last period was more marked than in output. This was due to the opposite movement in the figures on standard yield shown earlier in the course of the discussion on the quality of crop data.

TABLE 2.16   *Trends in cash crop acreage*
1920–46

Regions	Average annual rate of increase			
	Unrevised series	Revised series	Popula-tion	Percentage distribution of the acreage
All-Bengal	0.2	0.1	0.8	100
Presidency	2.0	1.7	1.2	11
Burdwan	−0.8	−0.7	0.8	3
Rajshahi	0.5	0.5	0.3	38
Dacca	−0.3	−0.7	0.9	39
Chittagong	−0.6	−0.9	1.3	9
British India	0.03			
Madras	0.7			
Greater Bengal	0.0			
Punjab	0.5			
United Province	0.4			
Central Province	−1.4			
Bombay–Sind	0.1			

Source: For Blyn's estimates shown in the lower half of the Table see Blyn, *op. cit.*, pp. 131–2.

TABLE 2.17   *Index of cash crop acreage in the quinquennia*
(1920/21 to 1922/23 = 100)

Regions	1920–24	1925–29	1930–34	1935–39	1940–44
All-Bengal	108(111)	136(135)	116(114)	122(124)	132(120)
Presidency	110(112)	161(157)	123(119)	147(145)	203(178)
Burdwan	95(94)	104(104)	90(89)	78(77)	97(92)
Rajshahi	106(108)	127(127)	115(112)	120(119)	137(128)
Dacca	109(113)	135(133)	116(114)	123(126)	117(102)
Chittagong	117(118)	165(154)	122(116)	128(126)	129(109)

Note: Estimates based on the revised series are shown in brackets.

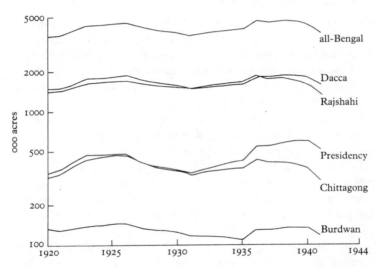

FIGURE 2.7   *Cash crop acreage (official series), five years' moving average (log scale).*

2.12. REGIONAL TREND RATES IN CASH CROP ACREAGE

The near-zero provincial rate of expansion in cash crop acreage was not typical of any of the regions (Table 2.16). In three regions – Burdwan, Dacca and Chittagong – acreage under cultivation declined during the period as a whole. (It may be recalled here that the rate of expansion in food crop acreage in Burdwan and Chittagong was the lowest.) In the two other regions cash crop acreage expanded and once again the average annual rate was the highest in Presidency Division. As indicated by the provincial average the picture that emerges in the revised series remains more or less the same.

This stands in sharp contrast to the marked changes effected in the trend rates of food crop acreage.

With regard to the trends in the quinquennial periods two main features may be pointed out. The general trend in the acreage under cultivation in the successive periods was the same as indicated in the provincial average. It is only in Burdwan in the fourth and Dacca in the last period that the trend was different. Secondly, though the general trend was the same the magnitude of change was considerably dissimilar. In this respect Burdwan and Presidency Divisions belonged to opposite extremes. Thus, while the rate of change was the most marked in the latter, it was the least so in the former.

2.13 PROVINCIAL TRENDS IN YIELD PER ACRE OF ALL CROPS

Increased agricultural output can be obtained either by the extension of the acreage under cultivation or by increasing the intensity of cultivation, or by raising yield or by combination of all three. It has been seen that during the period as a whole there was hardly any extension of cultivation. This is not, however, surprising in view of the fact that at the beginning of the period under investigation Bengal had the densest population in the sub-continent, and it is reasonable to believe that this pressure had already pushed cultivation almost to the natural limits. Under the circumstances increased production could be obtained only from intensive cultivation, i.e. raising yield per acre. The scope in this direction was very good as, at the beginning of this period, yield in Bengal was much lower than in the advanced agricultural countries.[1] But from the discussion that follows it is clear that at the end of the period the discrepancy remained as wide as before, and in some cases became wider.

Thus, during the period as a whole yield per acre for all the crops taken together increased at the rate of 0.1 per cent per year (Table 2.18). Clearly this implies that virtually the whole of the increase in all-crop output was obtained from the expansion of cultivation.

As pointed out later this rate was not typical of either of the groups of crops or of any individual crops. Does it imply that increase in the yield of one crop entailed decline in another? This question is discussed later on. But at this stage it may be pointed out that this near-zero trend in the productivity

---

[1] In spite of the considerable overestimation in yield as discussed earlier it is found that compared to Bengal at the beginning of our period the productivity of rice per acre was 260 per cent higher in Japan, 200 per cent higher in the USA and 300 per cent in Egypt. In the case of wheat it was 263 per cent higher in Japan, 284 per cent in the UK and 160 per cent in the USA. Even the productivity of a plantation crop like tea was 167 per cent higher in Japan. These estimates are based on figures available from the *Estimates of Area and Yields of Principal Crops in India* (annual).

TABLE 2.18   *Trends in all-crop yield per acre*
1920–46

Regions	Annual rate of increase	Percentage distribution of acreage
All-Bengal	0.1	100
Presidency	0.2	17
Burdwan	−0.2	15
Rajshahi	0.4	26
Dacca	−0.1	30
Chittagong	−0.3	12
British India	−0.2	
Madras	0.2	
Greater Bengal	−0.5	
Punjab	0.9	
United Province	0.2	
Central Province	−0.9	
Bombay–Sind	0.4	

Source: For Blyn's estimates presented in the lower half of the Table see Blyn, *op. cit.*, pp. 165–6.

per acre of all the crops seems to strengthen the opinion of the Royal Commission that a stable state had been reached in agriculture and no further decline was likely to take place in yield.[1] Increased yield involves the use of improved technology. But as there was hardly any progress in this direction the picture seems to conform to what could be expected for an underdeveloped agriculture – equilibrium at a low level of productivity.

However, in the quinquennial periods there were considerable variations in yield (Table 2.19). Thus, yield was increasing during the first 15 years, though gradually at a slower rate, and declined in the last quinquennium. So

TABLE 2.19   *Index of all-crop yield in the quinquennia*
(1920/21 to 1922/23 = 100)

Regions	1920–24	1925–29	1930–34	1935–39	1940–44
All-Bengal	99	104	107	107	101
Presidency	100	104	109	100	108
Burdwan	94	86	92	98	84
Rajshahi	102	115	123	121	114
Dacca	99	109	107	109	100
Chittagong	96	95	91	94	92

[1] *Report of the Royal Commission on Agriculture in India* (London, 1928), p. 76.

far as crop output is concerned this drop partly neutralised the effect of the upward revision in acreage data during the last five years. In this connection it may also be pointed out that the sudden increase in the standard yield for the quinquennium beginning 1932/33 did not have much effect on the yield per acre of all-crops as the 'annawari' estimates of the seasonal condition were lower during these years.

2.14 REGIONAL TRENDS IN YIELD PER ACRE OF ALL-CROPS

Among the five regions the trend in all-crop yield was positive in the Presidency and Rajshahi Divisions (Table 2.18). In the three other regions – Burdwan, Dacca and Chittagong – yield per acre declined during the period as a whole. This drop in yield in Burdwan and Chittagong Divisions is of particular significance as the revised series indicates that there was also a considerable decline in cropped area. However, in the Presidency and Rajshahi Divisions the rate of improvement in yield was higher than indicated by the provincial average. With regard to the quinquennial trends in Burdwan and Chittagong the decline in yield started at the outset. But while in the former there was some improvement during the third and the fourth periods, in the latter there was a slight rise only during the fourth. In the Presidency and Rajshahi Divisions improvement in the yield of all the 13 major crops taken together started at the beginning of the period under study and continued up to the third quinquennium. The fourth quinquennium witnessed some decline in yield in both these regions, but the trend was different in the last period.

2.15 PROVINCIAL TREND IN YIELD PER ACRE OF FOOD CROPS

For the period as a whole the average annual rate of decline in food crop yield was 0.2 per cent (Table 2.20). As acreage under food crops accounted for more than 80 per cent of the total acreage it is clearly this decline which depressed the rate of increase in all-crop productivity. The trends in the quinquennial periods indicate that this decline started at the outset and, except for a break during the third quinquennium, continued up to the end (Table 2.21). The drop in the yield per acre in food crops during the last quinquennium was wholly caused by the two lean years of 1940/41 and 1942/43 in the productivity of winter and autumn rice. The similarity of the level of yield per acre in the third and fourth periods merits particular mention. There was considerable decline in the standard yield estimated for the fourth period. But a run of favourable weather conditions seems to have kept the actual yield per acre at about the level of the first quinquennium.

TABLE 2.20   *Trends in yield per acre of food crops*
1920–46

Regions	Annual rate of increase	Percentage distribution of acreage
All-Bengal	−0.2	100
Presidency	0.1	18
Burdwan	−0.3	18
Rajshahi	0.0	24
Dacca	−0.4	28
Chittagong	−0.5	13
British India	−0.4	
Madras	−0.03	
Greater Bengal	−0.7	
Punjab	0.5	
United Province	−0.3	
Central Province	−0.8	
Bombay–Sind	−0.4	

Source: For Blyn's estimates presented in the lower part of the Table see Blyn, *op. cit.*, pp. 165–166.

TABLE 2.21   *Index of yield of food crops in the quinquennia*
(1920/21 to 1922/23 = 100)

Regions	1920–24	1925–29	1930–34	1935–39	1940–44
All-Bengal	96	93	97	96	90
Presidency	99	96	105	95	101
Burdwan	94	85	90	97	82
Rajshahi	97	99	110	106	95
Dacca	94	96	93	95	88
Chittagong	94	86	84	85	83

2.16 REGIONAL TRENDS IN FOOD CROP PRODUCTIVITY

With regard to the trends in the yield of food crops the five regions may be said to have belonged to two groups. While in the Presidency and Rajshahi Divisions yield per acre remained more or less static throughout the entire period under review, in the three other regions the trend was one of decline (Table 2.20). It may be mentioned that except in Dacca these rates of decline (or of increase) are the same as for winter rice. As shown in the following chapter there was some rise in the yield of other food crops. But the share of winter rice in the total food crop acreage was so high (65 per cent) that these increases could make only a little difference.

The decline in the yield of food crops started at the beginning of the period under review (Table 2.21). In three regions – Burdwan, Chittagong and Dacca – this drop continued during the next five years. But in the two other regions there was an improvement. During the depression years yield increased in all regions except Dacca and Chittagong. In the next period there was improvement only in Burdwan, Dacca and Chittagong. The difference between the two neighbouring regions of Presidency and Burdwan was mainly caused by opposite trends in the yield of winter rice. During the last five years it was only in Presidency Division that there was some increase in productivity.

2.17 ALL-BENGAL TRENDS IN CASH CROP YIELD

Two main features may be pointed out with regard to the trends in the productivity of cash crops. In sharp contrast to a decline in the yield of food crops productivity in this group increased at the rate of 1.2 per cent per year (Table 2.22). This is particularly remarkable in view of the fact that productivity per acre of jute which accounted for more than 50 per cent of the non-food crops improved at the rate of only 0.3 per cent per year. Among

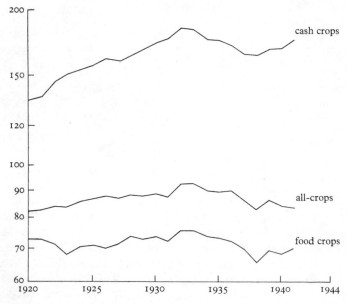

FIGURE 2.8   *Yield of food crops, cash crops and all-crops (all-Bengal), five years' moving average (log scale; weighted by price).*

78

TABLE 2.22   *Trends in cash crop yield per acre*
1920–46

Regions	Annual average rate of increase	Relative importance of acreage under cultivation
All-Bengal	1.2	100
Presidency	1.0	11
Burdwan	1.4	3
Rajshahi	1.4	38
Dacca	1.2	39
Chittagong	1.1	9
British India	1.2	
Madras	0.6	
Bombay–Sind	2.1	
Punjab	1.7	
Greater Bengal	0.8	
United Province	0.9	
Central Province	−0.02	

Source: For Blyn's estimates presented in the lower half of the Table see Blyn's *op. cit.*, pp. 165–6.

other provinces with positive trends it was only in Bombay–Sind and the Punjab that the rate was higher.

Secondly, though the rate of increase for the period as a whole was impressive, it is clear from the quinquennial trends that the pace of improvement was slowing down during the first 20 years and this was followed by some decline during the last five (Table 2.23). But this drop was much less marked than in the productivity per acre of food crops. The only other period in which the trend in cash and food crop productivity was the same was the third quinquennium, but once again the rate of increase in the latter was much slower.

2.18 REGIONAL TRENDS IN CASH CROP YIELD PER ACRE

The average rates of improvement in productivity were almost identical with that of the all-Bengal average (Table 2.22). This stands in sharp contrast to the wide variations in the regional trends in the acreage under the cultivation of food crops and cash crops and partly in the yield of the former. In the course of the discussion on the trends in cash crop output it was pointed out that the variations in the rates of acceleration or retardation at the regional level do not seem to have necessarily depended on the relative importance of the particular group of crops in each region. This is brought

TABLE 2.23   *Index of yield of cash crops in the quinquennia*
(1920/21 to 1922/23 = 100)

Regions	1920–24	1925–29	1930–34	1935–39	1940–44
All-Bengal	106	123	136	138	133
Presidency	109	132	138	134	136
Burdwan	96	101	129	133	116
Rajshahi	105	122	135	136	136
Dacca	109	128	139	145	134
Chittagong	105	122	128	133	129

out more clearly by the opposite pattern in the two determinants of output—acreage and yield. The proportion of area under cash crops was the highest in Rajshahi and Dacca and the lowest in the Presidency and Burdwan Divisions. But these regions had opposite trends or widely dissimilar rates of increase or decrease in the area under cash crops. Conversely in the present case all the regions had almost identical rates of improvement in yield though the relative importance of the area under cash crop in each region was widely different.

The quinquennial trends reveal the same pattern as already noted for all-Bengal. The rate of increase in yield was slowing down during the period from 1920 to 1940 and this was followed by some drop in the last period. The only exceptions were Burdwan where the rate of improvement was accelerating during the first 10 years and Presidency Division which had some drop in yield in the fourth period as against some increase in the last. The drop in Presidency Division was almost entirely due to a marked decline in the productivity of jute.

In the previous chapter it was pointed out that it seems reasonable to assume that the trends in the revised series are more reliable. Now it is clear that this assumption is strengthened by the fact that the actual findings are more in conformity with the experience in the other parts of India. The picture of the agricultural economy of Bengal which is thus presented may be summarised as follows. Firstly, during the period as a whole there was hardly any increase in the yield of all-crops and only a marginal expansion of the acreage under cultivation. The resultant increase in all-crop output was much lower than the growth of population. Secondly, the experience between the two groups of crops was widely dissimilar. In the case of food crops a small increase in the acreage under cultivation (0.2 per cent per year) was neutralised by a corresponding decline in yield per acre. But in cash crops a still smaller increase in acreage (0.1 per cent per year) was accompanied by a fairly impressive improvement in yield per acre

(1.0 per cent per year). Thirdly, agricultural trends in the different regional units were considerably dissimilar.

This chapter may be concluded by an attempt to explain this contrast between the productivity of food crop and cash crops. What caused this difference? Once again this raises the question of the quality of the official data on yields considered in the preceding chapter. How far was this difference a real one? Obviously nothing definite can be said on this question. Therefore, the purpose here will be to see if there could be any conceivable explanation for this divergent experience as indicated by the official statistics. In this connection it may be recalled that of the individual crops responsible for the stagnation in the productivity of food crops the most important was the decline in the yield of winter rice. The yield of other food crops increased, but since winter rice alone accounted for 65 per cent of the total acreage under this group of crops the rates of increase could only neutralise the effect of this decline in winter rice. Thus, the question raised above is essentially a question as to the cause of the decline in the yield of winter rice as against an increase in that of cash crops.

One possibility referred to by Blyn is that jute and rice are alternative crops and the decline in rice yield was caused by the transfer of better land from the cultivation of rice to that of jute.[1] Another suggestion, made by Spate, is that jute and rice are associated in rotation planting and this might have caused the lowering of rice yield since jute is a soil-exhausting crop.[2] These explanations seem to be fairly convincing at first sight. But looked at more closely it seems that these suggestions do not fully explain the decline in rice yield.

Of the three varieties of rice it is only autumn rice which is a direct alternative to jute in the sense that these two crops are sown and harvested in the same season. In the case of winter rice its transplanting season coincides with the harvesting season of jute. After the jute harvest, planting of winter rice on the same land mainly depends on favourable weather conditions. Thus, winter rice is alternative only under favourable weather conditions. During the period as a whole the productivity of jute and autumn rice increased at the annual rate of 0.2 per cent and 0.3 per cent per year respectively. Now the questions that have to be asked are: if better land were transferred from the cultivation of rice, why did the productivity of autumn rice not decline? Secondly, why did the productivity of jute increase so marginally as against a much higher growth in the other cash crops. This is particularly important in view of the fact that by the late 1930s 50 per cent

[1] G. Blyn, *op. cit.*, p. 158.
[2] O. H. K. Spate, *India and Pakistan: A General and Regional Geography* (London, 1954), p. 527.

of the total acreage under jute was sown with improved seeds. In this connection it may also be mentioned that jute and winter rice accounted for respectively 9 per cent and 59 per cent of the total crop acreage. Clearly the impact of the transfer of better land should have been limited or even neutralised by the fact that 6 per cent of the rice acreage was sown with the improved varieties of seeds. Thus, it would appear that the decline in the yield of winter rice cannot be explained as mainly due to the transfer of better land or as due to rotation planting with jute.

A more important explanation may lie in the remarkable expansion of double cropping. It is reasonable to argue that most of this expansion took place on land under the cultivation of winter rice. This is suggested, firstly, by the importance of this crop in terms of acreage under cultivation. Secondly, the sowing and transplanting season of winter rice is such that it allows considerable scope for raising a second crop in the same agricultural year. It is well-known that different 'rabi' crops such as mustard, linseed, sesamum, gram are grown on land released by the harvest of winter rice. It is possible that there was an increase in the proportion of land transplanted with winter rice after the harvest of autumn rice and jute. It may be argued that the yield per acre of the crops so grown would also tend to decline. But there are reasons which suggest that this may not have happened. In the case of jute there was one upward force against the tendency for a drop in the yield resulting from double cropping. This was the use of the improved varieties of seeds. These seeds could not raise productivity by 25 per cent as was believed by the Agricultural Department, but it cannot be denied that they had some effect. Secondly, crops like wheat, barley, gram, sesamum, linseed and mustard accounted for only 8 per cent of the total acreage under cultivation. It is conceivable that the small size of the area under cultivation enabled the cultivators to take greater care of manuring, ploughing and weeding. This possibility is particularly applicable in the case of tobacco and sugarcane. In this connection it may also be mentioned that improved seedlings were used for these two crops. By the late 1930s more than half of the acreage under the latter was planted with the new varieties of seedlings.

Thus, the explanation for the contrast in the yields of these two varieties of crops as indicated by the official data seems to lie in the effect of the transfer of better lands from winter rice, the extension of double cropping, the use of improved varieties of seeds and perhaps the greater care in the cultivation of certain cash crops.

The variations which have been pointed out at the regional level with regard to the trends in acreage under cultivation and yield per acre raise a number of important questions. This is particularly so in view of the fact that the two neighbouring regions of Burdwan and Presidency Division had such divergent experience. But these can best be appreciated with reference to the trends in the individual crops which are taken up in the next chapter. At this stage it need only be recalled that these variations do not seem to have necessarily been due to the difference in the relative importance of the two groups of crops in each region.

3

TRENDS IN OUTPUT, ACREAGE AND YIELD: INDIVIDUAL CROPS

Percentage rates of change presented in the preceding chapter reveal the picture of a stagnant agricultural economy characterised by the near-constancy of both acreage under cultivation and yield at the aggregate level. In the present chapter the analysis is taken a step further by examining whether this picture was representative of all the individual crops. There are several questions that need resolving. For example, if the trends were dissimilar, what was the significance of this difference? Again, it is imperative to seek some possible explanations for these dissimilarities. The mode of presentation is more or less the same as in the previous chapter. In the discussion on the quinquennial trends the emphasis is on the provincial average. In order to facilitate the interpretation of the rates of change in the 13 crops selected for analysis their weights in the all-crops acreage and all-crop output at the all-Bengal level are shown in the respective tables. The analysis of the changes is followed by an attempt to explain the differences in regional trends.

3.1 PROVINCIAL AND REGIONAL RATES OF CHANGE IN THE CROP OUTPUT

Considerable variations are noticed in the trends of the output of individual crops (Table 3.1). In both series the annual rates of growth were highest for sugarcane and gram. In the case of the former this has to be attributed to the introduction of a protective tariff against the import of sugar and the consequent expansion of local manufacture.[1] The remarkable expansion in the output of gram started in the middle of the 1930s despite the fact that exports of this crop had been declining since the beginning of the period under review.[2] This would thus indicate, at least partly, a tendency towards in-

---

[1] The number of sugar mills in Bengal increased from only two in 1933 to nine in 1939 with a daily crushing capacity of nearly 4000 tons. For details, see, Government of India, *Report on the Marketing of Sugar in India* (Delhi, 1939), p. 12. Working in the same direction was the introduction of the improved varieties of seedlings as discussed in the preceding chapter.

[2] All the export figures are available from the *Annual Statement of the Sea-Borne Trade and Navigation of British India*, published by the Director General of Commercial Intelligence and Statistics, Government of India, Delhi (annual).

TABLE 3.1   *Annual percentage rates of change in individual crop output*
1920–46

Crops	Relative importance	All-Bengal	Presidency	Burdwan	Rajshahi	Dacca	Chittagong
Winter rice	53	0.4	1.7	−0.1	0.6	0.1	−0.4
		(−0.3)	(0.8)	(−1.2)	(0.3)	(−0.2)	(−0.6)
Autumn rice	15	1.6	1.6	0.4	2.0	2.8	−0.2
		(0.9)	(0.8)	(1.4)	(0.5)	(2.7)	(−1.7)
Jute	17	0.7	2.4	2.0	1.2	0.0	0.3
		(0.2)	(2.0)	(1.7)	(0.7)	(−0.4)	(−0.1)
Mustard	1	0.1	3.1	0.3	0.5	−0.8	0.1
		(0.3)	(3.3)	(1.1)	(0.6)	(−0.5)	(0.2)
Summer rice	2	1.8	3.4	0.5	2.3	1.8	0.1
		(1.0)	(2.2)	(−3.3)	(1.2)	(1.5)	(2.7)
Gram	1	6.6	7.8	2.6	5.4	3.6	3.1
		(5.0)	(6.5)	(0.6)	(3.3)	(1.2)	(0.0)
Wheat	1	2.6	4.6	2.4	1.1	3.8	–
		(2.3)	(4.6)	(0.7)	(1.1)	(3.3)	
Sesamum	1	1.5	3.9	−0.6	1.8	1.2	2.9
		(1.5)	(3.9)	(−0.6)	(1.8)	(1.2)	(2.9)
Tobacco	2	0.7	0.3	−2.2	0.1	3.4	2.4
		(1.9)	(−0.7)	(−0.6)	(1.8)	(3.3)	(2.0)
Linseed	0	2.1	4.3	−0.6	0.3	−1.5	1.0
		(2.1)	(4.3)	(−0.6)	(0.3)	(−1.5)	(1.0)
Sugarcane	4	4.3	7.1	0.1	4.3	5.6	1.4
		(4.3)	(7.1)	(0.1)	(4.3)	(5.6)	(1.4)
Tea	4	2.9	–	–	2.9	–	1.1
Barley	0	2.8	5.3	−2.6	3.2	1.4	–
		(1.1)	(4.7)	(−3.0)	(0.1)	(0.7)	
All-crops	100	0.9	2.0	0.0	1.4	0.8	−0.2
		(0.3)	(1.1)	(−1.0)	(0.5)	(0.4)	(−0.7)

Note: Figures in brackets in this table refer to the revised series. Differences in the relative importance in the two series are not marked and therefore only the weights in the official series are presented.

creased consumption of the inferior foodcrops. Conversely, the rates of increase in the official series were the lowest for mustard, winter rice, jute and tobacco. The revised series reveals a completely different picture for winter rice. This crop accounted for more than half of the total crop output in Bengal and evidently this decline of 0.3 per cent per year was of the greatest importance for the economy at large. Jute was the most important of the cash crops, but the revised series indicates a very much lower rate of increase. As almost the whole of the jute production was exported, either in raw or manufactured form, this may indicate the effects of the restrictive practices of the local manufacturers,[1] the drastic fall in world consumption during the depression years and the increased needs of food production beginning from the middle of the 1930s. The very low rate of increase in mustard could have been due to the gradual decline of the export trade in this crop from the outset of the period. Autumn rice and summer rice belonged to one group and, in sharp contrast to the experience in winter rice, output of these two crops was increasing considerably. In both the series the trends were much better for crops like barley, wheat, sesamum, linseed and tea which together accounted for only 6 per cent of the all-crop output. Thus, it was the output of only the minor crops which was increasing during the period as a whole and evidently the rates were much higher than those indicated by the weighted average of all the crops.

For almost all the crops the provincial rate of change was not representative of any of the five regions. Presidency Division formed a category by itself in that the annual rates of increase were the highest in all the individual crops except autumn rice and tobacco. Burdwan and Chittagong belonged to the extreme opposites in almost all the crops. Of particular importance in the latter was the marked decline in winter rice and autumn rice. In Burdwan the drop in winter rice was marginal and there was some improvement in autumn rice, gram and wheat. But these were offset by the very high rates of decline in barley and tobacco. The contrast between these three regions becomes more marked in the revised series. In the former the rates of increase still remain impressive and in many cases as high as in the official series. But in Burdwan and Chittagong the position further deteriorates. In both the series Dacca and Rajshahi occupy a somewhat middle position. They had the same trend in almost all the crops though the rates of change were different.

3.2 PROVINCIAL AND REGIONAL TRENDS IN THE QUINQUENNIAL PERIODS

For the province as a whole the level of output of nine crops was lower during the first five years than in the base period (Table 3.2.). Among the remaining crops production of tea and jute was increasing, though at low rates. Thus, it was only on the production of these two crops that the post-war recovery in the market conditions was beginning to have some effect.[2] This provincial picture in the first quinquennium was typical of all the regions

---

[1] See *Report of the Bengal Jute Enquiry Committee*, Vol. i (Calcutta, 1939), p. 22.

[2] The supply response of the major crops for the period as a whole is examined in a separate chapter. The purpose in the present chapter is to emphasise, in a straightforward way, the pattern of shifts in the quinquennial periods.

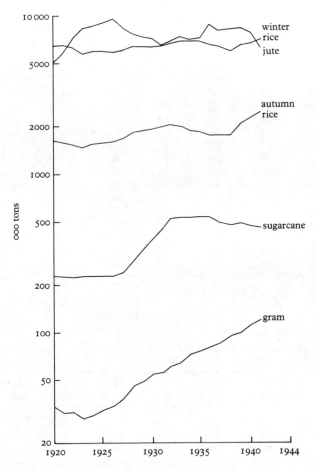

FIGURE 3.1   *Individual crop output (official series, all-Bengal), five years' moving average (log scale).*

in most of the crops including winter rice and autumn rice. The most marked exception was the drop in jute production in Burdwan.

For the province as a whole the trends in the output of the 13 crops were slightly different in the second quinquennium (Table 3.3) when prices were at their highest level. Apart from jute and tea the output of linseed and tobacco also responded to these favourable market conditions. However, the pattern of the last two crops was not the same in all the regions. This was true also with regard to the crops with negative trends during these

TABLE 3.2 *Index of output 1920/21 to 1924/25*
(1920/21 to 1922/23 = 100)

Crops	All-Bengal	Presi-dency	Burd-wan	Raj-shahi	Dacca	Chitta-gong
Winter rice	94	98	92	93	94	93
Autumn rice	94	95	88	95	94	95
Jute	131	136	85	129	131	136
Mustard	93	95	110	95	89	105
Summer rice	97	94	97	100	98	95
Gram	94	95	90	90	102	98
Wheat	97	97	98	97	104	–
Sesamum	92	89	96	93	89	104
Tobacco	100	86	92	101	99	103
Linseed	100	106	105	98	89	101
Sugarcane	97	90	92	102	97	96
Tea	104	–	–	104	–	101
Barley	94	93	96	93	97	–
All-crops	98	99	92	100	101	98

TABLE 3.3 *Index of output 1925–29*
(1920/21 to 1922/23 = 100)

Crops	All-Bengal	Presi-dency	Burd-wan	Raj-shahi	Dacca	Chitta-gong
Winter rice	87	89	74	91	96	83
Autumn rice	91	97	125	97	79	78
Jute	215	281	174	204	206	248
	(192)	(251)	(155)	(182)	(184)	(221)
Mustard	86	101	116	87	78	112
Summer rice	89	204	47	94	94	46
Gram	87	85	80	90	105	75
Wheat	102	119	112	92	121	–
Sesamum	82	93	77	114	62	134
Tobacco	134	75	137	147	83	132
Linseed	102	114	174	92	73	80
Sugarcane	96	77	78	106	108	76
Tea	140	–	–	141	–	92
Barley	89	123	76	61	116	–
All-crops	104	104	80	114	113	96
	(100)	(101)	(77)	(107)	(112)	(93)

Note: Figures in brackets in this table, as in the later ones, refer to the revised series.

years. For example, in Dacca and Rajshahi output of raw sugar increased as against a decline in linseed. Among the three crops with a positive trend the highest acceleration took place in jute production. Conversely, the decline in output was the most marked in winter rice and the least so in autumn rice. This clearly suggests that the expansion in jute production in this quinquennium was mostly at the cost of winter rice.

The picture completely changed during the depression years. Of the several crops which had responded positively to the rise in price level in the past, now it was only the production of jute which dropped with the fall in prices (Table 3.4). It may, however, be of significance that the rate of decline was much less than the rate of increase in the preceding quinquennium. Output of tobacco, linseed and tea continued to increase though there was a considerable fall in prices. The increase in the production of tea as against a drop in jute is important as it underlines how, in the absence of an alternative product, the highly capitalised estates could not adjust their production to the fall in the price level.[1]

Similarly, the output of other crops, including winter rice and autumn

TABLE 3.4   *Index of output 1930–34*
(1920/21 to 1922/23 = 100)

Crops	All-Bengal	Presidency	Burdwan	Rajshahi	Dacca	Chittagong
Winter rice	92	100	81	103	92	85
Autumn rice	111	119	131	120	119	73
Jute	170	190	146	158	174	181
	(156)	(174)	(135)	(145)	(158)	(165)
Mustard	110	139	156	120	94	119
Summer rice	106	100	60	105	121	65
Gram	148	162	108	136	137	122
Wheat	140	149	164	125	226	–
Sesamum	104	101	85	149	84	155
Tobacco	150	69	169	162	114	154
Linseed	130	161	216	126	77	59
Sugarcane	163	157	98	197	193	88
Tea	142	–	–	143	–	86
Barley	104	181	83	71	120	–
All-crops	109	112	88	123	115	91
	(105)	(110)	(84)	(116)	(111)	(89)

Note: Estimates based on the revised series are presented in brackets.

[1] This was also the experience in Malaya and the Dutch East Indies. See P. T. Bauer, *The Rubber Industry* (London 1948), p. 30.

rice (which declined in the earlier years in contrast with the increase in jute production), improved considerably during these years. The sudden spurt in the production of sugar reflects the timing of the introduction of the protective tariff and the consequent beginning in the expansion of domestic industry. Thus, the finding of the preceding chapter that there was an upward shift in all-crop output during the depression years was also characteristic of all the individual crops. The only exception was jute – a fully marketed crop. Trends at the regional level were almost uniformly the same as indicated by this provincial average. In this respect, also, the experience in the third quinquennium was different. This may suggest that the effect of falling prices is more pervasive than that of rising ones.

During the post-depression years there was a considerable improvement in market conditions. But the recovery in jute production, even in the revised series, was small (Table 3.5). The output of other crops, including winter rice, continued to increase. Since there were two lean years in the yield of autumn rice – the other alternative crop to jute – and this held down output despite some expansion of acreage it may be suggested that the trend was much the same as for other crops. This was in sharp contrast to the experience in the first and second quinquennia. This new pattern is of considerable importance as it indicates that the increased needs of food supply

TABLE 3.5 *Index of output 1935–39*
(1920/21 to 1922/23 = 100)

Crops	All-Bengal	Presidency	Burdwan	Rajshahi	Dacca	Chittagong
Winter rice	96	105	85	103	100	84
Autumn rice	107	102	117	109	130	74
Jute	171	199	102	150	178	194
	(166)	(193)	(99)	(145)	(172)	(187)
Mustard	111	165	151	121	93	117
Summer rice	115	175	37	123	128	64
Gram	204	246	111	165	145	77
Wheat	148	216	137	115	212	–
Sesamum	124	108	77	158	114	165
Tobacco	151	68	98	158	154	152
Linseed	145	194	170	122	75	118
Sugarcane	225	254	102	284	272	113
Tea	152	–	–	153	–	103
Barley	115	209	64	88	121	–
All-crops	113	115	86	125	125	92
	(109)	(114)	(86)	(117)	(122)	(91)

Note: Figures in brackets refer to the revised series.

curtailed the production of jute and expanded that of rice. It is true that the recovery in the price level was slow to come, but the underlying trend is fairly clear.

As pointed out in the discussion on the nature of the official statistics there was a sudden acceleration in the output of all the crops except mustard, tea, tobacco and sugarcane during the last five years (Table 3.6). Clearly the difference between food crops and cash crops has to be attributed to the 'Grow More Food Campaign' launched during these years by the provincial government. Consequently, the changes effected by the revision of statistics are more marked in these crops. The sharpest drop takes place in winter rice and output stands at a considerably lower level than in the base period. In the context of the Bengal famine of 1943 this seems to have been of the greatest importance. Autumn rice still shows some increase along with the two marginal crops of gram and barley.

TABLE 3.6 *Index of output 1940–44*
(1920/21 to 1922/23 = 100)

Crops	All-Bengal	Presidency	Burdwan	Rajshahi	Dacca	Chittagong
Winter rice	98	134	81	99	98	84
	(85)	(111)	(65)	(83)	(93)	(83)
Autumn rice	131	137	105	146	152	88
	(109)	(116)	(131)	(102)	(143)	(62)
Jute	187	304	204	207	155	190
	(148)	(242)	(159)	(163)	(123)	(148)
Mustard	96	188	123	104	74	114
	(93)	(176)	(128)	(104)	(74)	(111)
Summer rice	134	228	102	190	130	83
	(114)	(176)	(52)	(124)	(126)	(64)
Gram	305	372	141	252	208	195
	(231)	(295)	(98)	(166)	(130)	(102)
Wheat	156	238	147	118	215	–
	(147)	(230)	(108)	(118)	(187)	
Sesamum	116	202	79	140	94	189
Tobacco	133	95	70	129	175	168
	(152)	(76)	(92)	(155)	(166)	(159)
Linseed	153	244	115	100	60	111
Sugarcane	197	302	82	212	258	109
Tea	197	–	–	199	–	120
Barley	164	270	57	165	136	–
	(120)	(244)	(52)	(89)	(121)	
All-crops	120	153	85	136	122	96
	(101)	(126)	(69)	(108)	(108)	(93)

Note: Revised estimates are presented in brackets.

The regional picture once again brings out the contrast between Presidency Division on the one hand and Burdwan and Chittagong on the other. While for the former even the revised series shows some increase in the output of all the crops the trend is the opposite for the latter two regions.

3.3 PROVINCIAL AND REGIONAL TRENDS IN ACREAGE UNDER CULTIVATION

With regard to trends in acreage the 13 crops may be classified under several groups (Table 3.7). In both the series the rate of expansion was the highest in gram. However, this expansion of acreage was accompanied by only a marginal improvement in yield. Acreage under the three crops of sugarcane,

TABLE 3.7 *Trend rates in acreage under individual crops*
1920–46

Crops	Relative weights	All-Bengal	Presidency	Burdwan	Rajshahi	Dacca	Chittagong
Winter rice	58	0.7	1.6	0.2	0.7	0.7	0.4
		(0.0)	(0.7)	(−0.8)	(−0.2)	(0.4)	(0.2)
Autumn rice	22	1.5	1.2	0.6	−0.2	1.6	1.1
		(0.8)	(0.5)	(1.6)	(−4.1)	(0.5)	(0.8)
Jute	9	0.3	2.1	1.1	0.9	−0.2	−0.8
		(−0.1)	(1.6)	(0.7)	(0.4)	(−0.6)	(−1.2)
Mustard	3	−0.6	1.5	−0.6	0.3	−1.8	−1.5
		(−0.4)	(1.7)	(0.1)	(0.4)	(−1.5)	(−1.4)
Summer rice	2	1.1	2.7	−0.2	1.6	1.1	−0.6
		(0.2)	(1.6)	(−4.1)	(0.5)	(0.8)	(2.0)
Gram	1	6.1	6.8	2.7	5.5	3.8	3.2
		(4.5)	(5.5)	(0.8)	(3.4)	(1.4)	(0.1)
Wheat	1	2.1	3.7	2.1	0.9	2.4	−
		(1.8)	(3.7)	(0.4)	(0.9)	(1.8)	
Sesamum	1	0.4	2.2	−1.6	0.1	0.3	1.5
Tobacco	1	−0.5	−1.0	−3.3	−0.9	1.3	1.3
		(0.7)	(−1.9)	(−1.7)	(0.8)	(1.2)	(0.9)
Linseed	1	0.9	2.6	−1.8	−0.9	−2.5	0.5
Sugarcane	1	2.4	4.3	−2.2	3.0	3.7	−0.9
Tea	1	0.5	−	−	0.5	−	0.5
Barley	0	2.5	5.0	−2.9	2.9	1.1	−
		(0.9)	(4.4)	(−3.3)	(−0.2)	(0.4)	
All-crops	100	0.9	1.7	0.2	1.0	0.9	0.1
		(0.2)	(0.9)	(−0.7)	(0.1)	(0.6)	(−0.6)

Note: Figures in brackets refer to the revised series.

barley and wheat also increased at high rates, but together these crops accounted for only two per cent of the total cropped area. Among the other minor crops the trends were one of some expansion in tea, sesamum and linseed and some decline in mustard and tobacco in the official series. The high rates of expansion of acreage under barley and wheat, despite the fact that yield per acre in Bengal was one of the lowest in the sub-continent, underlines, as in the case of gram, the increased necessity of raising a second food crop in the dry season, though this generally meant the consumption of inferior cereals. The slow rate of expansion of the acreage under tea, even though productivity was increasing at 2.3 per cent per year, could have been due to the limited scope for the extension of tea plantation in undivided Bengal. According to the official series acreage under the two major crops of winter and autumn rice increased and in the latter the rate of expansion was double the rate of population growth. Area under autumn rice has a positive trend also in the revised series, but in winter rice the picture is one of stagnation. Clearly this stagnation was responsible for the near-zero trend in all-crop acreage.

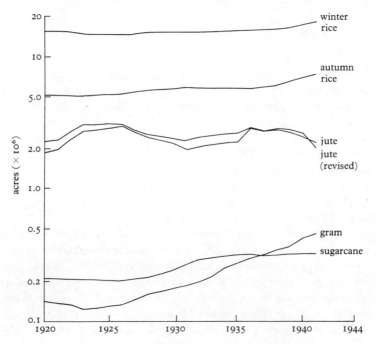

FIGURE 3.2 *Individual crop acreage (official series, all-Bengal), five years' moving average (long scale).*

The regional trends reveal the same pattern as noticed in the case of output – the all-Bengal average rates were not representative of most of the component units. On the contrary, the contrast between Presidency Division and the two regions of Burdwan and Chittagong was more marked in crops like sesamum, linseed and tobacco. Obviously this was due to the similarity of the trends in the yield of these crops as shown in the relevant section. The problem of discerning the possible explanations for the variations in the trends of the individual crop acreage at the regional level is discussed at the end of this chapter. But at this stage it may be pointed out that the pattern in the individual crop confirms the finding of the previous chapter that the rates of change in a crop did not necessarily depend on its relative importance in each region. Thus, for example, while the relative importance of autumn rice was more or less the same in Rajshahi and Dacca the rates of change in both the series were completely different. Again, Presidency and Burdwan Divisions accounted for one fifth and one sixth respectively of the total acreage under winter rice. But while the rate of expansion was 1.6 per cent in the former it was only 0.2 per cent per year in the latter.

3.4 PROVINCIAL AND REGIONAL TRENDS IN THE QUINQUENNIAL PERIODS

The quinquennial trends in acreage under the cultivation of individual crops were in general similar to those in output. Thus, during the first five years it was only in the case of the two minor crops of linseed and wheat that the trends were different from those in output (Table 3.8). Otherwise the general pattern was the same – the acreage under tea and jute was expanding with the recovery in the market conditions and this was accompanied by a decline in the acreage under the remaining crops. It may, however, be pointed out that the rate of expansion of the acreage under jute and the rates of decline in the other crops were slower than for output. Secondly, at the level of the regional units the variations were more marked.

The trends in the second period were more or less similar. As market conditions continued to improve, the acreage under the cultivation of jute, tobacco and tea expanded and this was accompanied by some decline in the other crops (Table 3.9). It is, again, important that the rates of decline, particularly in winter rice, were not as high as in output. Conversely, in jute and tobacco the pace of expansion was slower. This indicates that yield per acre was perhaps an important factor in the magnitude of response of the various crops to the changes in the price level. Thus, while a drop in the productivity of autumn rice was accompanied by some expansion of acreage

TABLE 3.8   *Index of acreage 1920–24*
(1920/21 to 1922/23 = 100)

Crops	All-Bengal	Presi-dency	Burd-wan	Raj-shahi	Dacca	Chitta-gong
Winter rice	99	99	98	96	100	100
Autumn rice	97	97	89	96	99	100
Jute	121	127	90	118	123	125
Mustard	95	95	108	97	91	106
Summer rice	101	98	101	105	102	99
Gram	95	95	93	95	97	100
Wheat	101	102	96	100	100	–
Sesamum	94	86	92	95	92	100
Tobacco	100	86	92	101	78	103
Linseed	98	100	99	96	92	99
Sugarcane	99	93	93	103	101	97
Tea	101	–	–	101	–	100
Barley	97	95	98	95	99	–
All-crops	100	99	97	98	102	102

TABLE 3.9   *Index of acreage 1925–29*
(1920/21 to 1922/23 = 100)

Crops	All-Bengal	Presi-dency	Burd-wan	Raj-shahi	Dacca	Chitta-gong
Winter rice	93	90	88	90	99	97
Autumn rice	98	104	122	97	89	93
Jute	187	241	158	176	183	196
	(167)	(215)	(141)	(157)	(163)	(175)
Mustard	86	91	109	91	76	125
Summer rice	99	222	52	104	104	51
Gram	88	84	89	93	116	100
Wheat	102	118	96	93	101	–
Sesamum	83	102	62	106	71	106
Tobacco	103	70	119	110	73	111
Linseed	97	107	149	83	80	89
Sugarcane	95	82	73	109	106	75
Tea	108	–	–	108	–	108
Barley	90	122	77	62	117	–
All-crops	101	100	92	99	104	101
	(98)	(98)	(89)	(96)	(103)	(99)

Note: Figures in brackets refer to the revised series.

during these years the pattern was just the opposite for linseed. So far as the regional picture is concerned these provincial trends were most representative in the case of winter rice, gram and jute. In the other crops there were considerable variations.

During the depression years the acreage under cultivation expanded for all the crops except tobacco, linseed and jute (Table 3.10). It may be recalled here that with regard to output it was only in the case of jute that the impact of the depression was felt. However, since the decline in the acreage under linseed and tobacco was so marginal it may be suggested that the nature of the impact of the depression on the acreage under the cultivation of individual crops was similar to that on output. The provincial pattern was most representative of the regional trends once again in the case of winter rice, autumn rice, wheat, barley, gram and jute.

The expansion of acreage under all the individual crops during the period from 1935 to 1939 confirms the earlier findings on the end of substitution between jute and the two varieties of rice; and, secondly, confirms the increased emphasis on minor cash crops (mustard, linseed, sesamum and tobacco) for cash needs (Table 3.11). There was a considerable increase also of acreage under wheat, barley and gram. This increase in the cultivation of

TABLE 3.10   *Index of acreage 1930–34*
(1920/21 to 1922/23 = 100)

Crops	All-Bengal	Presidency	Burd-wan	Raj-shahi	Dacca	Chitta-gong
Winter rice	97	97	90	93	102	106
Autumn rice	107	106	129	106	118	84
Jute	140	156	117	129	146	136
	(128)	(143)	(108)	(118)	(133)	(124)
Mustard	87	96	110	97	75	102
Summer rice	100	94	56	96	112	60
Gram	120	122	97	130	121	100
Wheat	120	121	121	115	159	–
Sesamum	85	95	58	110	74	109
Tobacco	102	57	120	108	83	114
Linseed	96	106	142	90	65	74
Sugarcane	112	101	63	137	138	66
Tea	113	–	–	113	–	111
Barley	99	172	79	68	115	–
All-crops	102	102	94	100	108	100
	(101)	(102)	(92)	(98)	(107)	(98)

Note: Figures in brackets refer to the revised series.

TABLE 3.11   *Index of acreage 1935–39*
(1920/21 to 1922/23 = 100)

Crops	All-Bengal	Presidency	Burdwan	Rajshahi	Dacca	Chittagong
Winter rice	99	107	86	97	107	103
Autumn rice	109	113	110	105	128	82
Jute	144	183	86	130	150	140
	(140)	(177)	(83)	(126)	(145)	(136)
Mustard	89	114	112	104	71	96
Summer rice	104	158	34	111	117	58
Gram	183	207	104	158	140	100
Wheat	129	176	108	108	140	–
Sesamum	99	95	56	116	97	121
Tobacco	110	58	76	116	103	119
Linseed	106	128	117	85	62	110
Sugarcane	149	162	60	182	194	76
Tea	114	–	–	114	–	108
Barley	110	198	60	84	115	–
All-crops	105	115	89	104	115	98
	(105)	(115)	(87)	(102)	(114)	(96)

Note: Figures in brackets refer to the revised series.

these minor crops clearly reflects the expansion of the double cropped area which took place during these years. For these crops are grown during the interval between the harvesting and sowing of the major crops – winter rice, autumn rice and jute. Another feature of the trends in this quinquennium is that even in the case of these crops the rates of increase were higher for food crops. This would again indicate the emphasis on increased food production.

The trends in the last quinquennium bring out more clearly the effects of the upward revision of statistics during these years (Table 3.12). For reasons already referred to, the rates of increase were highest for the food crops. Acreage under the other crops remained either stagnant or increased at a slower pace. With regard to the rates of acceleration among the individual food crops the expansion of acreage under minor crops like wheat, barley and gram was much higher.

As to the effects of the revision of statistics, winter rice and jute fall under one group in that the trend is reversed. The near-zero trend in autumn rice during these years has to be interpreted with reference to the relatively simple method of revision. Thus, it is only in the case of minor crops that the revised series indicates some expansion of acreage.

TABLE 3.12   *Index of acreage 1940–44*
(1920/21 to 1922/23 = 100)

Crops	All-Bengal	Presidency	Burdwan	Rajshahi	Dacca	Chittagong
Winter rice	110	132	99	106	113	107
	(97)	(111)	(81)	(89)	(107)	(104)
Autumn rice	130	125	114	136	157	96
	(109)	(107)	(142)	(96)	(149)	(68)
Jute	167	268	183	184	143	142
	(132)	(211)	(143)	(146)	(113)	(111)
Mustard	89	138	103	107	66	86
	(87)	(130)	(108)	(103)	(65)	(85)
Summer rice	126	213	97	177	123	78
	(107)	(164)	(49)	(116)	(119)	(60)
Gram	283	311	157	276	231	210
	(214)	(245)	(108)	(185)	(142)	(110)
Wheat	149	215	139	117	150	–
	(140)	(208)	(100)	(117)	(132)	
Sesamum	95	132	60	100	89	133
Linseed	122	176	87	77	54	113
Tobacco	99	72	55	99	114	130
	(113)	(58)	(72)	(119)	(109)	(124)
Sugarcane	150	194	57	181	192	77
Tea	114	–	–	114	–	108
Barley	157	258	55	157	130	–
	(115)	(234)	(50)	(85)	(116)	
All-crops	119	141	101	120	123	105
	(103)	(119)	(84)	(97)	(114)	(91)

Note: Figures in brackets refer to the revised series.

3.5 ALL-BENGAL AND REGIONAL RATES OF CHANGE IN YIELD PER ACRE

The near-zero trend in the yield of all the crops taken together may be said to be most representative of autumn rice, which accounted for one fifth of the total acreage under cultivation (Table 3.13). The annual rates of increase of the most important cash crop (jute) and the three minor food crops of gram, wheat and barley were better, but still low. In the case of the last three crops this, however, conforms to what could be expected, as the climatic conditions of Bengal are less suitable for the cultivation of these crops than other parts of India. With a moderate annual growth of 0.7 per cent, mustard and summar rice belonged to one group followed by linseed, tobacco and sesamum in another. The trends in these three crops were fairly high but their combined relative importance was small. The three other crops belong to two opposite extremes. Thus, the productivity per acre of sugarcane and tea increased at the rates of 1.8 per cent and 2.3 per cent respectively per year. Conversely the yield of winter rice declined at the annual rate of 0.3 per cent. As pointed out in the previous chapter this was of the greatest importance for the agricultural economy at large and may perhaps explain at least a part of the much better trends of some of the minor crops. Thus, generally, the trends in yield per acre reveal the same pattern – productivity increased only for the minor crops.

At the regional level the rates of increase of the yield of linseed, tobacco, sesamum and the rates of decline in gram were more or less the same in all the component regions. In the case of the other crops there were considerable variations – most markedly for winter rice. Thus, while the trend in the Presidency Division was still positive, the rates of decline varied from 0.1 per cent in Rajshahi to as high as 0.8 per cent in Chittagong. Rajshahi and Dacca accounted for three quarters of the acreage under the cultivation of sugarcane and jute, but the rates of increase in these two regions were much slower. As in the case of the trends of acreage this indicates that the trends of yield did not necessarily depend on the relative importance of a crop in each region. The rates of increase in barley and summar rice have to be interpreted with reference to the fact that yield per acre has been assumed to be uniform in all the regions.

3.6 PROVINCIAL AND REGIONAL TRENDS IN YIELD PER ACRE IN THE QUINQUENNIAL PERIODS

During the first five years the yield per acre of nine crops which accounted for nearly nine tenths of the all-crop acreage was declining (Table 3.14). Of the individual crops the most marked drop took place in the productivity of winter rice. The yield of the three other crops of jute, linseed and tea was increasing but at slow rates. Thus the general pattern was the same as in acreage under cultivation. At the regional level the picture was mostly similar to this provincial average. The fall in the yield of jute in Burdwan Division was mainly due to four consecutive bad years in the Midnapore District. This was, however, partly neutralised by some improvement in the productivity of wheat, mustard and sesamum.

The decline in the three important food crops of winter rice, autumn rice and gram continued during the second quinquennium (Table 3.15). Conversely, the rates of increase in the productivity of jute and tea accelerated. In the case of the former this seems to reflect the greater use of the improved variety of seeds during these years of relative prosperity. The radical jump in the productivity of tobacco has to be understood with ref-

TABLE 3.13   *Annual rates of change in individual crop yield*
1920–46

Crops	Relative weight	All-Bengal	Presi-dency	Burd-wan	Raj-shahi	Dacca	Chitta-gong
Winter rice	58	−0.3	0.1	−0.3	−0.1	−0.5	−0.8
Autumn rice	22	0.2	0.4	−0.2	0.3	0.2	0.1
Jute	9	0.3	0.4	0.9	0.3	0.2	1.1
Mustard	3	0.7	1.5	1.0	0.2	1.0	1.6
Summer rice	2	0.7	0.7	0.7	0.7	0.7	0.7
Gram	1	0.5	1.0	−0.1	−0.2	−0.2	−0.1
Wheat	1	0.4	0.9	0.3	0.2	1.4	−
Sesamum	1	1.2	1.7	1.0	1.7	0.9	1.4
Tobacco	1	1.2	1.2	1.1	1.0	2.1	1.1
Linseed	1	1.2	1.7	1.3	1.3	1.1	0.4
Sugarcane	1	1.8	2.8	2.4	1.3	1.8	2.3
Tea	1	2.3	−	−	2.4	−	0.6
Barley	0	0.3	0.3	0.3	0.3	0.3	−
All-crops	100	0.1	0.2	−0.2	0.4	−0.1	−0.3

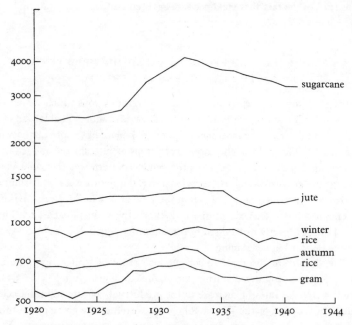

FIGURE 3.3   *Yield of individual crops (all-Bengal), five years' moving average (log scale).*

TABLE 3.14   *Index of yield per acre in the quinquennium 1920–24*
(1920/21 to 1922/23 = 100)

Crops	All-Bengal	Presidency	Burdwan	Rajshahi	Dacca	Chittagong
Winter rice	95	99	94	96	94	93
Autumn rice	97	98	98	99	95	95
Jute	105	107	94	108	104	105
Mustard	98	100	102	98	98	100
Summer rice	96	96	96	96	96	96
Gram	99	101	97	94	95	98
Wheat	97	95	101	96	104	–
Sesamum	98	92	105	97	97	105
Tobacco	100	100	100	100	100	100
Linseed	103	106	106	103	96	102
Sugarcane	98	96	99	99	96	98
Tea	103	–	–	103	–	101
Barley	98	98	98	98	98	–
All-crops	99	100	94	102	99	96

TABLE 3.15   *Index of yield per acre 1925–29*
(1920/21 to 1922/23 = 100)

Crops	All-Bengal	Presidency	Burdwan	Rajshahi	Dacca	Chittagong
Winter rice	94	99	84	99	97	86
Autumn rice	93	95	100	100	88	85
Jute	113	120	117	114	110	121
Mustard	100	111	106	96	103	93
Summer rice	91	91	91	91	91	91
Gram	97	98	90	96	90	75
Wheat	101	98	115	98	122	–
Sesamum	99	91	123	108	88	124
Tobacco	130	107	115	134	113	119
Linseed	103	106	116	112	91	90
Sugarcane	101	94	106	97	102	102
Tea	129	–	–	130	–	84
Barley	99	99	99	99	99	–
All-crops	104	104	86	115	109	95

erence to the straightforward method of adjustment made in the absence of the official yield figures for the first five years. Productivity of the three other minor crops of wheat, barley and mustard increased but at slow rates.

The trends in the yield of jute, wheat and barley were the same in all the regions. The drop in the productivity of jute for Burdwan in the preceding quinquennium was followed by a higher rate of acceleration during these years. In this respect the marked drop in the productivity of winter rice in this region may be of some significance. The pattern for the remaining crops was not always the same in all the regions. In this respect Chittagong seems to have formed a category by itself in that the yield per acre of winter rice, autumn rice, tea and linseed declined at higher rates.

During the depression years there was an increase in the productivity of all the crops except tea (Table 3.16). In course of the discussion on the nature of the official crop statistics it has been pointed out that the transfer of the crop-cutting experiments to the Agricultural Department resulted in an upward revision of the figures on standard yield for the quinquennium 1932/33 to 1936/37.[1] Now from the index of the actual yield per acre it is clear that it was only in the case of winter rice that the full effect of this bias was completely neutralised by the lower 'annawari' estimates of the seasonal condition. For the other crops the effect of the lower condition factor was partial. The magnitude of the individual crop output during the depression years noted in the earlier section must be interpreted in the light of this bias in the yield statistics. However, since the assumption in this study is that the trends in the acreage are more reliable these shortcomings do not affect the findings that

TABLE 3.16   *Index of yield per acre 1930–34*
(1920/21 to 1922/23 = 100)

Crops	All-Bengal	Presidency	Burdwan	Rajshahi	Dacca	Chittagong
Winter rice	95	103	90	100	91	80
Autumn rice	104	112	101	113	101	87
Jute	119	124	132	121	115	128
Mustard	127	145	141	124	127	118
Summer rice	108	108	108	108	108	108
Gram	123	134	112	105	113	122
Wheat	116	123	135	108	144	116
Sesamum	124	107	145	136	115	143
Tobacco	147	121	141	150	137	135
Linseed	135	152	153	138	117	78
Sugarcane	144	153	157	143	138	133
Tea	126	–	–	127	–	77
Barley	105	105	105	105	105	–
All-crops	107	109	92	123	107	91

[1] These figures (Table 3.16) do not fully reflect the upward shift in the standard as the quinquennium starts from 1930/31.

during the depression years there was a downward shift only in the production of jute. For, if it is argued that the yield per acre during these years remained more or less the same as in the preceding quinquennium the expansion of the acreage under cultivation would imply an expansion of production as well.

At the regional level the general pattern was the same as indicated by the provincial average, though in general the rates of change in Presidency Division were higher than in the other regions. The most marked exceptions were the reduction of the yield of winter rice in Burdwan and Chittagong. Almost the whole of this drop in the former region was caused by the lean year of 1935/36.

Productivity per acre of winter rice, sugarcane and linseed continued to improve during the fourth quinquennium, but only at marginal rates (Table 3.17). Conversely the yield of the remaining crops declined. This drop was much smaller than the drop in the figures on standard yield for the quinquennium beginning 1937/38. Obviously it is difficult to determine how far the reliability of the trends in individual crops was affected by this downward revision in the standard. But for reasons already pointed out this again does not affect the finding that the increased production of winter rice, autumn rice and minor commercial crops like linseed, tobacco and sugarcane was at the cost of jute.

Trends during the last five years were in sharp contrast to those in the third

TABLE 3.17   *Index of yield per acre 1935–39*
(1920/21 to 1922/23 = 100)

Crops	All-Bengal	Presidency	Burdwan	Rajshahi	Dacca	Chittagong
Winter rice	96	97	96	107	94	82
Autumn rice	98	91	105	104	101	91
Jute	117	111	124	116	116	132
Mustard	125	142	143	118	131	122
Summer rice	111	111	111	111	111	111
Gram	112	118	107	104	102	77
Wheat	114	122	127	106	153	114
Sesamum	125	112	136	137	119	138
Tobacco	137	114	128	137	150	128
Linseed	136	144	143	143	119	107
Sugarcane	151	157	170	156	140	148
Tea	133	–	–	134	–	81
Barley	105	105	105	105	105	–
All-crops	107	100	98	121	109	94

quinquennium (Table 3.18) – the yield of almost all the crops declined. The highest drop was in the productivity of winter rice despite the fact that the standard was more or less the same as in the preceding quinquennium. This was mainly due to the two lean years of 1940/41 and 1942/43. The unfavourable weather conditions of 1940/41 were a common factor in the reduced yield of gram, wheat and barley. There was some improvement in the productivity of autumn rice but clearly this was too marginal to offset the decline in the other food crops. Among the five regions the rate of decline in these crops was much higher in Rajshahi and Burdwan. The consequent drop in food production in Burdwan was further aggravated by the fall in the productivity of autumn rice. The negative trend in the case of the minor cash crops was mainly due to the lower standard yield used for the quinquennium beginning 1942/43.

Thus, the percentage rates of change of the acreage and yield of the thirteen individual crops were not the same as indicated by their weighted average. While the acreage and yield of the major crops remained either stagnant or declined, those of the minor crops improved considerably. As most of these crops were grown on double cropped land in the dry season this expansion of acreage conforms to what could be expected against a background of the near-constancy of the net cropped area.

The conceivable explanations for the contrast between the trends in the yield of winter rice and the minor cash crops have been discussed in the pre-

TABLE 3.18   *Index of yield per acre 1940–44*
(1920/21 to 1922/23 = 100)

Crops	All-Bengal	Presidency	Burd-wan	Raj-shahi	Dacca	Chitta-gong
Winter rice	88	101	81	92	87	79
Autumn rice	99	109	91	106	96	91
Jute	110	119	116	111	105	127
Mustard	108	136	118	97	112	132
Summer rice	107	107	107	107	107	107
Wheat	105	110	107	100	143	–
Gram	109	121	90	90	91	93
Sesamum	121	134	130	140	107	142
Tobacco	134	131	128	131	153	129
Linseed	125	139	132	129	111	99
Sugarcane	131	156	142	116	135	142
Tea	173	–	–	174	–	111
Barley	104	104	104	104	104	–
All-crops	101	108	84	114	100	92

ceding chapter. The present chapter may be concluded by an attempt to examine what factors might have caused the wide variations at the regional level. Of particular importance in this respect is the variation between Presidency Division and the two regions of Burdwan and Chittagong. With regard to the former region it has been pointed out that the shifting of the main Ganges flow'from the Bhagirathi–Hooghly River to the River Padma had caused a decrease, or a slowing down in the growth of population and a fall in soil fertility.[1] But clearly this is contradicted by the evidence presented in this chapter. This strengthens Blyn's suspicion that the effect of the change of the course of the Ganges was not an active force during the period under review.[2] It could, therefore, be argued that the physical conditions of Presidency and Burdwan Divisions were more or less the same. This is not, however, to deny that the conditions of some of the districts of Burdwan Division resemble those of Bihar more than those of other parts of West Bengal. But it is possible that the impact of these adverse conditions was mostly neutralised by the fact that the proportion of irrigated area was greater in this region. Considered in this context the marked contrast between these two regions seems to be perplexing. For if it is argued that the effect of the irrigation was marginal the question still remains why the gap was so marked. This is particularly relevant in view of the fact that the extension of the crop acreage in Presidency Division was mainly due to the reduction of fallow land and the increase of double cropping. It seems that in the absence of any technological innovation this would tend to lower yield per acre. Some qualitative assessment of yield per acre with reference to the conditions of the rivers, 'Khals' and 'Beels' was made in 1944–45.[3] But this does not throw much light on the issue. Nor are the Settlement and Survey Reports of the districts under these two regions of much help. The usefulness of the information otherwise available is affected by the fact that these operations were made at different times.

The trends for Chittagong seem to present a less difficult problem. Of the four districts in this region the soil conditions of Chittagong proper and Chittagong Hill Tracts are much different from those of the other parts of Eastern Bengal. It is very likely that in the absence of technological improvements the productivity in these two districts was declining and led to the shrinkage of area under cultivation. This argument may

[1] A. Geddes, *Au Pays de Tagore* quoted by G. Blyn, *Agricultural Trends in India, 1891–1947: Output, Availability and Productivity* (University of Pennsylvania Press, 1966), p. 199. This view was repeated in the *Agricultural Statistics by Plot to Plot Enumeration* (Calcutta, 1946), Part II, p. 2.

[2] Blyn, *op. cit.*, p. 198.

[3] *Ishaque Report, op. cit.*, pp. 10–86.

perhaps partly apply to certain parts of Noakhali district, which are inundated by the saline waters of the sea.

What could have caused the difference between Dacca and Rajshahi with regard to the trends in the yield per acre of winter rice? Again nothing definite can be said on this question, but some possibilities may be suggested. The revised series indicates some expansion of acreage under winter rice in Dacca and some retardation in Rajshahi. The extension of cultivation in Dacca was mostly due to the increase of double cropping and the reduction of fallow land. Conversely the proportion of double cropped area was much smaller in Rajshahi – only 13 per cent as against 25 per cent in the former. In the preceding chapter it has been pointed out that the extension of double cropping coupled with the pressure on fallow land could have produced an adverse effect on the yield per acre. If this possibility is accepted the difference in the rates of decline in the productivity of winter rice in these two regions would seem to lie in the difference of acreage trends itself. The effect of the increased intensity of land use could have been offset by the use of commercial fertiliser and improved varieties of seeds. But clearly there was little progress in this direction during the period under review.

PART TWO

4

PRICE ELASTICITY OF ACREAGE
UNDER CULTIVATION

The question as to whether a policy of providing price incentives to cultivators should be a part of the general policy of modernising the agricultural sector in the underdeveloped countries has led to a controversy as to the applicability of the concpet of supply response in a traditional agriculture. Thus, while some authors have ruled out the possibility of the play of the price-mechanism from agricultural production decisions, others have argued that peasant producers respond normally and significantly to changes in the price level.[1] To a certain degree this controversy has been confused and intensified by the failure to make explicit the three different aspects of the supply response: (1) the response of total agricultural production to changes in the terms of trade with the non-agricultural sector; (2) the response of individual crops to a change in price relative to the prices of alternative crops; and (3) the response of the marketed surplus to changes in the price. In the recent past it has been found in a number of econometric works that the acreage (in some cases output) of individual crops (category (2) above) is fairly responsive to changes in relative price.[2] But two other aspects of the problem have hardly been examined yet.[3] In the present chapter an attempt is made to investigate whether changes in the price level had any effect on the supply of total agricultural output and the produce of individual crops (categories (1) and (2) above). As the relevant data are not available no attempt is made to estimate the price elasticity of the marketed surplus of food crops.

This chapter is divided into five sections. In the first two sections hypotheses are framed with regard to the supply response of total crops and indi-

[1] See, for example, T. W. Schultz, *Economic Crises in World Agriculture* (Michigan, 1965), p. 49. J. W. Mellor, *The Economics of Agricultural Development* (Ithaca, 1966), pp. 199–200. Authors who believe that the concept of supply response is not applicable are referred to later.

[2] For a summary of these findings see J. R. Behrman, *Supply Response in Underdeveloped Agriculture: A Case Study of Four Major Annual Crops in Thailand, 1937–1963* (Amsterdam, 1968), pp. 15–18.

[3] The supply response of the marketed surplus has been examined by Behrman, pp. 281–315; and Raj Krishna, 'The Marketable Surplus Function for a Subsistence Crop', *Economic Weekly*, XVII (February 1965), pp. 309–20; 'A Note on the Elasticity of the Marketable Surplus of a Subsistence Crop', *Indian Journal of Agricultural Economics* XVII (1962), pp. 79–84. But there does not seem to be any work at all on the price elasticity of total agricultural production.

vidual crops. The procedural problems of estimating the supply response are taken up in section 4.3. This is followed by a discussion on the estimating formula in the fourth section and an analysis of the estimated elasticities in the last.

4.1 THE SUPPLY RESPONSE OF TOTAL OUTPUT

What is the usual response of total supply when prices are falling? During the world-wide depression of 1929–32 total world industrial production fell by 37 per cent, but agricultural production by only one per cent. In the United States the price index of non-agricultural commodities fell by 38 per cent from 1929 to 1932, while for agricultural production it fell by 54 per cent. In the same period industrial production dropped by 47 per cent, but agricultural production was actually higher in 1932 than in 1929.[1] It is a fact that such figures do not directly reflect the real magnitude of the price inelasticity of agriculture, as the impact of other non-price variables has not been considered and these years included some bumper crops. But the general pattern of the inflexibility of total production during a period of falling prices is fairly clear. When considered in the context of traditional agriculture like that of Bengal the possibility of such production behaviour becomes stronger.

The basic factor which creates this presumption that the aggregate volume of agricultural production will not decline during a period of depression is the composition of costs involved in agricultural operations. However, it is not 'cost' in the ordinary sense of the term. 'In dealing with the specific bearing of agricultural costs upon production behaviour during depression,' as Messrs Galbraith and Black point out, 'we must use the term "cost" in an inclusive sense, passing over all quibbles as to what are and are not costs, and including all disbursements of the farmer – monetary or otherwise – which may have a bearing on his activity.'[2] Considered in this context it is clear that in agriculture the proportion of fixed costs is much higher than in industry. Thus, the needs of food consumption of the cultivators' family – the single largest item of cost – partakes of the character of fixed expenditure. An adverse man–land ratio and a low productivity from the soil create conditions in which a large majority of the agricultural population have to live at the margin of subsistence. Now obviously during a period of depression the food requirements of the cultivators' family are not reduced. Conversely the possibility is that food requirements are increased as agriculture, in its traditional role as the 'shock-absorber', has to accommodate a part of industrial labour (though by definition very small in a predominantly agricultural country like Bengal)

[1] These figures are cited by A. Martin, *Economics and Agriculture* (London, 1968), p. 32.
[2] J. K. Galbraith and J. D. Black, 'The Maintenance of Agricultural Production During Depression: Explanations Reviewed', *Journal of Political Economy*, Vol. XLVI.

thrown out of employment. These considerations naturally preclude the possibility of a positive impact of falling prices on the production decision of the cultivators – in so far as it relates to the needs of domestic consumption. If there is a response at all it is likely that there will be an expansion of food production. In a traditional agriculture, production for subsistence needs is the dominant pattern. This suggests that even if there is a drop in the production of cash crops in response to a fall in the price level total agricultural output will not be price elastic.

But there are certain considerations which create the presumption that the supply of cash crops will also increase. Thus, firstly, while money income from the same volume of produce shrinks, the cultivators have to pay more for the goods they buy from the market as farm prices tend to fall faster and with bigger amplitudes than the prices of other products. Secondly, as pointed out in the preceding discussion, there is the paradox that at a time when the supply of agricultural labour is expected to be cut down in response to the changes in the market conditions it is actually increased. This results in an additional need for cash income. Thirdly, the cash expenditure involved in agriculture – rent, local taxes and interest on debt – remain fixed and thus their burden becomes heavier as a result of the drop in the price level. Such annual charges magnify the marginal utility of every unit of produce and thus outweigh the discouragement from the fall in the price level. The possibility that the output of cash crops would thus tend to increase is strengthened by the low opportunity cost of the other production inputs apart from labour – land, agricultural implements and bullock power. Thus, it would seem that, in view of the increased needs for a marketed surplus to meet fixed charges and other cash expenditures and the lack of an alternative use for the production inputs, the cultivators would devote all the available land to the production of cash crops after ensuring a supply of food for domestic consumption.

From the preceding discussion it is clear that family farms have two special characteristics which distinguish them from 'pure' firms. The latter 'purchase' almost all their inputs and sell almost all their output in the market at market prices and against money payments. As against these, on family farms a substantial or even the greater part of the output is meant for consumption by members of the family. On the input side the greater part of the inputs are supplied directly by the producers' household and their transfer-earnings are low or negligible.[1] In such a situation the aim of the producers will be to maximise the total return from the available land irrespective of a drop in the price

---

[1] These are discussed by Raj Krishna, 'Models of the Family Farm' in C. R. Wharton, Jr. (ed.), *Subsistence Agriculture and Economic Development* (Chicago, 1970), pp. 185–90; 'The Theory of the Farm: Rapporteur's Report', *Indian Economic Journal*, Vol. XIX, No. 4 (1964), pp. 514–25.

level. Thus, the utility functions of the cultivators preclude the possibility of an adverse effect from falling prices on the level of their production.

What would be the response of farmers who employ a considerable volume of wage labour and sell the larger part of their produce in the market? At first sight it would appear that they would reduce production when there is a drop in the price level. It is true that in general the production behaviour of this class of farms conforms to that of the pure firm,[1] but a closer scrutiny suggests that their production is also likely to remain inflexible. Firstly, the surplus farmers have to retain a part of their production for domestic consumption. Secondly, they have to bear certain fixed costs. To the extent that production is meant to pay for these the behaviour of the surplus farmers would be the same as that of the small farmers. Thirdly, the other important cost item – the cost of labour – is likely to drop along with a drop in the price level. Thus, on the whole, the response of the surplus producer is not likely to be significantly different from that of the subsistence farmer.

Thus, to summarise this part of the discussion, it seems that falling prices would not lead to a drop in the level of agricultural production. Conversely, if it is believed that cultivators try to improve or at least to maintain their present standard of living then it follows that such a tendency would be strengthened during depressions and this would be reflected in those rates of growth in total production compatible with the given technological and institutional framework.

Two other forces which also have some bearing on the inelasticity of supply when prices are declining (as also at times of rising prices) are uncertainty as to future prices and weather conditions. In low income countries seasonal fluctuations in prices tend to be highly erratic and can be large. Similarly the year to year fluctuations are unpredictable and can be large. Being accustomed to such swings in prices, even in normal business conditions, the cultivators tend to ignore the sharper price movements of the earlier years of boom or depression. To this is added the significant effect of weather conditions. In Bengal agricultural produce depends so much on rainfall that it is regarded as a 'gamble in monsoon'.[2] Considering the magnitude of risk and the penalty

[1] That considerations of making a profit as understood in its usual sense constitute an important determinant of the production decision of the larger farmers is shown by the findings in Indian agriculture. These findings are summarised by, among others, R. Krishna, 'Land Reform and Development in Southern Asia', in W. Froelich (ed.) *Land Tenure, Industrialisation and Social Stability* (Milwaukee, 1961).

[2] In the USA a 10 per cent change in weather conditions has been found to imply a 4 per cent change in both the total farm output and the output of all-crops. See Z. Griliches, 'Estimates of the Aggregate United States Farm Supply Function', *The Journal of Farm Economics*, XLII (1960). For the importance of the same in the agriculture of the Punjab see R. S. M. V. Unakar, 'Correlation between Weather and Crops with special reference to Punjab Wheat', *Memoirs of the Indian Meteorological Department*, Vol. XXV, Part IV.

for error it is not surprising that the cultivators should strive to maintain a steady volume of production. However, in attempting to explain the inflexibility or upward trend in agricultural production when prices are falling too much emphasis should not be laid on these two forces alone.[1] Actually these two factors seem to play only a subsidiary, though important, role in the sense that they only add to the rigidity, which is essentially caused by the considerations described above.

Thus, it is not 'perversity' or the 'obtuseness on the part of the farmers',[2] but certain rational considerations which account for high aggregate production irrespective of the character of the market. Such a steady performance from the agricultural sector has rightly been regarded as a 'major national asset',[3] and this is one of the considerations why in the recent past agrarian reform in the underdeveloped countries has sought to create individual peasant holdings. The underlying motive in this respect is to maximise total agricultural output before a part of the labour force is withdrawn to the other sectors.

From the preceding discussion it follows that 'perversity' will be a feature accompanying falling prices. What would be the reaction of the cultivators when the prices of their produce are increasing? This raises the wider and the much-discussed question of whether the material values of the West are foreign to the people of the under-developed countries. An extreme stand in this controversy has been taken by Boeke who maintains that the social systems of the underdeveloped countries (moulded by fatalism and conservatism) are fundamentally different from the social systems of the Western countries (dominated by common sense, reason, and practical considerations) and as such require a different economic theory.[4]

Very few scholars support this extreme thesis, but there are some who believe that certain institutional and cultural constraints such as a spirit of 'resigned contentment', 'survival-mindedness', 'natural conservatism' stand

---

[1] Messrs Galbraith and Black (*op. cit.*) seem to overemphasise the importance of these two forces by giving them the same weight as the other factors mentioned earlier.

[2] B. D. Giles, 'Agriculture and the Price Mechanism' in T. Wilson and P. W. S. Andrews (eds.), *Oxford Studies in the Price Mechanism* (Oxford, 1951), p. 173.

[3] T. W. Schultz, *Agriculture in an Unstable Economy* (New York, 1945), p. 13. For a discussion on the importance of the creation of peasant holdings see, Georgescu-Roegen, 'Economic Theory and Agrarian Economics' in C. K. Eicher and L. W. Witt (eds.), *Agriculture in Economic Development* (New York, 1964), pp. 144–69.

[4] J. H. Boeke, *Economics and Economic Policies of the Dual Societies* (New York, 1953), pp. 3–5. His thesis is based on his personal experiences in Indonesia, but he claims their general applicability to all the under-developed countries. For a critical review of his work see B. Higgins, 'The Dualistic Theory of the Underdeveloped Countries', *Economic Development and Cultural Change*, Vol. IV (January 1956), pp. 99–112. For such opinions directly relating to India, see Vera Anstey, *The Economic Development of India* (London, 1957); K. Davis, *The Population of India and Pakistan* (Princeton, 1951), pp. 213–20; Max Weber, *The Religion of*

in the way of a positive response by the cultivators to rising prices.[1] Thus according to Kusum Nair

> in a situation of limited and static aspirations if a man should feel that his requirements are just two bags of paddy per year, he works for two bags, but not more. If he looks up to the stars, it is only to worship them, not to pluck them . . . in fact often the peasant does not consider it moral to want more. . . . He may and often does disdain to engage in activities yielding the highest net advantage even within the available opportunities and the restrictions imposed on him by the society to which he belongs.[2]

Evidently such contentions are based on the assumption that in underdeveloped societies the income elasticity of demand for leisure outweighs the cross elasticity of demand between leisure and additional income and this results in a backward bending supply curve. Obviously it is not possible here to review the different points raised by different authors in the debate on whether the supply curve of labour is really backward in the underdeveloped countries.[3] What has, however, to be pointed out is that most of the discussion has been speculative in character and is based on *a priori* considerations of peasant behaviour and institutional constraints. Price responsiveness is essentially an empirical phenomenon and it is difficult to accept any thesis which is not backed by evidence. There is no denying the fact that among the peasants there are many for whom additional leisure is more important than additional income, but the realities of life of the great majority of

---

India (Glencoe, Illinois, 1958); *Report of the Royal Commission on Agriculture* (London, 1928), p. 6.

[1] See, for example, J. P. Lewis, *Quiet crises in India: Economic Development and American Policy* (New York, 1964), p. 157; W. C. Neale, 'Economic accounting and family-farming in India', *Economic Development and Cultural Change*, Vol. VII (April 1952), pp. 286–305; R. O. Olson, 'The impact and implications of foreign surplus disposal on underdeveloped economies', *Journal of Farm Economics*, Vol. XLII (December 1960), pp. 1042–5. B. P. Misra and S. P. Sinha, 'Agriculture and its terms of trade with special reference to India', *The Indian Journal of Agricultural Economics* (1958), pp. 191–2; Mahesh Chand, 'Agricultural Terms of Trade and Economic Growth', *The Indian Journal of Agricultural Economics* (1958), pp. 201–2.

[2] K. Nair, *Blossoms in the Dust: The Human Factor in Indian Development* (New York, 1965), p. 193.

[3] Thus, for example, Anne Martin confuses this issue with marketed supply, *op. cit.*, p. 29. T. W. Schultz accepts such a contention but defends it on the grounds of lack of stamina and low marginal return. See his *Transforming Traditional Agriculture* (New York, 1962), pp. 26–8.

Among many other works on the debate see also S. Rottenberg, 'Income and Leisure in an Underdeveloped Economy', *Journal of Political Economy*, Vol. LX (1952), pp. 95–101; and E. J. Berg, 'Backward-Sloping Labour Supply Functions in Dual Economies – 'The African Case', *Quarterly Journal of Economics*, Vol. LXXV, (1961).

the agricultural population preclude the possibility of such production behaviour. The large volume of rural indebtedness, which was estimated at one hundred crores of rupees[1] in 1929 and one hundred and fifty crores of rupees in 1945,[2] is symptomatic of the fact that the needs of a large section of the cultivators far exceeded their income – a fact which cannot be reconciled with the possibility that they had been content with their current income. Even in the case of those to whom additional leisure was more important than additional income, it is reasonable to argue that their desire for more leisure should have led them, instead of leaving a part of the land fallow, to let it out to others. In other words, in a situation where everybody was bidding for more land, even under normal market conditions, it is hard to believe that the effect of rising income would be that less land were cultivated. These considerations create a strong presumption that an increase in the price level will be followed by an expansion of the total supply.

However, the assumption that the supply response will be positive in the face of rising prices has to be interpreted with reference to two important limitations which may 'obscure' the degree of response expected of cultivators. In the densely populated countries the supply of land is inelastic. When cultivable land was available more and more of it was brought under cultivation not only to meet the food requirements of the growing population but also the demand for commercial crops (mostly for exports). The aggregate output expanded in response to prices, thus reflecting the peasants' 'capacity to respond positively to economic incentives'.[3] But as a result cultivation was extended almost to the possible limits. This was particularly so in Bengal where by the beginning of our period 90 per cent of the total cultivable area was already under cultivation. The scope for the extension of cultivation in the remaining area was limited by the complex land revenue system and the known incapability for capital investment by the cultivators.

It is reasonable to assume that the cultivators of Bengal, through their long acquaintance with the cultivation of the same type of land, sowing the same crops and the use of the same techniques of production, had attained a fairly

[1] *Report of the Bengal Provincial Banking Enquiry Committee* (Calcutta, 1930), Vol. 1, pp. 69–70.
[2] Government of Bengal, *Agricultural Statistics by Plot to Plot Enumeration in Bengal 1944/45*, Part 1 (Calcutta, 1946), p. 57.
[3] H. Myint, *Economics of the Developing Countries* (London, 1973). To substantiate his argument he shows that rice exports from Burma and Thailand (produced by peasants) had increased by 10 to 13 times from 1873 to 1913 and 20 times by the late 1920s. This rapid expansion of peasant exports is all the more interesting because, unlike that of mining and plantation, it seems to owe little or nothing to outside economic resources. In the case of Bengal the rapid expansion of jute cultivation indicates the same pattern.

high degree of efficiency in the allocation of the factors of production.[1] In such a situation, when the scope for the expansion of output within the given institutional and technological framework was so limited, the response to price incentives should have been reflected more through the use of such purchased inputs as raise the yield per acre than through the extension of the acreage under cultivation. The necessity for the use of such improved inputs was realised by the Government of India and of Bengal and from 1918 the Agricultural Department devoted most of its otherwise limited resources to the popularisation of the improved varieties of seeds evolved at the experimental centres.[2] Due to the shortage of farms and trained staff the activities of the Department of Agriculture in the sphere of demonstration and propaganda were far from sufficient. But even then the demand for the improved seeds far exceeded the available supply. This readiness by the cultivators to make use of the new inputs for increasing their total output suggests that in general the peasant producers were not really 'survival-minded'. Thus, since the scope of increasing output either by the extension of cultivation to new areas or by the use of new inputs was limited, it is very likely that the response of total agricultural production to rising prices would remain concealed.

The second limitation to be emphasised is transport; coupled with imperfect marketing conditions. For areas more or less isolated for lack of transport and communication facilities the question of price elasticity is less significant. Considering that the means of transport were backward and the marketing system so defective in Bengal these limitations have to be regarded as of considerable importance.

4.2 THE SUPPLY RESPONSE OF INDIVIDUAL CROPS

Having examined all-crop supply responses the problems of inter-crop shifts of acreage in response to changing relative price may be discussed. The discussion will suggest that a traditional agriculture both has points of weakness and of strength which may respectively impede or facilitate shifts in land use in response to changing relative prices.

To begin with, the basic input of land with its components of soil and topography may be more suitable for the production of a particular crop than others. This would imply that even wide shifts in relative profitability may have little or no effect. Similarly, the allocative function of price will break down when several crops are sown alongside one another, provided the area is

---

[1] Schultz, *op. cit.*, pp. 35–52; W. D. Hopper, 'Allocation Efficiency in a Traditional Indian Agriculture' *Journal of Farm Economics*, Vol. 47 (1965), pp. 611–24.

[2] *Annual Report of the Department of Agriculture*, Government of Bengal for 1918 and the subsequent years.

so specific that it cannot be transferred to alternative uses. However, specificity is usually a matter of degree and, therefore, in the generality of cases this 'may effect the extent of area shifts between crops, or the promptness with which they occur, rather than preclude their occurrence altogether'. [1]

Non-land inputs, however, afford a great advantage for a changing price relationship to cast its influence on the distribution of areas under different crops. In sharp contrast to advanced agriculture the capital components in traditional agriculture usually consist of livestock, labour and simple tools which are relatively unspecific to any particular crop or production pattern. Similarly, although managerial skill has some specificity it is not as fixed as in an advanced agriculture. For example, the same cultivator who can produce jute can also grow other crops such as rice with equal efficiency. This flexibility in the use of non-land inputs is a great strength of traditional agriculture in so far as the problem under investigation is concerned.

In the preceding discussion it has been assumed that cultivators based their production decisions on changes in relative market prices. So far as they market a part of each crop this would be a valid assumption. But in underdeveloped countries subsistence production not only comprises a high proportion of what is produced, but output of a particular crop is often retained for domestic consumption. This simultaneous production for domestic consumption and cash needs introduces a discontinuity in the play of the impact of changing relative price as the cultivators naturally attach a higher price to production which is meant for family consumption. Thus, for a cultivator who markets only a small proportion of the rice he grows a relative fall in its price may make it profitable to reduce the cultivation of this crop and increase the area under jute – the alternative crop. The cultivator may respond to this by transferring only that portion of the acreage under rice which is sold in the market. He cannot be expected to transfer from the production of rice any area beyond this point, as in that case he will have to pay the retail price for the purchase of rice while getting the wholesale price for the sale of jute.

The effect of the above considerations on the allocative function of price is magnified by the two other factors referred to earlier – uncertainties of future prices and weather conditions. These two factors being so unpredictable the cultivator will naturally attach still greater importance to production for domestic consumption. In other words, he will hesitate to put under the cultivation of subsistence crops an area less than he considers sufficient to meet his requirements, as the penalty for under-attainment of a given level of food

[1] Dharm Narain, *Impact of Price Movements on Areas under Selected Crops in India, 1900–39* (Cambridge, 1965), p. 5.

crops is much greater than the benefits of over-attainment. Thus, it seems that relative prices would be a relevant factor only in the case of that proportion of individual food crops which is marketed. But since the proportion of marketed surplus is by definition small in an underdeveloped country the price elasticity of such crops is likely to be insignificant.[1]

How far could the specific conditions in Bengal be expected to conform to this general pattern? It is difficult to obtain reliable estimates of the proportion of food crops sold in the market. However, the available estimates and the wide disparity in the distribution of both operational and ownership holdings of agricultural land in Bengal[2] clearly show that at least a section of the cultivators could produce a marketable surplus. This would create the presumption that, given the scope for substitution with alternative crops, the price elasticity of food crops would also be positive, though very low. The importance of the availability of alternative crops is obvious as the cultivators cannot be expected to respond to a shift in the price level if there is no scope for substitution. The sowing season of a particular crop may be such that the cultivators cannot sow their land with an alternative crop which is more profitable. Obviously in such circumstances the question of changing prices is not of much significance. It seems that winter rice – the largest single crop – belongs to this category. On the other hand, autumn rice is directly alternative to jute. These considerations suggest that the expectation that the supply response will be normal but low will be fulfilled only in the case of autumn rice.

Thus, to sum up this part of the discussion, it seems that (*a*) total supply would not be responsive to changes in relative price, but (*b*) there would be considerable impact from changing relative price on the production of individual crops, and (*c*) such impact would be more marked in the case of crops which are wholly or mainly sold in the market.

4.3 PROCEDURAL PROBLEMS OF ESTIMATING SUPPLY RESPONSE

In the preceding discussion reference has mostly been made to the price elasticity of total output and the output of individual crops. But there are certain difficulties in correlating price with subsequent supply in estimating

---

[1] This part of the discussion is based on the work by Mellor, *op. cit.*, pp. 36–41.

The wider question of the price elasticity of the marketed surplus of a subsistence crop which also involves the problem of the price elasticity of the demand for food is not examined in this study. The purpose here is only to emphasise the restricted relevance of the price mechanism in the production of food crops.

[2] According to the information available from the *Agricultural Statistics* (*op. cit.*), 24 per cent of the rural households held more than 50 per cent of the total area, p. 51; According to the *Report on the Marketing of Rice in India and Burma* (Delhi, 1941), 44 per cent of total rice output, the largest single food crop in Bengal, was marketed, p. 35.

the response of cultivators to changes in market conditions. Reference has been made to the importance of weather conditions in Bengal agriculture. Since the cultivators have no control over natural forces they have no control over a yield per acre either. Therefore, the mere fact that a change in output follows a change in price cannot indicate the level of the cultivators' intended production. To obviate such a complication it is usual to correlate price with acreage, over which the cultivators have greater control. A similar procedure has been followed in the present work.

The question that now arises is: what is the price to which the acreage under total cultivation and the cultivation of individual crops can be expected to respond? The actual production process in agriculture introduces a lag between the decision with regard to the utilisation of land, and realised production. So at the time of decision making the cultivators have to form expectations about the price which they think is likely to prevail in the next season. Expectations of future prices are shaped by a multitude of influences, but no specific information about them is available. Nor can many of them be quantified. Therefore, it is usual, merely as a convenient way of summarising the effects of these diverse influences, to represent actual price as a function of past price.[1] Some authors have used the harvest prices, while others have used the prices prevailing during the pre-sowing season. But it is clear that each of these particular past prices represents only a, very short-run market phenomenon reflecting the equilibrium of the manifold forces present in the market at that time. These considerations render inadequate an attempt at approximating expected price to a particular price in the past. This inadequacy may be removed by assuming a Nerlovian approach of estimating 'expected normal price' on the basis of prices over a number of years in the past, supposing that the influence of more recent prices will be greater on them than the influence of less recent prices.[2]

Expressed in mathematical terms

$$P_t^* = A_1 P_{t-1} + A_2 P_{t-2} + \ldots + A_n P_{t-n} \qquad (1)$$

where P_t^* is the expected price for year t and $P_{t-1}, \ldots, P_{t-n}$ are the observed prices of the previous periods and

$$A_1 > A_2 \ldots > A_n$$

$$A_1 + A_2 + \ldots + A_n = 1.$$

---

[1] Marc Nerlove, *The Dynamics of Supply: Estimation of Farmers' Response to Price* (Baltimore, 1958).

[2] Nerlove, *op. cit.*, pp. 50–5. The formulation that follows is quite similar but not identical with that of Nerlove.

Such a dynamic model represents a distinct improvement on all past approaches. But, for reasons discussed later on, in the present study it is proposed to use a particular past price as a proxy for the expected price.

The next question that has to be dealt with is: should this particular price be the harvest price of the previous year or the pre-sowing price? The expectation formations are not influenced by the same set of prices for all classes of cultivators. The retention power for the bulk of small-scale producers is very limited and they market their produce soon after the harvest and they know that whatever prices were in the pre-sowing period they would fluctuate around the level of the current harvest prices during the next season. On the other hand, because of their greater retention power the big cultivators market a considerable portion of their produce at a time when prices are higher. In this connection it has to be added that the bulk of the cultivated area is usually held by this class of cultivators and their production decisions are more market-oriented.[1] However, there are two considerations which would seem to suggest that the harvest prices would be a better approximation of the expected price. Firstly, it seems that on the whole the larger part of the produce sold during the year is marketed during and immediately after the crops are harvested. Secondly, in the case of certain crops, such as sugarcane, this is the time when plans are made for the next season. Pre-sowing prices may come at a time so close to the actual sowing that the cultivators find it difficult to shift areas between crops in the same season. In view of these considerations harvested prices of the previous year have been taken as an indicator of the expected price on which to base the production decisions for the current year. In the construction of the composite price index against which all-crop acreage is expected to respond the harvest price of every crop has been weighted by the proportion of the total area under its cultivation.

The theoretical supply curve is drawn on the assumption that other prices remain the same. But as other prices do not really remain unchanged it would be pointless to correlate only the crude market prices with the subsequent acreage under cultivation of all the crops. This necessitates correction to give the real purchasing power of the cultivators' produce. Therefore, the composite index of the prices of all the crops has been deflated by an index of the prices of the daily necessities of life as constructed by the Government of India.[2]

---

[1] That the proportion of area under commercial crops increases with the increase in the size of holding has been found in India. Source: *The National Sample Survey*, 8th round, No. 30, *Report on Land Holdings* (2) (Delhi, 1960), cited by Narain, *op. cit.*, p. 161.

[2] Director General of Commercial Intelligence and Statistics, *Index Number of Indian Prices* (annual). The harvest prices of the crops are taken from the *Agricultural Statistics of India*, Vol. I (annual).

The problem of selecting the value of a crop whose variations will be positively correlated with those of its area is more complicated. Some attempts have been made to correlate the acreage under one crop with the price of that crop only. Clearly such a procedure suffers from serious limitations. If it is expected that the variations of area under crops will be a function of changing profitability, the prices of other crops must also be taken into consideration. But this raises another problem: what will be the composition of the 'other crops' the prices of which will be used to 'correct' the prices of the crop in question? Should they include all the single crops produced in a country or the prices of alternative crops only? Evidently the former method is likely to introduce some bias into the estimated price elasticity of a particular crop. But in spite of this shortcoming this procedure has been widely used in the United States. This could be due to the fact that most of the major crops are grown over a wide area and the number of relevant alternatives to a particular crop is very large. But in Bengal the scope of such substitution is somewhat limited. Thus, the crop which directly determines the opportunity cost of growing jute is autumn rice as these are the only two crops sown during the months from March to May. The other variety of rice – winter rice – is an alternative crop in a somewhat restricted sense in that the transplanting season of this crop (July to September) overlaps with the harvesting period of jute. After an early jute harvest 'Aman' paddy may be transplanted on the same land if the weather conditions are favourable, but this involves a loss of yield for both the crops. The other crops like mustard, linseed, sesamum, wheat, barley and gram are usually sown during the months from November to January. Thus, clearly these crops cannot be treated as alternatives to jute or autumn rice. The cultivators cannot be expected to plan the production of either jute or autumn rice on the basis of the relative price of one of these crops. It is true that the pattern of rotation among different crops sometimes makes the task of selecting the various alternative crops rather difficult. But this does not seem to justify the procedure of treating all 'other crops' as alternative to every individual crop. Therefore, in the present study price relatives of the different crops have been constructed on the basis of the prices of those specific crops which seem to directly determine opportunity cost. In certain cases when a straghtforward selection is difficult different combinations have been tried. These are elaborated in the course of the discussion on the estimated elasticities.

Apart from price the two other explanatory variables included in the model are yield and the mean of the quantum of rainfall during the sowing season. The inclusion of the former is justified by the fact that it is not only the price per unit of produce but also the volume of produce per unit of land which may influence the decision of the cultivators. Rainfall is included on the assumption that this may interfere with the actual sowing of the planned acreage with crops.

4.4 ESTIMATING MODEL

Prior to Nerlove's work it was usual to approximate the desired planted area to the actual sown area, and the expected relative price to the prevailing price in the previous period, in the studies of United States' agriculture and in studies of underdeveloped countries even subsequent to Nerlove's work. Nerlove tackles the obvious limitations of such 'crude' approximations in his adjustment and expectational model. The area adjustment model states that the area actually sown with a crop in production period *t* equals the area actually sown in the previous period plus a term proportional to the difference between the desired planted area in the *t*th period and the actually sown area in the previous period. According to his expectational model the expected relative price in production period *t* equals the expected relative price in the previous period plus a term proportional to the difference between the expected relative price and the actual relative price in the previous period. Thus, while the latter is supposed to reflect the manner in which past experience determines the expected value of the variable such as price or yield which in turn determines intended production, the former reflects the technological/institutional restraints which allow the cultivators to realise only a fraction of the intended production. In the light of the uncertainties of price and yield and many other restraints already referred to it is clear that both these types are of great importance in an underdeveloped agriculture. Therefore, ideally a model should be developed specifying a separate lag coefficient and different adjustment lag coefficient for each expectational variable, but such a model involves serious estimation problems.[1] Therefore the model used in this study provides for only an adjustment lag. This is as follows:[2]

$$A_t^* = a + bP_{t-1} + cY_{t-1} + dR_t + U_t \tag{2}$$

$$A_t - A_{t-1} = B(A_t^* - A_{t-1}) \tag{3}$$

---

[1] Nerlove, *op. cit.*, pp. 236–40.

[2] A different method of estimating price elasticity has been suggested by Z. Griliches, 'Distributed Lag: A Survey', *Econometrica*, Vol. 35, No. 1. An attempt to follow this method raises two main difficulties. Firstly, the volume of computation will be more complicated and much larger. Secondly, since this method is not followed by other authors, it will not be possible to compare the estimated elasticities. For a criticism of Nerlove's model see also F. M. Fisher, *A Priori Considerations and Time Series Analysis* (Amsterdam, 1962), pp. 21–58; H. W. Watts, 'Review of Nerlove, Distributed Lags and Demand Analysis for Agricultural and other Commodities', *Journal of Farm Economics*, Vol. XLI; G. E. Brandow, 'A Note on the Nerlovian Estimate of Supply Elasticity', *Journal of Farm Economics*, Vol. XL. (1958).

A_t^* is the acreage the cultivators would sow with crops in the year t if there was no difficulty of adjustment. A_t is the actually sown area.

P is the relative price of the crop in question, i.e. the harvest price of the crop deflated by the prices of the alternative crops.

Y is the relative yield of the crop.

R is the quantum of rainfall during the sowing season.

U is the error term.

B is the Nerlovian coefficient of adjustment.

It is assumed that the cultivators are able to vary the acreage under a crop in any year only to the extent of a fraction B of the difference between the acreage they would like to sow and the acreage actually sown in the previous period.

Equations (2) and (3) yield the following estimating equation:

$$A_t = a_0 + b_2 P_{t-1} + b_3 Y_{t-1} + b_4 R_t + b_5 A_{t-1} + V_t \qquad (4)$$

where $a_0 = aB$, $b_2 = bB$, $b_3 = cB$, $b_4 = dB$, $b_5 = (1 - B)$ and $V_t = BU_t$.

It is, however, possible to build an expectational model on the assumption that the expectation lag coefficients of the different variables are identical. Thus,

$$A_t = a + bP_t^* + cY_t^* + dR_t^* + U_t \qquad (5)$$
$$P_t^* - P_{t-1}^* = B(P_{t-1} - P_{t-1}^*) \qquad (6)$$
$$Y_t^* - Y_{t-1}^* = B(Y_{t-1} - Y_{t-1}^*) \qquad (7)$$
$$R_t^* - R_{t-1}^* = B(R_{t-1} - R_{t-1}^*) \qquad (8)$$

This model yields the following estimating equation:
$$A_t = a_0 + b_2 P_{t-1} + b_3 Y_{t-1} + b_4 R_{t-1} + b_5 A_{t-1} + W_t \qquad (9)$$

where $a_0 = aB$, $b_2 = bB$, $b_3 = cB$, $b_4 = dB$, $b_5 = (1 - B)$ and $W_t = U_t - (1 - B)U_{t-1}$.

The two estimating equations (4) and (9) are the same except for the lag in R and the error term which is serially correlated in (9) but not in (4). If it is assumed that U_t in this second model is serially uncorrelated, then W_t in the estimating equation (9) is automatically serially correlated, since $W_t = U_t - (1 - B) U_{t-1}$. On the other hand, if W_t is supposed to be serially independent, U_t is serially correlated.[1] Secondly, the assumption of identical expectation may be questioned. Thirdly, if different coefficients of expectation are specified for each of the additional lagged explanatory variables, the number of variables in the estimating equation becomes very large. Even

---

[1] US Department of Agriculture, *Distributed Lagos and Demand Analysis for Agricultural and Other Commodities* (Agricultural Handbook No. 141, 1958), p. 76.

for a model with two variables the estimating equation will have six explanatory variables.[1] With only twenty to thirty observations available in most of the cases, many degrees of freedom are lost in estimation. Lastly, the more serious objection is that the estimates of the regression coefficients thus obtained are not unique.[2] In view of these considerations the 'adjustment' model is used in this study though it has to be admitted that this over-simplifies the expectational side of the problem.

The same model has been used for estimating the price elasticity of the all-crop acreage. In such a case P_{t-1}, Y_{t-1} and R respectively refer to the composite index of the price of all the crops, weighted yield of all the crops in the previous period and the quantum of rainfall throughout the agricultural season (March–February).

In order to obtain a direct estimate of the elasticity of acreage with regard to the different explanatory variables both the dependent and the independent variables have been transformed into their logarithms.

4.5 ESTIMATED ELASTICITIES

The *a priori* considerations for the inclusion of different explanatory variables have been discussed. The actual computations have been done with different combinations of variables in order to obtain an equation which explains the highest degree of variance in the acreage under the cultivation of individual crops and all the crops taken together. The estimated short-run and the implied long-run elasticities are presented in Table 4.1. Standard errors of these elasticities are shown in parentheses. All these estimates have, however, to be interpreted with reference to the quality of the crop statistics discussed in the first chapter.[3] Findings of other authors on the same or similar crops are also presented in order to facilitate comparison.

4.5a *Jute.* In equations (1) and (2) autumn rice, and in equations (3) and

---

[1] *ibid.*, p. 60.

[2] *ibid.*, p. 62.

[3] In the official explanations for the variations of 10 per cent or above in the acreage under cultivation as given in the *Agricultural Statistics of Bengal*, it was often pointed out that these were due to shifts in the price level. It is difficult to say definitely if these annual variations in the officially published data were influenced by the subjective judgement of the reporting agencies. This also applies to the price statistics used in this study. These prices represent the median of the district figures (reported in the *Season and Crop Report*) which often remained the same for several years. Price statistics for the province as a whole are available from the *Agricultural Statistics of India* (Annual), Vol. 1. The quality of these data is discussed by R. C. Desai, 'Consumer Expenditure in India, 1931–2 to 1940–1', *Journal of the Royal Statistical Society*, Vol. CXI (1948), pp. 261–98.

(4) both autumn and winter rice have been treated as alternative crops. In both the cases there is no significant elasticity either with regard to expected yield or the quantum of rainfall during the sowing season. Conversely all four equations indicate that two thirds of the variance in area sown with jute is positively associated with changes in the expected relative price and these estimates are significant at less than the 0.1 per cent level. The implied long-run elasticity is higher than that estimated by Rabbani and Stern, but the short-run elasticity is smaller than found by the latter. This may be due to the fact that while Stern deflates the wholesale prices of jute by the prices of all other crops including rice, Rabbani includes, apart from Bengal, other jute-producing areas of India (Assam, Bihar and Cooch Bihar). The acreage under cultivation revised on the basis of the discrepancies found between the official estimates of jute production and the 'actuals' as determined from the trade statistics indicates a slightly lower elasticity with regard to expected price. But even then both the long-run and short-run elasticities are much higher than for a similar crop (cotton) in the USA. This may be due to the lesser scope for substitution for the latter and perhaps due to the relative specificity of managerial skill and resources in an advanced agriculture.

4.5b *Sugarcane.* This crop occupies the land for most of the year, and, therefore, the three other major crops of winter rice, autumn rice and jute have been treated as alternative crops. In both equations (1) and (2) (see Table 4.1) the pattern is completely different from that for either jute or sugarcane in the other Indian Provinces[1] – there is no significant elasticity of acreage with regard to expected relative price. Conversely, the model indicates a fair degree of response to the improvement in yield. The implied long-run elasticity is, however, considerably higher than unity. The low elasticity of adjustment seems to be due to the fact that this crop is the most expensive in terms of the required intensity of cultivation, weeding, fencing and growing time. However, it is clear that since, despite this high cost, the cultivators were favourably responding to the use of the improved varieties of seeds, the total sale proceeds of planting sugarcane must have made the production of this crop more profitable in relation to alternative crops. Thus, it seems that it was not higher relative price as such, but the success of the Agricultural Department in making the relative product-price per unit of land (by the popularisation of the improved varieties of seedlings) more attractive, which led to the remarkable expansion of sugarcane cultivation in Bengal.

---

[1] A significant price-acreage relation has been found in the case of the Punjab, United Province and Madras. For details, see Narain, *op. cit.*, pp. 84–106.

TABLE 4.1 *Findings on the elasticity of acreage with regard to different variables.*

| Regions | Crops | Years | Short run elasticity with regard to | | | Elasticity of adjustment B | R_2 | Long run elasticity with regard to | | Standard error of regression | Serial correlation according to Durbin–Watson test |
			P_{t-1}	Y_{t-1}	R_t			P_{t-1}	Y_{t-1}		
Bengal	Jute (1)	1920–39	0.60 (0.14)	0.42 (0.37)	0.32 (0.14)	0.56	0.68	1.07	—	0.15	No serial correlation
Bengal	Jute (2)	1920–39	0.66 (0.12)	—	—	0.49	0.69	1.35	—	0.15	No serial correlation
Bengal	Jute (3)	1920–39	0.67 (0.13)	0.51 (0.30)	−0.05 (0.15)	0.57	0.67	1.21	—	0.15	No serial correlation
Bengal	Julte (4)	1920–39	0.64 (0.13)	—	—	0.52	0.65	1.20	—	0.16	No serial correlation
Bengal, Bihar and Orissa[a]	Jute	1911–39	0.50	—	—	0.53	0.80	0.93	—		
Bengal[b]	Jute	1911–39	0.75	—	—						
Punjab[c]	Cotton (A)	1922–41	0.72			0.44		1.62			
Punjab[c]	Cotton (D)	1922–43	0.59			0.55		1.08			
USA[d]	Cotton	1909–32	0.34			0.51		0.67			

Price-elasticity of acreage under cultivation

Region	Crop	Period									
Bengal	Sugarcane (1)	1921–40	0.13 (0.15)	0.40 (0.11)	−0.005 (0.003)	0.32	0.89	—	1.25	0.07	No serial correlation
Bengal	Sugarcane (2)	1921–40	0.14 (0.13)	0.40 (0.11)	—	0.32	0.90	—	1.25	0.06	No serial correlation
Punjab[c]	Sugarcane	1915–43	0.34			0.56		0.60	—		No serial correlation
Bengal	Winter rice (1)	1921–40	0.08 (0.04)	−0.08 (0.10)	0.20 (0.09)	0.42	0.20	—	—	0.04	No serial correlation
Bengal	Winter rice (2)	1921–40	0.07 (0.04)	—	0.18 (0.08)	0.57	0.22	—	—	0.04	No serial correlation
Bengal	Winter rice (3)	1921–40	−0.14 (0.18)	−0.03 (0.11)	0.12 (0.10)	0.81	0.05	—	—	0.05	No serial correlation
Bengal	Winter rice (4)	1921–40	−0.14 (0.17)	—	0.11 (0.09)	0.87	0.10	—	—	0.05	No serial correlation
Undivided Punjab[c]	Rice	1914–46	0.31		0.52			0.59			
Punjab[c]	Wheat	1914–44	0.08		0.59			0.14			

127

TABLE 4.1 *Findings on the elasticity of acreage with regard to different variables (cont.).*

Regions	Crops	Years	Short run elasticity with regard to			Elasticity of adjustment B	R_2	Long run elasticity with regard to		Standard error of regression	Serial correlation according to Durbin–Watson test
			P_{t-1}	Y_{t-1}	R_t			P_{t-1}	Y_{t-1}		
Bengal	Autumn rice (1)	1920–39	0.14 (0.05)	−0.15 (0.12)	0.07 (0.05)	0.43	0.45	0.32	—	0.05	No serial correlation
Bengal	Autumn rice (2)	1920–39	0.12 (0.05)	—	0.08 (0.05)	0.43	0.43	0.30		0.05	No serial correlation
East Pakistan[f]	Autumn rice	1948–61	0.03 to 0.05								
Thailand[e]	Rice	1937–63	0.18					0.31			
Bengal	Mustard (1)	1921–40	0.43 (0.24)	0.14 (0.14)	0.00 (0.013)	0.29	0.39	1.51	—	0.04	No serial correlation
Bengal	Mustard (2)	1921–40	0.41 (0.23)	—	—	0.27	0.42	1.50	—	0.04	No serial correlation
Bengal	All-crops (1)	1921–40	0.02 (0.05)	−0.02 (0.12)	0.17 (0.08)	0.34	0.37	—	—	0.03	No serial correlation
Bengal	All-crops (2)	1921–40	0.02 (0.04)	—	0.17 (0.07)	0.37	0.41	—	—	0.03	No serial correlation

Sources: [a] A. K. M. Rabbani, *Jute in World Economy: A Statistical Study* (unpublished PhD thesis, University of London, 1964), p. 365.
[b] R. M. Stern, 'The Price Responsiveness of Primary Producers', *Review of Economics and Statistics*, XLIV (1962), pp. 202–7.
[c] R. Krishna, 'Farm Supply Response in India–Pakistan: A Case Study of the Punjab Region', *Economic Journal*, LXXIII (1963), pp. 477–87.
[d] Nerlove, *op. cit.*, p. 355.
[e] Behrman, *op. cit.*, p. 331 and p. 301.
[f] S. M. Hussain, 'A Note on Farmer Response to Price in East Pakistan', *Pakistan Development Review*, IV (1964), pp. 93–106.

4.5c *Winter rice.* In equations (1) and (2), jute and in equations (3) and (4), all the 'rabi' crops have been treated as competitive crops. The first formulation is suggested by the type of competition between these two crops shown in the elasticity of acreage under jute. 'Rabi' crops have been treated as substitutes in view of the fact that the harvesting of winter rice releases land at a time which is usually too late to enable the cultivators to raise a 'rabi' crop on the same land. There is no significant response of the acreage under this variety of rice in any of the four equations. This finding seems to conform to what could be expected in Bengal agriculture. As mentioned earlier, perhaps the larger portion of this crop was meant for domestic consumption by the members of the cultivators' family. Secondly, the planting season of winter rice is such that there is little scope for substitution with an alternative crop.[1]

As to the impact of the two other variables, winter rice is the only crop which shows a significant, though small, elasticity with regard to the quantum of rainfall during the sowing season (July to September). Again, this finding conforms to what could be expected for this crop. As winter rice is transplanted, the ploughing of the land is not enough; there must be a sufficient quantum of rainfall to facilitate the transplantation of the seedlings and their subsequent growth.

4.5d *Autumn rice.* The price and yield of autumn rice have been deflated by the corresponding figures for jute. The expectation that the cultivation of this crop, though mainly for domestic consumption, would be price elastic is borne out by the findings in both equations. The short run elasticity which is significant at the 5 per cent level, is similar to those found in Bangladesh. As in the case of winter rice and jute, there is once again no significant elasticity with regard to changes in relative yield. But so far as the impact of rainfall is concerned there is a significant difference between these two varieties of rice. However, this absence of any impact of rainfall on the acreage under autumn rice (as also under jute) conforms to what could be expected. While winter rice is transplanted, autumn rice and jute are sown. This creates the expectation that if in a particular season the quantum of rainfall is not too small or too heavy this would not stand in the way of sowing the desired area with autumn rice and jute.

4.5e *Mustard* In terms of acreage under cultivation mustard is the second largest commercial crop. As this crop is grown during the dry months from November to January its prices and yields have been deflated by the prices and

---

[1] In Thailand the magnitude of the price elasticities of rice cultivation has been found to be dependent upon the availability of economically attractive alternatives to rice cultivation. Behrman, *op. cit.*, pp. 303–5.

yields of all the 'rabi' crops. As in the case of jute and autumn rice there is once again no significant response to relative yield or rainfall. The elasticity of acreage with respect to expected relative price is more or less the same in both the equations, but these are significant at the 10 per cent level. Such a weak response may be attributed to two important factors. Firstly, three of the four alternative crops (gram, barley and wheat) are food crops and, therefore, it seems that their cultivation would remain more or less inflexible. This limits the desired level of increase in the acreage under mustard though there may be an improvement in the relative price. Secondly, mustard is grown as a second crop in the same agricultural year. Therefore, the level of production is likely to depend more on the scope offered by the desired rotation between the major crops than by the changes in relative price.

4.5f *All-crop acreage.* The actual findings seem to substantiate our hypothesis that in a traditional agriculture characterised by an adverse man/land ratio no significant response of all-crop acreage to changes in relative price can be expected. This relative inelasticity of total acreage under cultivation cannot, however, be interpreted as indicating that the total supply in Bengal agriculture was not positively related to an increase in the price level. As argued earlier, since the scope for further extension of cultivation was limited, the impact of rising prices could have been reflected in (a) the greater use of new inputs and (b) changes in the crop-mix as a result of the shift of acreage under individual crops in response to changes in relative price. In this latter respect it has been seen that acreage under three individual crops is price elastic and there is no systematically opposite trend in the case of the most important crop (winter rice). Therefore, it may be assumed that the total supply in Bengal agriculture was price responsive.[1]

To sum up, out of the five crops included in this study acreage under jute and autumn rice was responsive to changes in relative price and that of sugarcane to improvement in relative yield. In the case of winter rice, only rainfall had some impact on the acreage under cultivation. Therefore, it may be suggested that though the total acreage under cultivation was not price elastic the Bengal cultivators were trying to maximise their proceeds from the available resources by the shift of areas to such crops as were

---

[1] For further elaboration of this point see Raj Krishna, 'Agricultural Price Policy' in H. M. Southworth and B. F. Johnston (eds.), *Agricultural Development and Economic Growth* (New York, 1967). This author cites the significant evidence that in many countries – e.g. Spain, Egypt, Yugoslavia and Mexico – changes in the cropping pattern alone contributed 15 to 20 percent of the increase in total crop output during the period 1948–50 to 1960–62.

relatively more profitable, either due to an improvement in relative price or relative yield per acre. As indicated in the case of the price elasticity of autumn rice, such variations of area were not confined to cash crops only. In other words, they seem to have taken such rational production decisions as were desirable within the given technological and institutional constraints.

5

CAPITAL IN AGRICULTURE

Economic development is generally defined as the sustained growth of per capita output. Among the factors which account for the growth of output a crucial role is usually assigned to capital and capital formation.[1] Theoretically, this dominance of capital theory in the literature on growth economics is partly due to the popularity which the Harrod–Domar model has gained, especially through its application to the economic development of the underdeveloped countries. In this model the rate of economic development is a function of two factors: (a) capital formation and (b) the capital/output ratio; and accordingly development policies have been described as aiming to increase the former, reduce the latter or to achieve both. Much effort has gone into the estimation of the capital/output ratio and the measurement of the contribution of the physical capital stock to past economic growth and the requirements for future progress. Some investigations have shown considerable differences over time in the relation between physical capital and output, but none of them has suggested any ground for doubting the importance of capital formation in economic progress.

Along with this emphasis on the role of capital, another concept which has been widely discussed is that the underdeveloped countries are plagued by a 'vicious circle'.[2] The circle theory emphasises that since per capita income in these countries is low, little remains as a surplus after consumption needs are fulfilled. The low level of real income is, in turn, due to the lack of an adequate capital stock. From the findings presented in the preceding two chapters it is clear that in spite of the relative abundance of labour there was hardly any increase in yield per acre and, against a background of rapid population growth, this meant a decline in per capita output. Such a finding

[1] See, for examples, W. A. Lewis, *The Theory of Economic Growth* (London, 1955), particularly the chapter on capital. W. W. Rostow, *The Stages of Economic Growth* (Cambridge, 1971), pp. 39–44.
[2] This thesis is presented by different authors in several distinctly different variants. These are analysed by P. T. Bauer, 'The vicious circle of poverty' in I. Livingstone (ed.), *Economic Policy for Development* (London, 1971), pp. 19–36. See also Tamas Szentes, *The Political Economy of Underdevelopment* (Budapest, 1971), particularly pp. 50–60. For the present purpose only the supply aspect of capital formation is discussed.

creates a strong presumption that the agrarian economy of Bengal was characterised by the same 'vicious circle' of low income and the consequent low capital formation.

In the present chapter an attempt is made to investigate this aspect of the agricultural economy of Bengal, i.e. the trend of capital formation. The three specific questions raised are: (*a*) what was the trend of the stock of capital, (*b*) how does this trend compare with those in production, land and the labour force engaged in agriculture, and (*c*) did the weights of the different categories of physical capital change over time? These questions are analysed, in the light of the available materials, both at the all-Bengal and regional levels.

5.1 PROBLEMS OF DEFINITION

Such a study involves a good deal of difficulties. These arise partly from the controversies associated with capital theory and partly from the nature of the available data. With regard to the former the debate among economists is concerned with the two related problems of the definition and measurement of capital. It would be tedious to review this controversy in detail. However, some indication must be given of its nature in order to illuminate the subsequent discussion of our findings. The problem of definition is taken up first.

According to a United Nations publication capital goods are 'all goods produced for use in future production processes – machinery, equipment, plant, buildings, other construction and works, and producers' stock of raw materials, semi-finished and finished goods'.[1] Evidently according to this view only those goods are capital goods which are produced for use in future productive processes. On the other hand, some authors argue that the definition of capital should not be so narrow as to include only the physical assets. Thus, it is believed that if long-term increase in per capita income is described as economic growth the definition of capital should be broadened to include all uses of current output that contribute to such an increase. Thus capital formation should include, apart from additions to the physical stock, expenditure on health, education, recreation and material luxuries that contribute to the greater productive skill of the labour force.[2] Recently

[1] *Concept and Definition of Capital Formation*, UNO 1955, p. 7, cited by P. V. John, *Some Aspects of the Structure of Indian Agricultural Economy, 1947/48 to 1961/62* (Delhi, 1968), pp. 139–40.
[2] See for example Simon Kuznets, 'International Differences in Capital Formation and Financing' in National Bureau of Economic Research, *Capital Formation and Economic Growth* (Princeton, 1955), p. 21.

it has become usual to describe such non-physical development expenditure as 'human capital'.

One cannot deny the fact that ideally a study of capital formation should include such expenditure as makes the members of a community more productive. But over and above the problem arising from the non-availability of relevant data such an attempt to broaden the definition of capital creates many difficulties. Thus, conceptually it is difficult, if not impossible, to separate human capital on the one hand and physical output on the other. Secondly, there are problems of measurement, i.e. imputation and allocation of costs and valuation of returns. These difficulties have weighed heavily in the decision to exclude human capital even in major studies on capital formation.[1] Therefore, the present study is confined to an analysis of only the physical capital assets involved in Bengal agriculture.

The question that now has to be discussed is whether land should be regarded as an item of capital. Like buildings land is a durable physical asset, but in economic theory only the former is regarded as capital. This distinction is made on the grounds of what has been regarded as the fundamental differences in the origin and supply of land and other durable producers' goods. Thus, it has been argued that land is a free gift of nature and fixed in supply, whereas capital is a 'produced means of production' and its supply responds to the human decision of investment. As against this argument it has been pointed out that 'Granted that the gross acreage of a country or region cannot be altered, it is still possible to change greatly the productive acreage and the productivity of acreage already in use by means which closely resemble methods by which buildings and equipment are increased'[2] and, therefore, land should be included as an item of capital. It is difficult to differ from this line of argument, but it seems that land can be so treated only on recognition of the fact that this procedure does not take into consideration the expenditure of money and effort required from the cultivators. The increase of 'productive acreage' or the extension of cultivation to new areas may be achieved by the investment of money and effort in such things as clearing, drainage and irrigation. On the other hand, the productivity of land already under cultivation may be increased by, apart from the more intensive use of labour and implements, investment on fertilisers, prevention of soil erosion and soil depletion. Both process would involve investment in land, but no information is available on the volume of all such investments. Therefore, it is clear that new land which is brought under cultivation during

---

[1] See for example A. S. Tostlebe, *Capital in Agriculture: Its Formation and Financing* (Princeton, 1957); Kuznets, *op. cit.*; Henry Rosovsky, *Capital Formation in Japan* (New York, 1961).

[2] Tostlebe, *op. cit.*, pp. 4–5.
See also L. M. Lachmann, *Capital and its Structure* (London, 1956), p. 11.

a particular period of time should be treated as an item of capital. This will be an index of the investment of money and effort made by the cultivators for the creation of additional 'productive acreage'. From this it is also clear that this procedure does not take account of all the direct investments made in land already under cultivation. This follows from the fact that, along with other assets, land is valued at a constant price and, thus, all changes in the volume of direct investment are ignored. It is likely that in an economy where the scope for the extension of cultivation is limited but the supply of labour is abundant some improvement takes place at least in such investments as depend mainly on increased physical labour. Thus, it seems that in including land as an item of the cultivator's stock of capital it has to be specifically understood that this represents not the whole but only a part of the investment of money and effort made by members of a community within a particular period.

5.2 PROBLEMS OF MEASUREMENT

The controversy with regard to measurement concerns the selection of a unit in which to aggregate the heterogeneous mass of capital items into a homogeneous collection. Usually the following four methods are advocated to evaluate the different items of capital: (*a*) in terms of their value expressed in some unit of purchasing power, (*b*) their contribution to the future flow of product, (*c*) the cost of labour involved in the construction of capital goods and (*d*) the prices of the existing goods required to make them. It is not necessary to review the controversy relating to the merits of each of these procedures. The method followed in this study is to weight the different items of capital according to their market prices at a particular point of time, e.g. at t_1, and to keep the weight constant at periods $t_2, t_3, \ldots, t_n$.

There is, however, one point which merits particular attention. This procedure of taking the market value of the stock assumes the equality of marginal cost with marginal revenue, which under perfect competition equals the price. Does this assumption hold good over a period of time? In other words, it has to be asked if, in the estimation of the cultivators, the weights of the different items remain constant. Clearly nothing definitive can be said on this question. It would, therefore, be interesting to see if alternative estimates made on the basis of prices prevailing at different points of time show any significant differences. But no such attempt can be made in view of the non-availability of the relevant information.

Another problem is created by depreciation. When the stock of physical capital involved in an economy is compared at two points of time without making any allowance for depreciation, it is assumed that either the stock is equally new or equally depreciated. In other words, that the rates of depreciation and replacement balance each other. In the absence of any relevant data it is difficult to say whether this is a valid assumption regarding Bengal agriculture during the period under study. Therefore, the estimates presented in this chapter have to be taken as estimates of gross capital formation.

It is desirable that estimates are presented not only of the trends of capital formation, but also of its magnitude. In other words, since capital formation implies saving it is important to gain some idea about the proportion of income represented by such savings. But there are two difficulties which do not permit any such attempt. Firstly, as pointed out later, there is the non-availability of data on the working capital of the cultivators and no reliable price statistics of even the limited number of physical assets selected for this study. Secondly, even if these data were available there is the further problem created by intersectoral flows. If agriculture was a closed economy it could have been taken that all the investment outlays in this sector were financed by the rural households themselves. In other words, the annual flow of investments would have been matched by the flow of savings. But this equality is complicated by the flow of capital between the agricultural and the non-agricultural sectors – on which no data are available. In view of these difficulties no attempt can be made to relate capital formation to per capita income in the agricultural sector. Instead only the broad indications discernible are pointed out.

5.3 SOURCES OF DATA, THEIR COVERAGE AND ADJUSTMENTS

Capital assets selected for this study include: (*a*) land, (*b*) buildings, (*c*) animal labour and (*d*) farm implements. In view of the non-availability of relevant information no attempt has been made to estimate the trends in working capital involved in Bengal agriculture. Thus, clearly the concept of capital as used in this study becomes more restrictive than implied by the phrase 'physical capital'.

The sources and nature of crop statistics in Bengal have been discussed earlier. For the present purpose it has to be asked (*a*) what categores of land should be included and (*b*) should land to be included refer to a particular point in time? As to the first question the usual procedure has been to include only the net cropped area and the area currently left fallow by the cultivators.[1] But there is one consideration which suggests that this procedure of including net cropped area as against total cropped area (net cropped area + double cropped area) is defective. In an underdeveloped agriculture where the scope

---

[1] T. Shukla, *Capital Formation in Indian Agriculture* (Bombay, 1965), p. 64.

for the extension of cultivation to new areas is limited the increase in double cropped area represents the expenditure of money and effort by cultivators to increase total output. Therefore, in the present study land as an item of capital includes total cropped area and the area currently left fallow.

The second question is important because there were considerable year-to-year fluctuations in the acreage under cultivation. Therefore, the inclusion of the acreage of only the quinquennial Livestock Census years may introduce some bias in the estimates. In order to obviate this difficulty figures have been calculated on the basis of a three years' average centred on the census years. A similar procedure has been followed in the case of all-crop output.

5.4 DRAUGHT ANIMALS

Data on livestock labour are available from the *Quinquennial Cattle Census Reports*. In the first three reports published by the Government of Bengal separate estimates of 'plough cattle' were presented. It is common knowledge that the same livestock labour may be used for, apart from ploughing land, such purposes as carrying crops from the fields to the cultivators' houses or from the latter to the rural markets. Of greater importance is the fact that the same work animals may be used for non-agricultural purposes. Such uses are frequent, particularly during the relatively slack season of the year. In view of this flexibility in the use of livestock labour in the rural areas it is difficult to accept the official estimates as estimates of only 'plough cattle'. However, this would not have created a major problem if the method of classification was uniform during the entire period. But it seems that a change was introduced for 1940 and 1945. Firstly, whereas separate estimates of 'plough cattle' were provided in the first three census reports, no such category was maintained in the last two. Instead the number of bovine population 'kept for work only' was separately shown. In view of the pattern of use of livestock labour referred to earlier it is clear that this latter method of classification was an improvement on the earlier ones. Secondly, while according to the first three censuses 'plough cattle' included only bulls, bullocks and male buffaloes, in 1940 and 1945 the number of cows and female buffaloes (over and above the above three categories) 'kept for work only' was also presented. It is difficult to say how far conceptually these two categories are strictly comparable[1] but even if they are assumed to be so it is clear that the scope of the latter category was wider. In view of these difficulties, the available data

---

[1] Figures on bulls, bullocks and male buffaloes presented in Appendix VII in *Livestock Census Reports* and designated as 'plough cattle' are slightly smaller than the corresponding figures shown in Appendix IV. It is not known on what criterion the figures in the former appendix were determined.

on bulls, bullocks, cows and buffaloes (male and female) have been taken for present purposes to represent the total livestock labour available for crop production.

5.5 AGRICULTURAL IMPLEMENTS

Quinquennial cattle censuses up to 1930 provided information only for ploughs. From 1940 ploughs were divided into wooden and iron ploughs and items such as sugarcane crushers, oil engines, electric pumps and tractors were also included. Therefore, in order to obtain a uniform series only ploughs have been treated as agricultural implements.

Data on livestock labour and ploughs require two adjustments. Firstly, no census was held in Bengal in 1935. So figures for this year have been interpolated on the basis of the rate of growth between 1930 and 1940. The second adjustment is for the year 1945 when only the all-Bengal figures were published. The regional figures for this year have been estimated on the basis of the percentage distribution of livestock labour and ploughs in 1940.

Statistics on livestock population and agricultural implements were said to have been collected by the village panchayets.[1] In the light of the picture that emerges with regard to the crop statistics discussed earlier it is difficult to say whether the panchayets were really the primary source. However, since the same agency may have been responsible for compiling the data it would seem that the margin of error was more or less the same over the entire period.

5.6 OCCUPIED HOUSES

Data on 'occupied houses in the villages' are available from the Decennial Population Censuses. In the Census Reports no reference is made to the size, type and uses of these houses. Thus, ideally these data require three adjustments, but actually no adjustment is possible. The difficulty with regard to the different uses of the rural houses arises from the very nature of the problem of including houses as an item of capital stock. In a peasant agriculture it is not possible to estimate the number of houses used for purely residential purposes as against those used for 'productive' purposes only. For it is common knowledge that the same house may be used by a cultivator partly for residential purposes and partly for storing crops. In many cases it so happens that a portion of a house is shared by cattle. These considerations clearly preclude the possibility of making an estimate of the proportion of rural

[1] *Cattle Census Reports*, p. 1.

houses used for production purposes only. Changes in the types and sizes of houses at different points of time are less difficult to ascertain, but the relevant type of data are not available from the census reports. In a stagnant economy characterised by a fast rate of population growth it is very likely that there were considerable changes in the types of houses over a period of 25 years. Therefore, it would seem that the estimates presented in this chapter have to be interpreted with considerable reservation.

5.7 AVAILABILITY OF PRICE STATISTICS

It has been pointed out earlier that for the purpose of aggregation of the different items of capital stock these are weighted by their market prices. Such prices were compiled by the Banking Enquiry Committee[1] for all the categories included in this study except houses. How far are these price statistics reliable? This question is important, because prices of all these items differ widely not only in relation to their quality and position but also between different points of time within the same year. Statistics available from this source were not collected on the basis of any scientific procedure. As against this, price statistics available from an alternative source[2] were collected from randomly selected representative farms over a period of three years. It is true that these data refer to a later period and only to the West Bengal districts. But it would seem that the bias introduced by these limitations, if any, would be less marked. Therefore, data available from this latter source are used for purposes of aggregation. Weights given to the different items on the basis of these statistics are as follows: land: 0.625; houses: 0.196; work animals: 0.035; ploughs: 0.011.

5.8 AGRICULTURAL LABOUR

Data on agricultural labour present two problems. The first problem, which is more or less common to all the underdeveloped countries, is caused by imperfection in the occupational specialisation in these countries. In advanced economies the worker is engaged full-time in his listed occupations. But in the underdeveloped countries many of the cultivators generally move within a wide range of occupations in accordance with changes in prospective net advantages. These activities include various forms of small-scale trading, the supply of transport services and the provision of personal services generally.

[1] *Report of the Bengal Provincial Banking Enquiry Committee* (Calcutta, 1930), Chapter V, p. 26.
[2] Government of India, *Studies in the Economics of Farm Management in West Bengal* (Delhi, 1963), p. 52.

Many of them may remain idle during the slack season. Such an imperfect specialisation of labour may greatly affect the meaning and significance of occupational statistics.[1] It is, however, clear that though imperfect occupational specialisation affects the usefulness of the calculated magnitude of total labour supply at a particular point in time we may still gain some idea about time-trends if it can be assumed that the degree of imperfection remains more or less constant over time. This brings us to the second problem referred to earlier. Can it really be assumed that the degree of imperfection was more or less uniform in Bengal during the period under review?

The Census returns of 1931 showed a reduction of nearly two million in the total work force in Bengal and most of this decline was recorded in the category 'Exploitation of animals and vegetation'. It was only in the four occupational groups of 'Public force', 'Professional and liberal arts', 'Persons living on their income' and 'Insufficiently described occupation' that no reduction in labour was recorded.[2] The number of people engaged in different occupations was not calculated in 1941. Instead, some estimates of the labour force in agriculture were made on the basis of information obtained from every fiftieth slip from the census materials. Calculation on the basis of these estimates shows that the volume of agricultural labour remained at the 1931 level, though population increased by 5 million.

The Census Report of 1931 recorded some differences in the proportion of people belonging to different age-groups.[3] It is unlikely that these differences meant a marked increase or decrease in the volume of the total work force. Therefore, it may be assumed that if a uniform mode of classification had been followed the rate of change in the volume of the labour force in 1931 would have been more or less the same as in the total population. But it is clear that no uniform criterion was followed. Thus, while the classification in 1921 was simply between 'actual workers' and 'dependants', that of 1931 was between 'workers', 'working dependants' and 'dependants'. This change in the mode of classification must be treated as of fundamental importance. This is because the phrase 'working dependants' was so narrowly defined that a large number of persons who would have been returned as 'workers' by the standard adopted in 1921 were returned as dependants pure and simple in the Census of 1931.[4] It was admitted in the Census Report that the figures for 'earners' may be taken in general as being reasonably accurate, but in

---

[1] For a more detailed treatment of this problem see P. T. Bauer and B. S. Yamey, *The Economics of Underdeveloped Countries* (Cambridge, 1957), Ch. III.

[2] *Census of India, 1931* Vol. v *Bengal and Sikim, Part.* I (Calcutta, 1933), p. 260.

[3] *Ibid.,* Ch. IV.

[4] For details see B. G. Gate, *Changes in the Occupational Distribution of Population* (New Delhi, 1940).

view of this defect it is correct to say that the figures for 'working dependants' are considerably on the low side.[1] Thus it may be safely concluded that the work force involved in agriculture did not really decline in 1931.

In view of these considerations it is clear that the size of the agricultural labour force as shown in the Census Reports of 1931 and 1941 is not comparable with the size calculated in 1921. This means that data on agricultural labour need to be corrected if we are to gain some idea of the trends in the capital/labour and land/labour ratios. Therefore, in the present work it has been assumed that the ratio of the agricultural labour force to the total population in 1931 and 1941 was the same as in 1921. Evidently such a method of correction is somewhat crude because, though it may be confidently asserted that the total volume of agricultural labour increased with the growth of population, it is risky to assume that the rate of increase was the same. The findings on the trends in the capital/labour and land/labour ratios have to be interpreted with reference to this limitation of the data on agricultural labour.

It was admitted by the Census Commissioners of both India and Pakistan that in 1941 there was an overcounting of 5.4 million in the figures on total population.[2] Accordingly the all-Bengal figure has been deflated. To facilitate comparison the size of the labour force shown in the Census Report of 1921 has been assumed to represent the number in 1919/20 when the first cattle census was conducted.

5.9 METHOD OF PRESENTATION

On the basis of the data discussed in the preceding pages indexes of physical capital assets are presented for the period from 1919/20 to 1944/45. In all, 12 different indexes are presented for different combinations of capital assets and their relationship with labour, land and output. Indexes C1 to C4 refer respectively to the four items of land, houses, animal labour and ploughs. Index C5 represents the total volume of physical capital. Index C6 refers to all categories of capital excluding land. Land was the most important item and, therefore, this procedure has the merit of showing the combined trend in houses, livestock labour and ploughs. Similarly, in order to isolate the influence of both land and houses index C7 has been constructed only on the basis of the data on draught animals and ploughs. Indexes C8 and C9 respectively measure the changes in the availability of draught animals and implements per head of labour and per unit of cultivated land. Finally

---

[1] *Census of India, op. cit.*, p. 261. 'Working dependants' was not anywhere reported in the two occupational sub-groups of 'cultivating owners' and 'tenant cultivators'.

[2] *Census of India, 1951, Vol. I, Part 1–B* (Delhi, 1955), p. 104.

changes in the capital/output ratio are shown in indexes C10 to C12. These indexes are constructed for analysis of the trends in all the individual quinquennial periods. To facilitate comparison for the six quinquennia as a whole the average quinquennial rates are presented at the beginning.

5.10 OVERALL RATES OF CHANGE

Percentage rates of change in the different items of capital assets for all the quinquennial periods taken together are presented in Table 5.1. The total volume of farm capital shows an average quinquennial increase of 2.6 per cent in the unrevised series and 1.2 per cent in the revised series. It is needless to mention here that the entire difference in the two series is due to the revision of acreage statistics for the last six years. As it is believed that the revised series is more reliable it is clear that the rate of increase in durable physical assets involved in Bengal agriculture was much lower than the growth of total labour force. The picture further deteriorates when the trends in the individual categories are analysed as it becomes clear that almost the entire increase in the total volume was due to the expansion of acreage under cultivation. The number of occupied houses in the rural areas increased at a

TABLE 5.1   *Percentage rates of quinquennial change in capital assets*

Categories	All-Bengal	Presi-dency	Burd-wan	Raj-shahi	Dacca	Chitta-gong
Land (C1)	2.6	3.8	1.2	1.5	4.2	1.6
	(1.0)	(3.4)	(−4.4)	(0.0)	(3.2)	(−0.6)
Houses (C2)	4.4	1.8	4.9	3.7	5.0	7.5
Work animals (C3)	−1.6	−0.1	−2.3	−2.6	−0.9	−2.4
Ploughs (C4)	−1.4	−3.7	−4.1	−1.3	0.7	0.3
All assets (C5)	2.6	3.5	1.4	1.5	4.2	2.0
	(1.2)	(3.2)	(−3.8)	(0.2)	(3.2)	(0.0)
All assets minus land (C6)	2.9	1.3	2.9	1.8	3.7	5.6
All assets minus land and houses (C7)	−1.6	−0.3	−2.4	−2.5	−0.8	−2.1
Agricultural labour	4.2	5.9	3.9	1.4	4.3	6.3

Source: Govt. of India, *Livestock Census of India*; Govt. of Bengal, *Cattle census Neport*.

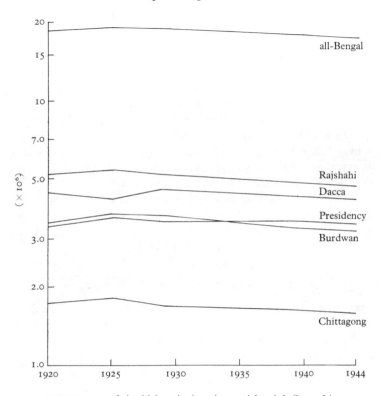

FIGURE 5.1 *Animal labour in the quinquennial periods (log scale).*

faster rate than the growth of population, though it is not known whether this was at the cost of change in the type and size of houses. Conversely, the number of work animals and ploughs declined during the period as a whole. These varying directions and rates of change in the different categories of durable assets and their relationship with the growth of labour force raise a number of questions of basic importance for the agrarian economy. However, before we proceed to deal with these questions the main features of the changes at the regional level and the trends in the individual quinquennial periods may be pointed out.

So far as the total volume of physical capital is concerned, Chittagong Division appears to have the closest resemblance with the all-Bengal rate of increase. The four other regions belong to two opposite extremes. Thus, while the rate was much higher in Presidency and Dacca Divisions, it was much lower in the two other regions.

As to the trends in the individual series the general picture is the same as indicated by the provincial average, i.e. in all the regions the rates of change in the total volume almost wholly reflect the trends in acreage under cultivation. Once again, the rate of increase in the number of occupied houses was impressive in all the regions except for Presidency Division. On the other hand, this latter region has the lowest rate of decline in work animals. Among the four other regions the rates of decline were highest in Burdwan, Rajshahi and Chittagong. The all-Bengal picture with regard to the trend in ploughs was representative of only three regions – Presidency, Burdwan and Rajshahi. In the two other Divisions the number of ploughs increased, though at low rates. These differences in the trends of work animals and ploughs at the regional level would indicate that at least a part of the animal labour in Presidency Division and ploughs in the other regions became underemployed or unemployed during the period under discussion. But from the explanation which is attempted in a later section it would seem that this may not necessarily have been the case.

5.11 TRENDS IN THE QUINQUENNIAL PERIODS

The overall trends in the different categories discussed above were not, however, the same in all the five individual quinquennial periods. Thus, during the first six years when the prices of agricultural produce had made a considerable recovery there was some increase in the number of animals, houses and ploughs. Conversely, the acreage under cultivation was below the level of the base period (Table 5.2). The obvious result of this drop in land – the most important item – was that the total volume of physical assets was lower than in 1919/20. The provincial trends in all the individual series were representative of almost all the regions.

The acreage under cultivation expanded during the years from 1926/27 to 1929/30, though this was yet to exceed the level of the base period (Table 5.3). The increase in the number of houses (C2) continued during these years, but again at a low rate. The trends in Series C7 are particularly important as these point out the timing of the decline in numbers of work animals and ploughs which continued during the next decade. Prices of agricultural produce during these years were higher than in the preceding quinquennium. The decline in C3 and C4 in spite of this relative prosperity stands in sharp contrast to the experience of the first six years. At the regional level it was only in Dacca that the trends in draught animals and ploughs were opposite to those indicated in the provincial average.

During the third quinquennium there was an acceleration in the rate of increase of houses (C2), but land still remained at the level of the preceding quinquennium (Table 5.4). The continuation of the decline in animal labour

TABLE 5.2 *Index of capital assets 1925/26*
(1919/20 = 100)

Categories	All-Bengal	Presidency	Burdwan	Rajshahi	Dacca	Chittagong
Land (C1)	97	96	89	98	105	93
Houses (C2)	103	101	103	102	104	107
Work animals (C3)	103	108	108	104	94	104
Ploughs (C4)	105	108	106	104	104	104
All assets (C5)	98	97	90	99	105	94
All assets minus land (C6)	103	103	104	102	101	106
All assets minus land and houses (C7)	103	108	108	104	95	104

TABLE 5.3 *Index of capital assets 1929/30*
(1919/20 = 100)

Categories	All-Bengal	Presidency	Burdwan	Rajshahi	Dacca	Chittagong
Land (C1)	100	101	97	99	105	93
Houses (C2)	105	102	105	103	107	112
Work animals (C3)	102	104	107	99	102	97
Ploughs (C4)	103	105	106	100	106	99
All Assets (C5)	100	101	98	100	105	94
All assets minus land (C6)	104	103	105	102	106	109
All assets minus land and houses (C7)	102	104	107	99	102	97

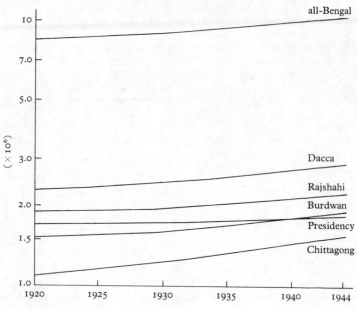

FIGURE 5.2   *Occupied houses in the quinquennial periods (log scale).*

TABLE 5.4   *Index of capital assets 1934/35*
$(1919/20 = 100)$

Categories	All-Bengal	Presi-dency	Burd-wan	Raj-shahi	Dacca	Chitta-gong
Land (C1)	100	97	86	102	109	99
Houses (C2)	111	104	111	108	113	122
Work animals (C3)	99	104	101	96	99	95
Ploughs (C4)	99	96	95	97	104	100
All assets (C5)	100	98	88	102	109	100
All assets minus land (C6)	108	104	108	104	109	116
All assets minus land and houses (C7)	99	104	101	96	100	96

and ploughs during these years has to be interpreted with reference to the fact that no census was held in 1935 and the relevant data have been interpolated on the basis of the rates of change between 1930 and 1940. In spite of the possible error in these two series (C3 and C4) it may, however, be asserted that during the 15 years from 1919/20 there was hardly any change in the total volume of durable physical assets involved in Bengal agriculture. The provincial trends with regard to the different categories were once again characteristic of all the regions except in the case of land.

As to the acreage under cultivation the fourth quinquennium was a turning-point as it was during these years that for the first time land exceeded the level of the base period (Table 5.5). The obvious result of this expansion – characteristic of almost all the regional units – was that for the first time the total volume (C5) was higher than in the base period. Among the three other categories the rate of increase in the number of houses slowed down. Conversely, the rate of decline in work animals was higher than in the preceding quinquennium. There was a considerable recovery in the price-level of agricultural produce during these years. The decline in C3 and C4 in spite of this recovery indicates the revival of the inverse relationship between price and these two categories which first started in the late 1920s.

TABLE 5.5   *Index of capital assets 1939/40*
(1919/20 = 100)

Categories	All-Bengal	Presidency	Burdwan	Rajshahi	Dacca	Chittagong
Land (C1)	105	109	96	102	116	97
Houses (C2)	117	107	118	114	120	132
Work animals (C3)	97	105	96	93	97	94
Ploughs (C4)	94	87	84	94	103	100
All assets (C5)	105	108	97	102	116	99
All assets minus land (C6)	111	106	112	107	114	124
All assets minus land and houses (C7)	96	104	95	93	97	94

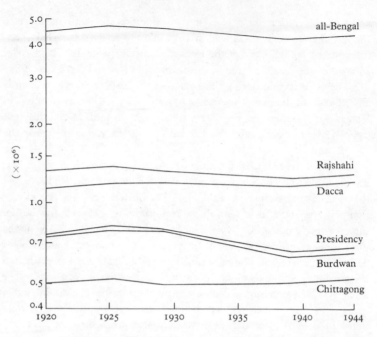

FIGURE 5.3   *Ploughs in the quinquennial periods (log scale).*

Trends in acreage during the last five years differ widely between the revised and unrevised series (Table 5.6). The decline in the revised series has to be understood with reference to the nature of the revision of acreage statistics. Among the three other component units, the decline in the number of ploughs during the years 1926/27 to 1939/40 was now reversed, though the actual number was still below the level of 1919/20. There was a considerable loss of work animals during the famine years.[1] It would, therefore, seem likely that the trend in the number of work animals would also be positive during this quinquennium. Prices of agricultural produce radically increased after 1940. This would indicate that the inverse relationship between price and the series C_3 and C_4 which was characteristic of the second and the fourth quinquennia had now changed.

To summarise the trends in the individual quinquennial periods, expansion of acreage seems to have started in the fourth quinquennium. Numbers of houses increased all throughout the period, though at varying rates. Conversely, the number of draught animals and ploughs declined during the years 1926/27 to 1939/40.

[1] P. C. Mahalanobis, 'A Sample Survey of the After-Effects of the Bengal Famine of 1943', *Sankhya: Indian Journal of Statistics*, Vol. 7, Part 4 (1946), pp. 337–400.

TABLE 5.6   *Index of capital assets 1944/45*
$(1919/20 = 100)$

Categories	All-Bengal	Presidency	Burdwan	Rajshahi	Dacca	Chittagong
Land (C1)	115	121	107	109	125	108
	(102)	(111)	(77)	(98)	(116)	(95)
Houses (C2)	124	110	127	120	128	143
Work animals (C3)	93	101	92	89	93	90
Ploughs (C4)	98	90	88	98	106	104
All assets (C5)	115	120	108	109	124	110
	(103)	(111)	(80)	(99)	(116)	(98)
All assets minus land (C6)	116	107	117	110	119	132
All assets minus land and houses (C7)	94	100	92	90	94	92

Note: Figures in brackets refer to the revised series.

5.12 RELATION BETWEEN LABOUR AND CAPITAL

How do we explain this decline in ploughs and draught animals (series C7)? This question is of particular importance as it is believed that an exogenous increase in the labour force engaged in agriculture provides an impetus for the growth of capital and this impetus works through the complementary relationship between labour and capital in crop production.[1] Since there was a substantial increase in the volume of agricultural labour in Bengal during the period under review, according to this view the number of ploughs and the quantity of animal labour should have also increased. But in the light of the available data it seems that the process was just the reverse.

In view of the lack of data on working capital, complexities in estimating physical assets and the nature of the data on agricultural labour it is difficult to be reasonably confident whether the decline in the capital/labour ratio was as high as 24 per cent (Table 5.7). However, it may be safely asserted that the underlying trend was one of decline. This decline in the capital/labour ratio indicates that by 1944/45 a considerable part of the total labour force in Bengal agriculture had become underemployed or un-

[1] See Shukla, *op. cit.*, Ch. III.

TABLE 5.7 *Index of the capital/labour ratio*
(1919/20 = 100)

Regions	1919–20	1925–26	1929–30	1934–35	1939–40	1944–45
All-Bengal	100	99	95	88	82	76
Presidency	100	104	97	90	84	76
Burdwan	100	104	100	90	82	76
Rajshahi	100	102	96	92	88	84
Dacca	100	91	95	88	82	76
Chittagong	100	97	86	79	73	67

Note: In the ratios worked out above we have ploughs and draught animals (series C_7) in the numerator and farm labour in the denominator.

employed. However, if it is believed that there was unemployment or under-employment at the beginning of the period under review, these trends would indicate that the problem had become more acute in 1944/45. It is needless to mention here that this finding is quite consistent with the widely-held view that underdeveloped agriculture is characterised by the presence of a considerable stock of surplus labour.

What then remains of the thesis that since there is zero substitutability between labour and capital the increased supply of labour will stimulate an autonomous increase in farm capital (series C_7)? The purpose in raising this question is not to doubt the validity of this relationship in an underdeveloped agriculture, but to point out that this complementary may not necessarily lead to an increase in ploughs and animal labour. If it is believed that this view about the impact of zero substitutability between labour and capital is correct, two other assumptions have to be made. From the supply side it has to be assumed that per capita income is constant though population is increasing or, if there is a decline, the deficit is met by an increase in the savings/income ratio, or the greater availability of borrowed funds, or both. From the demand side the assumption will be that along with the increase of labour there is a corresponding expansion of cultivation to new areas or that the marginal productivity of labour on existing land is remunerative, or both.[1]

Let us now examine if these are valid assumptions in the case of Bengal; it is convenient to start with the second. We have already seen that there was a marked disparity between the rates of expansion in acreage and the increase in the supply of labour (Table 5.1). The decline which thus took place

[1] It must, however, be recognised that the decline in C_7 may have been due to an increase in investments which increased the area under double cropping or in improved seeds or in the construction of additional houses or in all of these items. The purpose is to point out that even if these possibilities are not taken into consideration the hypothesis that the increased supply of labour will lead to an autonomous increase in capital may not be valid.

in the availability of land per head of labour in the agricultural sector is shown in Table 5.8. These trends in the land/labour ratio indicate that though the supply of labour increased there was no demand (induced by a corresponding expansion of acreage) for equipping all the additional labour with ploughs and work animals. In this connection it may be mentioned here that most of the expansion of acreage which took place during these years was due to the increase in double cropping. This is important as it shows that what was needed was not an increase in the number of work animals and ploughs, but the greater intensity in the use of the same ploughs and animal labour during the relatively slack season of the year.

It may, however, be argued that even if there was no corresponding extension of cultivation to new areas the additional labour could have been used on the land already under cultivation and this would have provided an incentive to a growth in farm implements and animal labour (C7). Clearly this argument would assume that the marginal productivity of additional labour was remunerative. In other words, the additional output to be obtained from the employment of additional labour was higher than the extra expenditure required to equip such labour.[1] Obviously it is not possible to say anything definitely as to whether conditions in Bengal during the period under review were so favourable as to fulfil this assumption.

Some idea may, however, be made from the findings of the survey of farm economics conducted in certain west Bengal districts during the three years from 1954/55 to 1956/57. Two features of these findings are of particular interest in the present context. Firstly, as many as 50 per cent of the farms are incurring losses.[2] Secondly, the use of additional inputs increases yield up to a

TABLE 5.8   *Index of the land/labour ratio*
(1919/20 = 100)

Regions	1919–20	1925–26	1929–30	1934–35	1939–40	1944–45
All-Bengal	100	93	93	89	89	93(83)
Presidency	100	93	95	84	88	92(84)
Burdwan	100	85	91	77	82	88(63)
Rajshahi	100	97	96	97	97	101(92)
Dacca	100	100	98	97	98	101(94)
Chittagong	100	86	82	82	75	79(70)

Note: Figures in brackets refer to the revised acreage statistics.

[1] This will be the consideration in the case of self-employed labour. In the case of hired labour the wage will have to be taken note of.

[2] See: *Survey of Farm Economics (op. cit.)*, pp. 72–3.

certain point, but this results in lower rates of profits and higher losses.[1] It may be safely asserted that the agrarian economy of Bengal hardly experienced any basic change in the decade following independence. It would, therefore, seem that the significance of these findings holds equally good for the period under review.

However, though the preceding discussion explains why the increase in labour supply did not result in an autonomous increase in series C7, it still remains to be explained why there should have been a decline. This calls for an examination of the first assumption. This examination is important as in our image per capita income in an underdeveloped economy is low and the long-term trend is one of stagnation, if not decline. In such a situation the very condition (increased supply of labour) which is supposed to provide an impetus to the growth of farm capital (C7) makes addition to capital stock more difficult. So far as Bengal is concerned, in the absence of relevant data, it is not possible to make any estimate of the trend in per capita income during the period under discussion. As an alternative some idea may be gained from the trend in per capita all-crop output, but this again raises the question of the reliability of crop statistics. However, if we accept these figures for whatever they are worth, it is clear that per capita income was declining. For whereas population was increasing at the rate of 0.8 per cent per year, the rate of increase in all-crop output was only 0.3 per cent per year (0.9 per cent in the unrevised series). This disparity between population growth and crop output indicates how the increased supply of labour is likely to have discouraged (not stimulated) further addition to the capital stock.

Could it be argued that there was an improvement in the availability of borrowed funds? Relevant data are available only on Co-operative Credit (discussed in the next chapter), but these funds accounted for such a small proportion of the total requirements that it is difficult to make any reliable guess about the underlying trend. However, there are three *a priori* considerations which would suggest that the availability of loanable funds declined, particularly from the beginning of the depression period. Firstly, the fact that the per capita income in the agricultural sector as a whole was declining suggests that the proportion of rural families with loanable surplus became smaller.[2] Secondly, as this section of the rural families are usually more affected by changes in market conditions it would seem that the slump in agricultural prices in the 1930s further aggravated the underlying trend of a decline in loanable funds. Thirdly, working in the same direction may have been the influence of the Money-lenders Act of 1933 and the Agricultural

---

[1] *ibid.*, pp. 87–90.
[2] This is obviously on the assumption that the distribution of income among the different classes of rural family remained unchanged.

Debtors Act of 1935. The influence of the second Act under which Debt Conciliation Boards were set up to scale down ancestral debts would seem to have
been of particular importance as it came at a time when there was as yet no
recovery in the price level. These considerations would suggest that the flow
of capital from the non-agricultural sector was also declining.

As already pointed out it is difficult to say how far this decline in series
C7 reflects a real drop in the level of total investment in inputs other than
land and houses. However, if any conclusion is to be drawn from the available
data, it is clear that there was hardly anything in the economy which could
allow the increased labour supply to lead to an increase, rather than a decline,
in farm implements and livestock labour.

5.13 CAPITAL/LAND RATIO

As a matter of fact it seems that in an under-developed agriculture the best
criterion on which to judge the trends in such traditional inputs as draught
animals and ploughs is to examine the capital/land ratio. In such an agriculture, where the scope for the extension of cultivation is limited and the
increase in labour supply is given, it is the change in the availability of
ploughs and animal labour per unit of land under cultivation which is most
important. In this respect the picture that emerges with regard to Bengal
agriculture is presented in Table 5.9.

During the first six years the capital/land ratio was increasing. This
was followed by a decline, which remained low during the second and the
third quinquennia and then accelerated during the fourth. During the
period as a whole the availability of farm capital (C7) per unit of land
declined by 9 per cent in the revised series. The real magnitude of this drop

TABLE 5.9 *Index of the capital/land ratio*
(1919/20 = 100)

Regions	1919–20	1925–26	1929–30	1930–34	1939–40	1944–45
All-Bengal	100	106	102	100	92	82(91)
Presidency	100	112	103	107	95	83(90)
Burdwan	100	122	110	117	99	86(120)
Rajshahi	100	105	99	94	91	83(91)
Dacca	100	90	97	91	84	75(81)
Chittagong	100	112	105	97	98	85(96)

Note: Figures in brackets refer to the revised series. Capital in this Table includes only
ploughs and work animals.

must have been smaller in view of the fact that most of the expansion of acreage was due to the increase in double-cropping. However, even if this latter aspect is not taken into consideration, it is clear that the disparity in capital/land ratio was much less marked than the decline in capital/labour ratio.

However, the fact that the total number of work animals and ploughs declined in spite of some expansion of acreage raises the question as to whether this had any impact on the yield per acre. It may be recalled here that the yield slightly improved in the first decade. This was followed by stagnation during the next two quinquennia and some drop in the last.

This constancy in yield during the years from 1929/30 to 1939/40 in spite of the decline in farm capital would imply that (*a*) animal labour and ploughs in this period were of a better quality and/or (*b*) there was a surplus stock during the initial years so that in spite of the decline in the latter years the intensity of cultivation remained more or less the same or (*c*) the stock of farm capital was reduced to finance investment in such inputs as improved seeds so that the level of productivity was not affacted. As already pointed out it is difficult to say anything definite on the first and the third score. So far as the second possibility is concerned the findings of the survey in the West Bengal districts referred to earlier would indicate that the decline in work animals did not mean a change in the intensity of cultivation, but an improvement in the intensity of capital utilisation – so that productivity per acre did not decline. The high level of unemployment of livestock labour in the various sizes of farms is shown in Table 5.10.

This study may be concluded by a reference to the trends in the amount of capital of various types that have been used over the years to obtain the supply of a unit of agricultural output. Opinions are divided as to the methods of estimating such costs in terms of capital. Thus, capital/output ratios may

TABLE 5.10 *Levels of unemployment of animal labour*

Size of farms (acres)	Percentage of unemployed bullock labour
0.01– 1.25	89.1
1.26– 2.50	84.8
2.51– 3.75	86.1
3.76– 5.00	81.9
5.01– 7.50	81.4
7.51–10.00	83.3
10.01–15.00	83.1
Above 15.00	80.0

Source: *Economies of Farm Management, op. cit.*, p. 46.

be estimated on the basis of both the numerator or denominator being gross or net. For the present purpose the estimates are made on the basis of gross output and gross physical capital. This procedure is clearly suggested by the nature of the available data. Moreover, since the capital/output ratio is a technical relationship gross output becomes relevant. Secondly, the estimates are presented only for all-Bengal. In Table 5.11 index C10 is obtained by dividing index C5 (aggregate volume of capital) by output. In constructing index C11 only land, and in index C12 both land and houses, are excluded from the stock of capital.

In interpreting these findings it has to be recalled that the output figures for the cattle census years have been estimated, as in the case of acreage data, on the basis of a three years' average centred on those years.

As expected from the quinquennial trends in series C7 it is clear that the underlying trend was one of decline (index C12) in capital per unit of output. This drop in the number of draught animals and ploughs per unit of output has to be attributed to the various possible changes discussed earlier. However, the picture that emerges when a 'statistical bias' is introduced by the addition of houses to the stock of capital is the reverse – except during the first 10 years the capital/output ratio was increasing (series C11). It has to be recalled here that no adjustment has been made for any possible change in the types and sizes of houses in the rural areas. The quinquennial trends in index C10 are less consistent, but compared to the base year the capital/output ratio was always lower. In other words, the aggregate volume of physical capital used to obtain a unit of output was smaller than in 1919/20. However, the total volume of decline in the capital coefficients was very low.

The scope of this study is obviously limited in that it is confined to an analysis of the trends only in durable physical assets involved in Bengal agriculture. It has not been possible either to include such items as working capital and investment in seeds or to relate even the limited number of

TABLE 5.11   *Trends in the capital/output ratio*
(1919/20 = 100)

Years	Index C10	Index C11	Index C12
1919/20	100(100)	100(100)	100(100)
1926/27	96(94)	100(99)	101(100)
1929/30	94(90)	97(94)	95(92)
1934/35	95(92)	102(99)	94(91)
1939/40	103(94)	108(100)	93(86)
1944/45	98(87)	109(88)	88(71)

Note: Figures in brackets are based on the unrevised series.

categories to the trends in per capita income and total savings. Moreover, the available data have certain limitations. However, if the findings presented above are believed to be of some significance the following conclusions may be drawn. Of the four categories selected for this study the acreage under cultivation and the number of houses increased. The trend in the former category substantiates our assumption that in an under-developed agriculture most of the increase in capital formation would be in such a form as would expand the productive acreage, and if the scope for the extension of cultivation to new areas is limited such increase would be achieved through an increase in the proportion of double cropped area. The increase in these two items was accompanied by some decline in draught animals and ploughs. The rate of increase of the total volume of durable assets was far below the growth of labour force. Secondly, the decline in the number of work animals does not seem to have had any adverse impact on the productivity per acre of land. Thirdly, this would imply that either there was a surplus stock of animal labour and ploughs at the beginning of the period under discussion or a slight shift towards the use of better inputs.

6

AGRICULTURAL CREDIT AND THE
CO-OPERATIVE CREDIT MOVEMENT

The purpose of the present chapter is to evaluate the performance of the
Co-operative Credit Movement during the period under review (1920–47).
However, in order to place the movement in its proper perspective, we
start with a brief reference to some general issues related to agricultural
credit. Finally, the opinions of some individual authors and committees of
enquiry about the limited success of the Co-operative Credit Movement
are briefly reviewed.

6.1 THE GENERAL BACKGROUND

A proper system of credit is of as basic importance to agriculture as it is
to industry. But agriculture has certain distinctive features which place it in
a disadvantageous position as against industry in respect of the availability
of finance from the usual credit agencies. First of all, the scale of production
in agriculture is small. 'While other industries tend to become concentrated in
units of ever increasing size, agriculture remains scattered, individualistic,
small-scale and chaotic.'[1] The problem is further complicated by the
simultaneous presence of production for domestic consumption and the
market. In these conditions a large part of the working capital which the
cultivators need has the character of being related to their consumption
rather than to production. Secondly, the risks and uncertainties involved in
agricultural production are greater than in manufacturing industry, as success in agriculture depends on factors outside the control of the cultivators.
A third distinctive feature of agriculture is that agricultural products are
often perishable or of such a nature that they cannot be properly stored.
Lastly, agricultural production involves a longer time scale than does industrial production – sometimes the cultivators have to wait a year for their
harvests. They cannot switch over to an alternative crop in response to a shift
in prices once the land has been sown with a particular crop. As a result of

---

[1] *Report on the Indian Central Banking Enquiry Committee* (Calcutta, 1931), Vol. 1 (Majority
Report), p. 45.

these factors the cultivators cannot make use of capital with the same degree of efficiency as does industry generally.[1]

However, it is not only the internal weakness of agriculture which prevents the cultivators from attracting the services of the external mechanism of banking. By its very nature agriculture is rural, whereas these external establishments are urban in respect of location, preferences and the interests of the individuals who share the power of dispensing credit. As a result agricultural credit is usually the least organised.[2]

The Indian conditions were not such as to make the situation any different either. In the nineteenth century the 'opening up' of the country to wider commercial intercourse with the world market marked the advent of a cash economy in the rural areas on a much larger scale than before. The use of money assumed greater prominence even in areas or among sections of population which remained relatively unaffected by the spread of commercialisation. But as the credit agencies which grew up in the changed circumstances almost exclusively catered for the needs of the export trade and domestic industries, the rural areas remained cut off from the organised sources of finance. Thus, with the functional mechanism of an economic structure remaining incomplete, a vacuum was created and this was filled by the money lenders.[3]

If we look at the problem of agricultural credit in India in this way, it is clear that the money lenders did in fact fulfil an indispensable economic function. But the price they charged for their services was very high and they often indulged in malpractices. Thus, during the period under review interest on loans to agriculturists given on the security of land generally varied from $18\frac{3}{4}$ per cent to $37\frac{1}{2}$ per cent per annum. Interests on loans given without security were much higher, sometimes as high as 300 per cent per year.[4] Why was the rate of interest so high? The determination of interest rates is one of the most complex theoretical issues in economics. But evidently this question has an important bearing on the problem under investigation in this

[1] Incidentally it may be pointed out that it is for some of these reasons that the cultivators need credit.
[2] For further elaboration of these aspects see Reserve Bank of India, *All-India Rural Credit Survey*, Vol. II (Bombay, 1954), pp. 151–5. Henceforth referred to as *Credit Survey*. See also *Central Banking Enquiry Committee, op. cit.*, pp. 44–54.
[3] Throughout this study money lenders are meant to include, apart from the residential and itinerant ones (Mahajans, Pathans and Kabulis), persons who had other occupations, but also lent money such as landlords, merchants and pensioners. It is not suggested here that the origin of money lenders was due or associated with the spread of commercialisation. As a matter of fact money lending seems to have been a much older institution. See, *Bengal Provincial Banking Enquiry Committee* (Calcutta, 1930), Vol. I, pp. 170–80. Henceforth referred to as *Banking Enquiry Committee*.
[4] *Banking Enquiry Committee.*, p. 198.

chapter. Therefore, a brief reference needs to be made to some of the basic issues even though this may mean an oversimplification of a complicated problem.

Economists distinguish between net ('pure') and gross rates of interest. The former is the rate which would emerge if there was perfect competition among the borrowers and the lenders. Gross interest is what is meant by interest in ordinary use, the amount actually paid by the borrowers. Thus, while net interest is that portion of gross interest which is simply paid for the use of capital in competitive conditions, gross interest includes, apart from net interest, the cost of management, a premium for risk and monopoly profits.

According to non-monetary theory, rates of interest are determined, on the demand side, by the marginal productivity of capital. In an underdeveloped agriculture where the supply of capital is scarce in relation to the other factors of production, investment in inputs like fertiliser, pesticides, improved varieties of seeds, are highly productive. But it is generally held that the major part of borrowings is spent for consumption purposes.[1] Secondly, it is true that a part of the capital is directly used for productive purposes, but investment in traditional factors hardly enables the borrowers to increase the existing low level of productivity. It would, therefore, seem to be fairly clear that the high rates of interest in the underdeveloped agriculture are not determined by the marginal productivity or efficiency of capital.

According to monetary interest theory interest is not the price paid for saving, but the charge made for parting with liquidity. In a poor agriculture the liquidity preference is very strong and it is believed that the 'liquidity complex' is one of the reasons for the high level of interest rates. The findings in India that the rates of interest are higher in areas where a subsistence economy prevails strengthen this opinion.[2] But again this does not explain why even in the more monetised and commercialised areas the price of borrowed funds is so high.

From these considerations it is fairly clear that the high price of capital in the rural areas represented gross interest.[3] It is not possible to estimate the

[1] According to the findings of the *Credit Survey* (Vol. I. Part I, pp. 260–321) 37 per cent of the borrowings were for expenditure on the farm and 50.2 per cent for family expenditure. However, it is found that in most cases it was capital expenditure which was the most significant variable (explaining 69 per cent of the variations) affecting the demand for credit. For details see, Dr S. Ghatak, *Rural Money Markets in India* (unpublished PhD thesis University of London, 1972), pp. 75–80.

[2] *Credit Survey*, Vol. II, pp. 190–6.

[3] It is believed that net rate may not account for more than a quarter of the gross rate prevailing in the rural areas. See V. T. Naidu, *Farm Credits and Co-operatives in India* (Bombay, 1968), p. 145.

extent to which each of the three components of gross interest – monopoly profits, premium for risk and administrative cost – was responsible for the high price. However, there is evidence to show that the first two factors were at work. Firstly, it was pointed out to the Bengal Banking Enquiry Committee that the rates of interest were lower in areas where Co-operative Credit Societies were formed.[1] This would clearly indicate how the failure of the regular financial establishments to fulfil certain essential functions left the money lenders in a strong position to take advantage of the monopoly control they enjoyed of a scarce factor (capital) in the rural areas.

Secondly, the rates of interest on secured loans were much lower than in the case of unsecured loans. Such a pattern would indicate that a part of the high rate of interest represented a premium for risk.[2] However, this clearly conforms to what would be expected in a poor agriculture. In essence the nature of the security depends on two factors: (*a*) the capacity of the borrowers to earn an income beyond the basic needs of subsistence which will determine their ability to meet interest charges and eventually to repay the loan, and (*b*) the market value of the asset pledged as security should it be necessary to acquire them because the borrowers cannot meet their obligations.[3] In both these respects the specific conditions in Bengal were unfavourable to the borrowers. As the larger section of the rural population lived at the margin of subsistence their repaying capacity must have been poor. As to land, which was the best asset to be offered as security, there were many peasants who were landless. On the other hand, the sale price of land which the owner–occupier could obtain was depressed as the landlords were entitled to a transfer fee. It may be argued that since the money lenders had a monopoly in the rural areas they could charge a higher price than otherwise possible,[4] but it cannot be denied that considerable risk was involved in lending to borrowers with inadequate credit and this led to money lenders charging a premium. The preceding discussion would suggest that it was not only monopoly profits as such, but the low level of per capita production of

---

[1] *Banking Enquiry Committee*, p. 136. The experience has been found to be the same in India. For details see *Credit Survey*, Vol. II, pp. 190–6.

[2] *Banking Enquiry Committee*, p. 198. Different rates of interest on secured and unsecured loans were provided for under the Bengal Money-lenders Acts of 1933 and 1940. In India it has been found that an estimated four fifths of the debt owed to the professional and agricultural money lenders was unsecured. See *Credit Survey*, Vol. II, p. 169. According to the findings of Dr Ghatak (*op. cit.*, p. 163) it seems that most of the cost of credit in the rural areas was due to the high risk and uncertainty involved in lending to small-scale peasant producers.

[3] For a useful discussion particularly on this aspect of the problem, see, A. Bottomley, *Factor Pricing in Underdeveloped Rural Areas* (London, 1970), Chapter 12; Food and Agricultural Organisation (UN), *Agricultural Credit in Economically Underdeveloped Countries* (Rome, 1959), pp. 30–2.

[4] *Report of the Agricultural Finance Sub-Committee* (Delhi, 1945), p. 59.

the borrowers which accounted for the high rates of interest in the agricultural sector.

For a long time during the nineteenth century the policy of the government was one of non-interference with these forces in the rural economy which pushed up the price of credit. Such a policy was embodied in the Promulgation of 1855 which provided that 'in any suit in which interest is recoverable the amount shall be adjudged or decreed by the court at the rate (if any) agreed upon by the parties' and in the absence of any such agreement 'at such rate as the court shall deem reasonable'.[1] The evils which followed in the subsequent years, particularly in the form of land transfer from the borrowers, led to the passing of protective legislation in two Provinces – the Deccan Agriculturists' Relief Act and the Punjab Land Alienation Act. Action taken at the all-India level, though in principle more positive than the protective legislation, fell far short of the establishment of an Agricultural Bank which was being discussed for a long time.[2] This was the Land Improvement Act of 1883 and the Agriculturists' Loans Act of 1884 under which the Provincial Governments were allowed to advance loans to the cultivators. But the effectiveness of these two enabling Acts was hardly better than that of the protective legislation – the supremacy of the money lenders remained undisturbed and the transfer of land also continued.[3] At the turn of the present century it was realised that this legislation would have to be supplemented by more organised efforts for the supply of credit at a reasonable price and the result was the inauguration of the Co-operative Credit Movement under the Credit Co-operative Societies Act of 1904. The underlying assumption seems to have been that this arrangement, by offering effective competition, would compel the money lenders to reduce the rate of interest and thus solve the problem of rural indebtedness.

The Act of 1904 provided for the formation only of credit societies in both the urban and the rural areas. The rural societies were to have unlimited liability and the urban societies were free to opt for either limited or un-

[1] Cited by the *Banking Enquiry Committee*, p. 164. Before 1855 the statutory limit on the rate of interest as provided for under the Regulation of 1774 was 12 per cent.

[2] For a discussion on the background of these Acts see I. J. Catanach, *Rural Credit in Western India, 1875–1930* (University of California Press, 1970), pp. 10–32; see also T. R. Metcalf, 'The British and the Money-Lenders in the Nineteenth Century India', *Journal of Modern History*, Vol. xxxiv, No. 4 (1962), pp. 390–7. The problem of agricultural indebtedness in Bengal in the second half of the nineteenth century is examined by B. B. Chaudhuri, 'Rural Credit Relations in Bengal, 1859–1885', *Indian Economic and Social History Review*, Vol vi, No. 3 (1969), pp. 203–57.

[3] For the effectiveness of the Deccan Act see Catanach, *op. cit.*, pp. 25–6; for the Land Alienation Act see, M. L. Darling, *The Punjab Peasant in Prosperity and Debt*. Fourth edition (London, 1947), pp. 197–200; loans advanced in Bengal under the Loans Act and Land Improvement Act averaged 6.24 lakhs per year during the period from 1919 to 1928. For details see *Report on the Land Revenue Administration of the Presidency of Bengal* (annual).

limited liability. However, in reality the main emphasis was on the formation of agricultural credit societies. This defect of confining the scope of co-operative activities only to a particular field was soon realised as societies with other purposes began to be formed. Secondly, the Act of 1904 did not provide for the formation of any central agencies, banks or unions. These deficiencies were remedied by the Co-operative Societies Act of 1912.[1] However, the pace of progress in the immediately following years both with regard to the formation of Primary Societies and Central Banks remained slow. Thus, in 1920 there were only 5.8 thousand Primary Societies and 71 Central Banks in Bengal.

The Primary Societies obtained their capital from the following sources: (a) Share Capital paid up by the members, (b) a Reserve Fund created out of profits, (c) deposits from the members and loans from (d) Central Banks, (e) non-members, (f) government and (g) other societies. Funds from the first three sources formed the owned and those from the last four formed the borrowed capital of the Co-operative Societies.

Though the scope of the Act of 1904 was widened to include societies for purposes other than credit, the main character of the Co-operative Movement in the Province, as in other parts of India, remained essentially agricultural. Thus, out of a total of 41.0 thousand Primary Societies even in 1943/44 as many as 35.7 thousand were agricultural credit societies. Evidently this high proportion underlines the importance which was assigned to the problem of agricultural credit.

The remaining part of this chapter is devoted to an analysis of the achievements of the Co-operative Credit Movement during the period from 1920 to 1944. The method of presentation is similar to that for agricultural output. Trends in the different sides of the Movement – the number of societies, membership, working capital, etc. – for the period as a whole and the quinquennia are presented for all-Bengal and the five regions. The quinquennial trends are once again indicated by index numbers and for this purpose 1920 is taken as the base year. As a matter of fact the fourth period comprises only four years, but for the sake of convenience this is also referred to as a quinquennium.

6.2 SOURCES OF STATISTICS

All the data relating to the different categories of Co-operative Societies are available from the *Report on the Working of the Co-operative Societies in*

---

[1] For a discussion on the background and the development of the Co-operative Movement see, Catanach, *op. cit.*, pp. 32–55; E. M. Hough, *The Co-operative Movement in India* (Bombay, 1959), pp. 40–51.

Bengal,[1] and the series is available for the period up to 1943/44. Statistics obtained from this series required two adjustments. Firstly, from 1934/35 'other funds' were separated from the Reserve Funds. Therefore, in order to make the series uniform for the whole period the two items have been added up for the period from 1934/35. Secondly, for the year 1941/42 only the all-Bengal statistics are available. Therefore, the regional data for this year has been calculated on the assumption that the rates of decline or progress were the same in all parts of the Province.

6.3 THE TOTAL NUMBER OF SOCIETIES AND MEMBERSHIP

The role of the Co-operative Credit Movement may be evaluated in its two aspects – external and internal. The former relates to the proportion of total borrowers among the cultivators covered by the Primary Societies. The latter includes such issues as the proportion of borrowings of the members from Co-operatives in their total borrowings, efficiency of repayment and the proportion of owned capital to the total working capital.

As to the external side data are available on the number of Societies and their membership. During the period as a whole the number of Societies at the all-Bengal level increased at the rate of 7.8 per cent per year (Table 6.1) and this was characteristic of almost all the regional units. This represents an increase of 29.9 thousand Primary Societies from 1920 to 1944. Trends in the quinquennial periods show that after a sharp expansion during the second quinquennium the rate of expansion slowed down during the next two periods. This was due to the severe strain imposed on the agrarian economy by the depression and the consequent liquidation of a considerable number of Societies during the years from 1932/33 to 1935/36. Moreover, a policy of consolidation as against expansion was pursued by the Co-operative

TABLE 6.1 *Annual percentage rates of increase and quinquennial index of Societies* (1920 = 100)

Regions	Rate of increase	1920–24	1925–29	1930–34	1935–38	1939–44
All-Bengal	7.8	128	264	346	371	611
Presidency	6.8	140	302	347	354	573
Burdwan	7.9	128	302	433	453	594
Rajshahi	7.8	120	207	260	296	587
Dacca	8.1	124	252	352	381	610
Chittagong	7.9	140	308	407	428	676

[1] Annual publication of the Government of Bengal. Henceforth referred to as *Annual Report*.

Department from 1929/30 to 1931/32. The marked expansion during the last five years, more or less equally witnessed in all the regions, was due to the formation of a large number of Societies for the distribution of loans under a revised scheme discussed later.

The role of the Co-operative Movement in its external aspect obviously does not depend only on the formation of new Societies, but also on the average size of membership and its long-term changes. In this respect two important features may be pointed out. Firstly, the size of membership per society remained small – only 26 at the all-Bengal level. Secondly, the annual rate of expansion in membership for the period as a whole was lower than in the formation of new societies (Table 6.2). The only exception to this general pattern was Chittagong Division. The discrepancies between the number of societies and membership which thus took place in the five quinquennia are presented in Table 6.2. Apart from its more important implications noted later, these discrepancies meant that per capita administrative and maintenance expenditure was increasing over time.

6.4 PROPORTION OF BORROWERS COVERED BY CREDIT SOCIETIES

We now turn to the question of what proportion of the total borrowers in the agricultural sector was covered by institutional credit. This involves an estimation of the total number of agricultural families in the quinquennial periods and the proportion of families borrowing from different sources. The unreliability of the census returns of 1931 and 1941 on the total labour force engaged in agriculture has been pointed out earlier.[1] Therefore, for present

TABLE 6.2 *Annual percentage rates of increase and quinquennial index of membership per Society*
(1920 = 100)

Regions	Rate of increase	1920–24	1925–29	1930–34	1935–38	1939–44
All-Bengal	6.9	95	87	83	78	82
Presidency	5.9	94	84	83	80	80
Burdwan	6.4	96	91	85	80	73
Rajshahi	6.2	98	89	83	77	73
Dacca	7.1	94	84	76	72	81
Chittagong	7.7	93	89	90	84	92

[1] Chapter v, pp. 139–41.

purposes it is assumed that the proportion of agricultural labour to the total population as returned in the Census Report of 1921 was the same in the subsequent years. What proportion of these families (assumed to be represented by the quantity of labour) may be said to have been in need of borrowing? No such information is available for the period under review. This problem may, however, be resolved by assuming that the proportion of borrowing families in 1951 in certain districts of West Bengal was representative of all the regions of Bengal during the period under consideration.[1] On this basis it seems that the proportion of borrowing families covered by the Co-operatives for the period as a whole was only 6.4 per cent at the all-Bengal level (Table 6.3).

The picture does not materially improve even if account is taken of only the last quinquennium, when the Co-operative Movement had completed four decades of its existence. The vast majority of the borrowers still remained outside the scope of institutional credit. The variations at the regional level have to be understood with reference to the fact that the proportions of agricultural families to the total families and the percentage of families in need of borrowings have been assumed to be uniform.

6.5 LOANS ADVANCED

The failure of the Credit Movement stands out more prominently when we examine its internal aspect. Thus, while both the number of Societies and membership were increasing the total amount of loans advanced to the members declined (Table 6.4). In other words the increase in membership was accompanied by an almost corresponding drop in the availability of average loans per member. At the all-Bengal level the only exception to this

TABLE 6.3 *Percentage of borrowing families covered by the Co-operatives in the quinquennia*

Regions	1920–24	1925–29	1930–34	1935–38	1939–44
All-Bengal	3.0	5.5	6.6	6.3	10.6
Presidency	3.0	5.7	6.2	5.7	8.6
Burdwan	2.8	6.0	7.7	7.3	8.5
Rajshahi	3.2	5.0	5.8	6.0	11.2
Dacca	3.0	5.3	6.5	6.3	11.1
Chittagong	2.8	5.6	7.1	6.6	10.8

[1] *Credit Survey*, Vol. I, Part 2, pp. 232–3. The simple average is 56 per cent. In this study it has been assumed to be 60 per cent.

TABLE 6.4 *Annual percentage rates of decline and quinquennial index of per capita loans*
(1920 = 100)

Regions	Rates of decline	1920–24	1925–29	1930–34	1935–38	1939–44
All-Bengal	5.4	98	128	33	15	16
Presidency	5.0	117	160	58	21	24
Burdwan	4.0	108	124	39	23	21
Rajshahi	4.8	87	110	32	12	19
Dacca	6.9	92	132	21	9	13
Chittagong	8.8	110	130	35	18	11

general pattern was the experience during the relatively prosperous years from 1925 to 1929. Conversely the loan operations came to a virtual stop from the beginning of the depression period. During the last five years the Provincial Government advanced financial assistance to revitalise the Credit Movement but as the proportion of overdue loans continued to increase these advances could hardly improve the situation as regards the availability of average loans per member.

The more important question that has to be asked in connection with the loan operations of the Primary Societies is: to what extent did these loans advanced by the Credit Societies meet the needs of the members? No information is available from the Annual Reports as to the amount received per borrowing member. In view of this difficulty, together with the fact that no estimate of the total borrowings from all sources is available, it is not possible to say anything definite on this question. Some idea may, however, be gained from the proportion of loans advanced by the Primary Societies to the total short-term and medium-term requirements of an agricultural family as estimated by the Banking Enquiry Committee.[1] On this basis the total credit requirements of the average number of members for the five years ending 1928/29 amount to Rs. 59.2 millions, but the amount actually paid by the Credit Societies during this period accounted for only 24 per cent. In other words, institutional loan amounted to only 1.3 per cent of the total borrowing needs of the agricultural sector.

6.6 TRENDS IN REPAYMENT

The efficiency with which the members repaid their loans may be judged by the extent of overdue loans. For the purpose of analysis we have data on

[1] The *Banking Enquiry Committee* estimated that per family requirements amounted to Rs 160. For details see pp. 76–82.

loans repaid every year, the amount outstanding and overdue. All loans outstanding at the end of a year were not necessarily due at that time as many loans were granted for more than one year. This need not be taken into consideration when analysing the overdue loans. If the overdues as a percentage of the total outstanding were increasing it may be assumed that the borrowers were not efficient in repayment.

The annual rates of increase in overdue loans for the period as a whole and its proportion to the total outstanding loans in the quinquennial periods are presented in Table 6.5. In view of the fact that the high proportion of overdues constituted the most fundamental weakness of the Primary Societies a fuller examination of the relevant factors is attempted later. At the present stage three general observations may be made as to the relative position in the different periods. Firstly, except in Chittagong the position even in the relatively prosperous years of the 1920s was not very promising. Secondly, the depression imposed such a strain that even a reduction in the rates of interest and the use of the whole administrative machinery for the collection of overdues could not prevent a deterioration of the situation. Thirdly, in advancing crop loans during the last five years the Provincial Government expected that this would help the recovery of the overdues, but this was not fulfilled. The proportion of overdue loans increased despite the fact that many loans were adjusted against the deposits and the share capital of the borrowers and the legal power of the Co-operatives with regard to the collection of overdues was improved by the Co-operative Societies Act of 1940. Clearly the impact of the famine outweighed the recovery in the prices of agricultural produce.

6.7 WORKING CAPITAL

Data on the working capital of the Primary Societies available from the Annual Reports bring out a redeeming feature of the Credit Movement. At

TABLE 6.5 *Annual percentage rates of increase of overdues and overdues as a percentage of outstandings*

Regions	Rates of increase	1920–24	1925–29	1930–34	1935–38	1939–44
All-Bengal	12.0	33.1	30.7	72.0	87.0	90.5
Presidency	12.4	43.1	38.6	77.1	90.1	93.2
Burdwan	11.6	35.6	35.4	73.5	86.4	86.6
Rajshahi	9.6	35.2	36.7	73.7	91.7	88.7
Dacca	12.7	34.3	27.4	70.6	85.9	92.3
Chittagong	15.9	18.1	19.2	67.5	81.1	85.1

the all-Bengal level the increase of working capital kept pace with the expansion of membership (Table 6.6). Indeed in three regions – Presidency, Burdwan and Dacca – the position was still better than that indicated by this Provincial average. The quinquennial trends have two main features. The increase in working capital took place during the first 20 years. Secondly, there was a gradual deceleration in the rate of improvement after 1924–25.

6.8 OWNED CAPITAL OF THE SOCIETIES

The owned capital of the Primary Societies increased at a much faster rate than the expansion of membership (Table 6.7). In other words, when the number of members per Society was declining per capita owned capital was increasing. But these trends have to be understood with reference to two reservations. Firstly, for reasons to be discussed later it is doubtful if the increase in one of the components of owned capital – Share Capital – really represents the actual payment made by the members from their own resources.

Secondly, even if this possibility is discounted it is clear that even at the end of the whole period owned capital constituted less than half of the total working capital. Such a picture clearly reflects the failure of an underlying expectation behind the inauguration of the Co-operative Movement, i.e. that through the inculcation of the ideal of 'self help' and thrift the members of the Primary Societies would be encouraged to create an adequate fund of their own.

Having thus observed the trends in the owned resources of the Credit Movement at the aggregate level, the relative weights and the rates of change

TABLE 6.6 *Annual percentage rates of increase and quinquennial index of per member working capital* (1920 = 100)

Regions	Rate of increase	1920–24	1925–29	1930–34	1935–38	1939–44
All-Bengal	6.9	106	132	161	169	95
Presidency	7.7	103	143	186	205	129
Burdwan	7.9	119	162	185	188	153
Rajshahi	4.9	101	115	135	139	71
Dacca	7.3	109	139	176	184	102
Chittagong	7.7	112	147	172	183	101

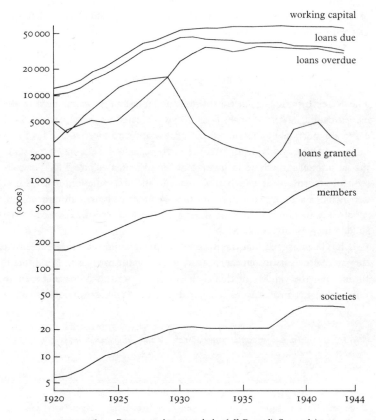

FIGURE 6.1 *Data on primary societies (all-Bengal) (log scale).*

TABLE 6.7 *Annual percentage rates of increase and quinquennial index of per member owned capital*
(1920 = 100)

Regions	Rates of increase	1920–24	1925–29	1930–34	1935–38	1939–44
All-Bengal	11.2	122	178	290	366	221
		(23.4)	(27.5)	(33.7)	(44.2)	(47.4)
Presidency	11.3	109	153	265	354	240
Burdwan	12.0	122	154	232	310	295
Rajshahi	9.0	121	172	267	322	169
Dacca	11.7	127	195	320	406	241
Chittagong	13.2	144	262	426	549	316

Note: Figures in brackets refer to the proportion of owned capital to total working capital.

of its three components – Reserve Fund, Share Capital and Members' Deposits – may now be taken up.

6.9 THE RESERVE FUND

The Reserve Fund, which constituted the largest single component of the owned capital of the Primary Societies, was created by the accumulation of a certain portion of the annual net profits and entrance fees.[1] This Fund increased from 15.7 lakhs in 1920/21 to 204.9 lakhs in 1943/44 – representing an annual growth of 12.9 per cent for all-Bengal (Table 6.8). The consequent improvement which took place in the accumulation of this Fund per member actually continued up to the end of the fourth quinquennium. As already mentioned the drop during the last five years was caused by the sudden increase in membership.

It has been argued that the Reserve Funds were illusory in the sense that they were created without making any provision for bad debts.[2] It is difficult to question the validity of this criticism. But from this it does not seem to follow that net profits were calculated in order to declare dividends on the

TABLE 6.8   *Annual percentage rates of increase and quinquennial index of per member Reserve Funds*
(1920 = 100)

Regions	Rate of increase	1920–24	1925–29	1930–34	1935–38	1939–44
All-Bengal	12.9	116	151	295	421	261
		(14.0)	(14.7)	(23.4)	(32.0)	(35.2)
Presidency	13.6	106	134	295	454	315
Burdwan	14.0	121	145	246	381	388
Rajshahi	10.2	115	152	273	362	189
Dacca	12.9	121	159	310	436	265
Chittagong	16.1	132	231	508	728	435

[1] Section 26 of the Rules framed under Section 43 of the Co-operative Societies Act of 1912 provided that in every Society not less than one half of the net profit in any year should be carried to a Reserve Fund until that Fund was equal to one half of the total liabilities of the Societies other than the Reserve Fund and Share Capital. Thereafter not less than one third should be added. If by an increase in the liabilities the proportion of the Reserve Fund to such liabilities was below one half the share of the net profit deposited into the Reserve Fund should be increased to one half until the proportion was restored. Under Section 56(2) of the Bengal Co-operative Societies Act of 1940 one fourth or such a share of the net profit as prescribed was to be credited to the Reserve Fund.

[2] A. I. Qureshi, *The Future of Co-operative Movement in India* (Bombay, 1947), p. 19.

Paid Up Share Capital of the members.[1] For almost all the net profits were added to the Reserve Fund. Thus, while Reserve Funds increased by 189.2 lakhs from 1920/21 the total net profits amounted to only 201.0 lakhs. In other words during a period of 24 years roughly 12.0 lakhs were declared as dividends.

6.10 SHARE CAPITAL OF THE SOCIETIES

Share Capital was first introduced in 1918 though this meant a deviation from the Raiffeisen Principle. It was normally of small values – Rs 10 to 15 each – payable in half yearly or annual instalments. The underlying hope in introducing this practice was that this would not only encourage thrift among the members, but also increase the Societies' financial strength and, by reducing its dependence on outside capital, should make possible lower interest rates to the members. From the published statistics it seems that this expectation was fulfilled as Share Capital increased again at a much faster rate than the expansion of membership (Table 6.9). However, the quinquennial trends show that the improvement in per capita Share Capital continued only during the first 15 years. The sharp drop during the last five years was due partly to the adjustment of overdue loans against Share Capital as noted earlier and partly to the less than proportionate increase in new payments. But as mentioned earlier there is one consideration which suggests that these increases were more apparent than real. The rates of interest on deposits varied between $7\frac{1}{2}$ per cent and 12 per cent in the different regions as against only $6\frac{1}{4}$ per cent on Share Capital. But, despite this, members' deposits increased

TABLE 6.9 *Annual percentage rates of increase and quinquennial index of share capital per member*
(1920 = 100)

Regions	Rate of increase	1920–24	1925–29	1930–34	1935–38	1939–44
All-Bengal	10.6	205	472	633	615	359
		(4.7)	(8.8)	(9.7)	(9.0)	(9.3)
Presidency	10.9	214	563	776	760	478
Burdwan	12.4	209	426	631	678	546
Rajshahi	8.7	178	68	481	453	253
Dacca	11.1	224	587	768	724	413
Chittagong	11.2	241	546	729	714	388

[1] J. P. Niyogi, *The Co-operative Movement in Bengal* (London, 1940), p. 21.

at much lower rates. It may be argued that the rural families paid the Share Capital only to join the Credit Societies and once they had done so they did not care much about making further contributions. But the suggestion which seems to be more plausible is that the funds shown as 'Share Capital Paid Up' were not really 'Paid Up' from the savings of the members, but mainly represented a deduction from the capital borrowed from outside sources.[1] It would, thus, seem that the internal strength of the Primary Societies was less satisfactory than appears from the published figures.

6.11 MEMBERS' DEPOSITS

The trends in members' deposits stand in sharp contrast to those in Share Capital and Reserve Funds in that the rates of increase were far slower than the expansion of membership (Table 6.10). This feature was typical of all the regions though the disparity was most marked in Presidency, Burdwan and Rajshahi Divisions. However, the quinquennial trends show considerable variations. Thus, as a matter of fact deposits were increasing at a faster rate during the years from 1924/25 to 1938/39. The improvement in the second period can be easily appreciated as these were relatively prosperous years. But what explains the continuation of this trend during the third quinquennium, which includes the depression years? Part of the explanation seems to lie in the marked improvement during the first two years of this quinquennium when the full effect of the slump in prices was yet to be felt. The sharp drop during the last five years seems to have been due to the haste with which Societies were formed to obtain the crop loans advanced by the Provincial Government, and the effects of the famine.

TABLE 6.10   *Annual percentage rates of increase and quinquennial index of deposits per member*

Regions	Rates of increase	1920–24	1925–29	1930–34	1935–38	1939–44
All-Bengal	4.2	97	103	112	107	54
		(4.7)	(4.0)	(3.6)	(3.2)	(2.9)
Presidency	0.8	79	48	41	48	32
Burdwan	2.6	92	66	57	52	44
Rajshahi	1.9	101	102	97	92	42
Dacca	6.8	100	132	150	170	87
Chittagong	5.7	120	188	212	169	79

[1] Qureshi, *op. cit.*, p. 19.

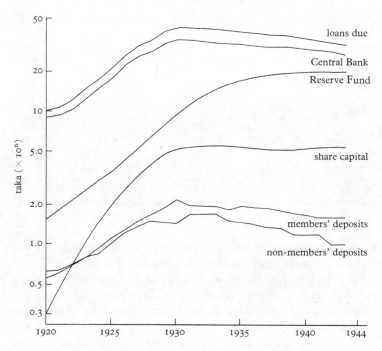

FIGURE 6.2   *Data on primary societies (all-Bengal) (log scale).*

6.12 BORROWED CAPITAL

The four sources of borrowed capital were the loans and deposits from the Government, other Societies, non-members and the Central Banks. As the contribution from the first two sources was very insignificant only the funds from the last two sources have been treated as borrowed capital. It may, however, be mentioned here that, while Central Banks contributed as much as 60.8 per cent of the total working capital, deposits from non-members accounted for only 3.1 per cent.

The annual rate of expansion once again fell short of the expansion of membership (Table 6.11). It was only in Presidency Division that the rates were more or less the same. Conversely, the disparity was most marked in Rajshahi. The quinquennial trends have the same features as for owned capital with the exception that borrowed capital per member started improving at the outset of the period. Moreover, the rates of increase were also higher. The sharp drop in the last quinquennium makes it clear that the

TABLE 6.11   *Annual percentage rates of increase and quinquennial index of borrowed capital per member*
(1920 = 100)

Regions	Rates of increase	1920–24	1925–29	1930–34	1935–38	1939–44
All-Bengal	4.7	102	121	129	120	63
		(75.8)	(72.3)	(63.1)	(55.7)	(47.4)
Presidency	5.6	102	140	158	153	91
Burdwan	5.6	119	166	170	148	106
Rajshahi	2.6	96	101	102	93	46
Dacca	5.3	104	128	144	134	70
Chittagong	5.1	107	127	123	117	62

financial assistance from the Government was far from being sufficient to keep pace with the expansion of membership.

From the preceding discussion it is clear that the Co-operative Movement in Bengal, as in other parts of India,[1] failed in its purpose of providing an effective alternative to the traditional sources of finance. At the end of four decades the Primary Societies could cover only one tenth of the agricultural borrowers, but the total credit needs of even this limited section remained unfulfilled. Of still greater significance, the Primary Societies mainly depended on borrowed capital and the proportion of overdue loans increased to such an extent that in the 1940s this accounted for more than two thirds of the total working capital. Thus, there remained a big gap between the high hopes and the actual performance of the Co-operative Movement in Bengal.

6.13 REVIEW OF OPINIONS ON THE LIMITED SUCCESS OF THE CO-OPERATIVES

Despite this record the importance of Co-operative institutions as an agency for the improvement of the socio-economic life of the rural people has been attracting increasing attention in the past two decades.[2] Therefore, it is important that an attempt should be made to isolate the main problems facing the Co-operative Societies in Bengal during the period under review. To

[1] T. Ghose and H. Sinha, 'Agricultural Co-operation in Bengal and the Rest of India', *Sankhya: The Indian Journal of Statistics*, Vol. 7, Part 2 (1945/46), pp. 189–203. See also *Credit Survey*, Vol. II, p. 167.

[2] The *Credit Survey* argues: 'co-operation has failed, but co-operation must succeed', Vol. II, p. 372.

begin with, some of the arguments put forward from time to time by various committees of enquiry, individual authors and persons directly connected with the Credit Movement may be briefly reviewed. Usually these relate to (a) the size of the Primary Societies, (b) the nature of liability, (c) the purpose of the Societies and (d) the lack of education and training in Co-operative Principles.

As to the size of the Primary Societies, as early as 1915 the Committee on Co-operation recommended that 'It is a good general rule that there should be one Society to one village and one village to one Society.'[1] It was subsequently argued that this 'was one of the reasons why the Co-operative Movement has not made any great progress in this country'.[2] It is arguably true that larger Societies would have had a larger membership, but it is difficult to see how this would have at all remedied the internal weaknesses discussed above. Moreover, when it is argued that organisers at the village level did not have sufficient knowledge of banking and supervision, it does not follow that larger Societies would have been more efficiently managed. In this respect the experience of the depression years when many Societies with larger membership had to be liquidated is particularly significant.

Another aspect of the Co-operative Movement which received considerable attention and was even held responsible for its failure, was the question of the nature of the liability of the Primary Societies. Thus, according to the Co-operative Planning Committee 'in most Provinces unlimited liability has not been very helpful to the progress of co-operative credit. Responsible people were kept out of the Movement by it and also it was largely illusory as there was no bar on the alienation of property by members.'[3] It is true that in providing for unlimited liability for the Primary Societies too much emphasis was laid on the moral aspect of the Movement as against its business side. Thus, it was easy to argue that the 'Movement is essentially a moral one and it is individualistic rather than socialistic. It provides as a substitute for material assets honesty and moral obligations and keeps in view the moral rather than the material sanctions',[4] but clearly such a sentiment did not take account of the socioeconomic realities of the rural life. From this, however, it does not necessarily follow that the principle of limited liability

---

[1] *Report of the Committee on Co-operation in India* (Calcutta, 1915), p. 16. Henceforth referred to as *Maclagan Committee*.

[2] Observation of a Co-operator from Utter Pradesh at the Fifteenth Conference of the Registrars of Co-operative Societies, 1947, cited by *Credit Survey*, Vol. II, p. 247.

[3] Government of India, *Report of the Co-operative Planning Committee* (Bombay, 1946), pp. 22–3. See also Qureshi, *op. cit.*, p. 96. He argued that the principle of unlimited liability meant a 'romantic' approach, p. 160.

[4] *Maclagan Committee*, p. x.

would have meant much difference to the picture of the Credit Movement which emerges in this study. This is clearly indicated by the fact that deposits from non-members accounted for only 2 per cent of the total working capital of the Primary Societies.

In this connection it is interesting that the advocates of limited liability who claimed to emphasise the 'business aspect' of the Credit Movement as against its 'romantic' aspect did not concern themselves with the legal situation regarding money lending. Before 1933 the main legislation regarding money lending was the Usurious Loan Act of 1918. Under this Act, where the rates of interest were excessive and the transaction substantially unfair the courts were empowered to reopen the transaction and relieve the debtors in respect of excessive interest. But in the absence of any statutory limits and various other defects this Act remained virtually a dead letter.[1] These limits were fixed by the Bengal Money-lenders Act of 1933, but it is interesting that these rates were higher than those on the deposits in the Credit Societies.[2] It was as late as 1940 when another Money-Lenders Act was passed that the statutory rates were fixed at about the same level.[3] From the evidence referred to later it is clear that this legislation also failed in its purpose of regulating the rates of interest. What is important at this stage is that the advocates of the supposed effectiveness of limited liability were also being partly 'romantic' in their approach.

The third question discussed at various levels was whether the Primary Societies should be single-purpose or multi-purpose. Thus, it was pointed out by one author that one of the main weaknesses of the Societies was that credit was not linked with marketing.[4] The idea was further extended by Nanavati to include the whole problem of rural rehabilitation by emphasising the ideal of 'Better Farming, Better Business and Better Living'.[5] It is true that as an ideal solution to the manifold problems of rural life multi-purpose societies are much better, though it has to be kept in mind that many of the more important aspects of rural rehabilitation by their nature were outside the limits of the resources of the Primary Societies. But again this does not fully explain why the Credit Societies made such poor progress. In this respect it is significant that the condition of the limited number of multi-

[1] *Banking Enquiry Committee*, pp. 165–7.
[2] The prescribed rates were 15 per cent in the case of secured and 25 per cent in the case of unsecured loans as against 7 per cent to 11 per cent paid by the Credit Societies.
[3] Respectively 8 per cent and 10 per cent for secured and unsecured loans.
[4] Qureshi, *op. cit.*, p. 63.
[5] See M. B. Nanavati, 'Re-organisation of the Co-operative Movement', *Indian Journal of Agricultured Economics* (August, 1952), pp. 33–4. See also Reserve Bank of India, Agricultural Credit Department, *Bulletin No. 2 – Co-operative Village Banks* (Bombay, 1937), pp. 29–30.

purpose societies was hardly different from that of the single-purpose societies.

The Royal Commission on Agriculture laid considerable emphasis on the lack of education and the inadequacy of the training in co-operative principles.[1] It has to be admitted that in certain respects these were important constraints on the progress of the Credit Movement. Formation of a Credit Society in a village required that at least some of the villagers had to be literate – a condition which it was difficult to fulfil when the rate of literacy was so low. But this does not explain why deposits from members constituted such as insignificant part of the working capital or why the proportion of overdue loans was so large.

Thus; these views do not fully explain, even if they are taken together, why the expectations of the Co-operative Movement were not fulfilled. The more fundamental causes lie elsewhere – mainly in the socioeconomic life of the rural areas and the inadequate realisation of the limited role which the provision for co-operative credit could play in such an environment when this was not conceived of as an integral part of an all-embracing plan for general reconstruction. Considered in this light it would seem that almost all the factors referred to above may at best be said to have played only a secondary role.[2]

Firstly, it may be explained why the Credit Movement made such poor progress in terms of its coverage of the rural families. The Banking Enquiry Committee argued that people in general had a preference for the loans available from money lenders.[3] There is considerable element of truth in this opinion. Loans received from money lenders were more flexible in their use and more readily available than those from the Credit Societies. It may further be argued that the consequent reliance on money lenders was strengthened by the fact that often they combined in themselves the role of landlord, merchant and village headman. It is conceivable that this factor in itself would have created an obstacle in the way of curtailing the power of money lenders even if outside finances were available at the required level and required time.

But it is interesting that the Committee did not see any difficulty from the supply side, i.e. from the opposition or at least the non-co-operation of

---

[1] *Report of the Royal Commission on Agriculture* (London, 1928), pp. 449–50. See also *Banking Enquiry, op. cit.*, p. 150.

[2] The *Credit Survey* goes a step further and argues that the functional and structural weaknesses of the Primary Societies and the technical and educational backwardness of the members were subsidiary forms of symptom rather than the main disease itself, Vol. II, p. 253.

[3] *Banking Enquiry Committee*, pp. 150–1.

the money lenders. Since they had a monopoly in the rural areas it was futile to expect that they would make their business less attractive by associating themselves with the Co-operative Movement and much less to take the initiative in the formation of Primary Societies. The money lenders were in a better position to safeguard their business when they were the only literate men in the village. In 1951 it was found that in 88 per cent of cases the money lenders were charging interest at rates higher than those stipulated by the protective legislation.[1] The ineffectiveness of legislation clearly indicates the futility of the expectation that the money lenders would, in general, voluntarily join the Co-operative Movement.

Another important factor which has to be taken into consideration in connection with the external coverage of the Credit Movement is the level of per capita income in the agricultural sector. The ideal of self-help basic to the success of the Co-operative Movement presupposes that the prospective members should have a surplus over their annual requirements. But given the low level of per capita income, and that the underlying trend was perhaps one of decline, it is clear that the larger section of the agricultural community did not have such a surplus. It would, thus, seem that poverty itself was a basic cause of why the coverage of the Credit Movement was so inadequate.[2] The possibility that in many cases the share capital 'paid up' by the members of the Primary Societies and 'paid up' by the latter to the Central Banks was actually the amount deducted from the loans to be advanced clearly indicates the importance of the point under discussion. Thus the overall position seems to have been such that the well-to-do section of the rural population did not join the movement in order to keep its business attractive and the general cultivators were not sufficiently enthusiastic because they did not have enough resources.

If this analysis of the socioeconomic life of the rural areas is accepted it is clear that this also largely explains why the owned capital of the Primary Societies constituted much the smaller part of their total working capital. For it follows that in areas where the Credit Societies were formed they mostly attracted prospective borrowers. The obvious result of this inadequacy

---

[1] *Credit Survey*, vol. I, part 2, p. 693. These findings vindicate the opinion of the *Central Banking Enquiry Committee* (*op. cit.*, p. 433) that 'In the present state of India he [money lender] is a necessity and, that being so, his calling will not be abolished by making it illegal.' The argument about the opposition or non-co-operation of the money lenders is not meant to apply to all money lenders. Since we have defined the term 'money lenders' to include all those who lent money in the rural areas, even occasionally, there is a strong possibility that many of these lesser money lenders joined the rural societies. There is also the possibility that some of the other money lenders joined the Primary Societies mainly to take an undue share of the available funds.

[2] Calvert, 'Prevailing Types of Rural Credit Societies' in *Indian Co-operative Studies*, p. 43, cited by Hough, *op. cit.*, p. 70.

of the internal resources of the Primary Societies was the dependence on borrowed funds, mainly from the Central Banks. But since the capital available from the latter was not sufficient to meet all the credit needs of the members they must have at the same time depended on the money lenders. It is likely that such a situation further added to the reluctance of the money lenders to join the Credit Societies.

Lastly, the question of overdue loans may be taken up. Why did the proportion of overdue loans account for nine tenths of the outstanding loans at the end of the whole period? From the available evidence it seems that this was mainly due to the type of objectives for which loans were made. The Co-operative Societies Act of 1904 was silent as regards the purpose for which loans could be advanced by the Primary Societies. It was open to the Provincial Governments to make the necessary rules. When the Bill was drafted the Government of India refused to accept a proposal that loans should be granted only for productive purposes. It was argued that it would be difficult to enforce such a provision. Moreover, in the Indian circumstances it would be unwise to confine loans to productive uses only – if the raiyats must borrow for other than productive purposes they should obtain the loans from the Credit Societies rather than from the money lenders. The Co-operatives took full advantage of this latitude in the law and it seems that 50 per cent of the loans were advanced for such long-term purposes as the repayment of old debts and the purchase of land.[1] Admittedly this was a sound idea to enable the members to get rid of their accumulated obligations to the money lenders, but the difficulty was that though most of these finances were raised by the Central Banks on a short-term basis the period within which to repay the loans was not accordingly fixed. It is not known whether loans so obtained were really used for the repayment of old debts or if these became an additional burden on the members. If, however, it is assumed that the borrowers did repay at least a part of their debts it is clear that all the overdue loans in the 1920s were not, properly speaking, overdues as such.

Obviously it should not be concluded that these procedural changes would have materially improved the repayment capacity of the borrowers. As pointed out by the Reserve Bank, where debt is a chronic feature of the cultivators' life 'it can only mean a perpetual disequilibrium between his income and expenditure. The disease thus is the deficit budget and if the symptom – debt – is to be removed, the causes of the deficit budget must be treated first'.[2] But since the Credit Movement was not conceived of as part of a co-

---

[1] The purposes for which loans were advanced by the Primary Societies were mentioned in the *Annual Reports* in the pre-1920 period.

[2] Reserve Bank of India, Agricultural Credit Department *Bulletin No. 1*, p. 12, cited by Hough, *op. cit.*, p. 38.

ordinated programme for increasing the per capita income of the cultivators the granting of loans for the repayment of old debts essentially meant the transfer of the obligation of the borrowers from the traditional money lenders to a kind of 'institutional money lenders'. Stagnation of the economy as against a background of population growth at a fast rate suggests that even short-term loans would accumulate over time. This was clearly indicated by the huge volume of agricultural indebtedness. The Primary Societies and the Central Banks went a step further in making long-term loans. It is true that the slump in agricultural prices imposed such a severe strain that it virtually paralysed the Co-operative Movement. But considered in the light of the inadequate realisation of the limited effectiveness of institutional credit in a backward economy it would seem that essentially the main contribution of the depression was greatly to accelerate a process which had already been started earlier.

The danger of advancing long-term loans was repeatedly pointed out in the Annual Reports, but the Central Banks and the Primary Societies did not pay much attention to these warnings.[1] This was made possible, to a considerable extent, by the lack of sufficient supervision by the Co-operative Department over their activities. The Maclagan Committee recommended that there should be one Auditor for every hundred Societies.[2] In itself this number seems to be far from sufficient, but even this minimum requirement was not fulfilled. Thus, whereas there were 40 Auditors in 1920/21 for roughly 5800 Primary Societies in 1942/43 there were 290 Auditors for 36,100 Societies. This was so in spite of the fact that the Primary Societies were regularly paying Audit fees to the Provincial Government and by 1935 there was a surplus of 10.4 lakhs.[3] Adequate supervision and direction was of considerable importance at the early stages of the Co-operative Movement, but this does not seem to have been realised.

It was pointed out that two of the reasons for the failure of the Co-operative Movement were that (a) the major part of the funds were taken by those who were in charge of the management of the Primary Societies[4] and that (b) these members were reluctant to repay their loans.[5] In the light of

---

[1] Thus, it was pointed out in the *Annual Report* of 1923/24 that until the difference between long- and short-term loans was realised 'the Central Banks and village Societies would move blindfold without looking under the surface and trying to discover what actually is being done with co-operative money'. p. 9.

[2] *Maclagan Committee*, p. 58.

[3] This question was raised in the Provincial Legislative Council by one member who alleged that the Government was 'misappropriating' the money. See *Proceedings of the Bengal Legislative Council*, Vol. XXVIII, No. 3 (1928), p. 473.

[4] Niyogi, *op. cit.*, pp. 30–1.

[5] *Ibid.* See also *Central Banking Enquiry, op. cit.*, p. 449.

the available evidence it is difficult to question the validity of the first charge.[1] Nor is it difficult to appreciate such a phenomenon as the unequal distribution of loans if we keep in mind the fact that the available funds were too inadequate to meet all the credit requirements of the members and that rural life is characterised by marked differences in the socioeconomic influence of the different classes of households. The fact that this latter aspect of the problem was not adequately recognised once again underlines that some of the basic assumptions behind the Co-operative Movement were unrealistic. As to the second charge it is very likely that some of the members were deliberately holding up the repayment of their overdue loans, though this is not always clear from the findings of the Co-operative Department as reported in the Annual Reports in the late 1930s. But it seems that in analysing the causes of the failure of the Credit Movement an exaggerated view was often taken about the impact of the role of influential members of the Primary Societies. Speaking from the point of view of agricultural development there was perhaps nothing wrong in the unequal distribution of loans. But as elaborated later, the problem was essentially due to the fact that provision for credit was not conceived of as part of a general plan for economic development. The role of a section of the members did aggravate this basic weakness of the Credit Movement.

Thus, from the side of the coverage of the rural families and the fulfilment of their credit needs the problem was essentially either to (*a*) incorporate the money lenders in the Primary Societies and to ensure that they could not misuse their powers[2] or (*b*) to eliminate them by effective competition.[3] With regard to the first point the efforts were far too insignificant – in one respect even contradictory – to be effective in inducing the traditional sources to surrender their profitable business. The alternative solution involved the flow of finance from outside sources. The establishment of Central Banks under the Co-operative Societies Act of 1912 was a sound decision in this direction, but as a federation of the Primary Societies lower down, these, in their turn, showed the same financial weakness. The Reserve Bank which was established in 1935 insisted that till the problem of rural indebtedness was solved and the cultivators were made credit-worthy it could not make any substantial financial accommodation.[4] Nor could the Co-operatives look up to the Government for much more than supervision, administration and

[1] *Annual Report*, 1918/19, pp. 4–5. See also Ghatak, *op. cit.*, pp. 88–9.
[2] This was proposed by B. V. N. Naidu, *Report of the Economist for Enquiry into Rural Indebtedness* (Madras, 1946), p. 35.
[3] *Report of the Agricultural Finance Sub-Committee, op. cit.*, pp. 31–2.
[4] Reserve Bank of India, Agricultural Credit Department, *Report Submitted to the Government of India under Section 55(1)(b) of the Reserve Bank of India Act* (Bombay, 1936).

advice. It was mainly during the last five years that some assistance was given, but this was hardly sufficient.

The problem was not, however, only to make provision for cheap credit, but also to emphasise its productive use. The evils of finance drawn from traditional sources were due partly to the high rates of interest and partly to the fact that it was not generally used to augment the per capita income of the borrowers, but to balance their deficit budgets.[1] Therefore, if the problem of rural indebtedness was to be solved what was needed was to emphasise the dynamic role of credit as against its static role – i.e. to use capital to promote a cumulative increase in per capita income. This required the integration of credit with assistance in applying new techniques, better farm management, adequate demand for increased production and facilities for marketing. In other words the overall problem was one of creating a climate for economic development.[2] Such an environment would have solved the problem of rural indebtedness and reduced the rate of interest by increasing the proportion of loanable funds and helping the cultivators to build up their security. In other words the forces which made credit a burden and so expensive in terms of its price would have been effectively challenged. But it would seem that the importance of such a dynamic role was not adequately realised either at the time of the inauguration of the Co-operative Movement or in the subsequent years.[3]

By 1944 the Debt Conciliation Boards established under the Agricultural Debtors Act of 1935 had reduced 50.0 crores of rural indebtedness to 18.00 crores.[4] But despite these efforts and the fact that money lending was statutorily regulated total agricultural indebtedness in 1945 was estimated at 150.0 crores[5] as against 100.0 crores in 1928/29.[6] It is difficult to deter-

---

[1] One of the explanations often put forward for rural indebtedness was that the cultivators were extravagant. This explanation was not accepted by the *Deccan Riots Commission* (Para. 54 of the Report, cited by B. B. Chaudhuri, *op. cit.*, p. 338) and *Banking Enquiry Committee*, pp. 71–2.

[2] Such a role of credit is emphasised by the publication of the Food and Agricultural Organisation referred to earlier. See also, by the same organisation, *Agricultural Credit Through Co-operatives and Other Institutions* (Rome, 1965).

[3] Thus, for example, the *Banking Enquiry Committee* (*op. cit.*, p. 450) believed that 'The only remedy for these unsatisfactory conditions which appears to offer any prospect of success is the patient and persistent education in the principles and meaning of co-operation of the members of Primary Societies by teachers competent to perform the task efficiently under adequate supervision.' Again the *Report Submitted to the Government of India* (*op. cit.*) made some recommendations for the liquidation of the existing debt of the cultivators, but as to the prevention of the accumulation of debt it contended that education would seem to be the only real and lasting corrective (pp. 14–16).

[4] *Agricultural Finance Committee*, *op. cit.*, p. 22.

[5] Government of Bengal, *Agricultural Statistics by Plot to Plot Enumeration in Bengal* (Calcutta, 1946), Part 1, p. 55.

[6] *Banking Enquiry Committee*, pp. 69–70.

mine how far this really represents (in money terms) an increase in the total amount of indebtedness, as the two estimates are not comparable as regards coverage of the different classes of rural families. Secondly, the basis on which the estimate of 1929 was made is of doubtful validity. However, it may be safely concluded that the problem of agricultural indebtedness was far from being solved and the prominence of the money lenders as a source of agricultural credit was still unchallenged.

7

BENGAL LANDLORDS AND AGRICULTURE

One argument that featured prominently in the discussion leading to the introduction of the Permanent Settlement in Bengal was that such an institutional arrangement would act as a radical incentive to agricultural development. Since the zamindars would have proprietary rights to the land and the demands of the government on them would not increase, the landlords would, it was believed, in their own interest invest their profits in land. Thus, Cornwallis asserted, 'Land property will acquire a value hitherto unknown in Hindustan and the large capital possessed by many of the natives in Calcutta which are now employed in usury or monopolising salt and other necessaries of life will be appropriated to the more useful purposes of purchasing and improving land'.[1] There were critics of this plan even at the time of its introduction and the experience of the subsequent years, when the failure of the expectations of Cornwallis became more and more clear, added both to the number of critics as well as to the severity of their denunciation. The Government of India believed that the desired effectiveness of the permanent settlement was not 'supported by the experience of any civilised country' and that under this system the 'cultivator was rack-rented, impoverished and oppressed'.[2] Again, according to the Land Revenue Commission the 'Permanent Settlement imposed on the province an iron-framework which has had the impact of stifling the enterprise and initiative of all classes of people'.[3] It has been generally held that the Bengal 'monied class' invested their capital in buying or taking leases on land from the old landed class and that this practice assumed such proportions as to dry up capital for commercial or industrial enterprise.[4] Thus, to some extent the process was the same as

---

[1] Cited by R. Guha, *A Rule of Property for Bengal: An Essay in the Idea of Permanent Settlement* (Paris, 1963), p. 172.

[2] *Land Revenue Policy of the Indian Government* (Calcutta, 1902), p. 8. This was said in reply to a series of letters by R. C. Dutt in which he was alleged to have advocated the extension of permanent settlement to the other parts of India.

[3] Government of Bengal, *Report of the Land Revenue Commission* (Calcutta, 1940), Vol. I, pp. 35–6. Henceforth referred to as *LRC*.

[4] Barrington Moore, Jr, *Social Origins of Dictatorship and Democracy* (London, 1967), pp. 345–70; N. K. Sinha, *The Economic History of Bengal*, Vol. I (Calcutta, 1961); Morris D. Morris, 'Values as Obstacles to Economic Growth in South Asia: An Historical Survey', *The Journal of Economic History*, Vol. XXVII, No. 4 (December, 1967), *LRC*, p. 35; see also the evidence of

expected by Cornwallis in Bengal and experienced in England. But, in spite of this over-capitalisation, agricultural productivity in Bengal remained one of the lowest in the world.

The present chapter is an attempt to investigate why the expected capitalistic development did not take place in Bengal. Was it due to their inherently 'negative attitude' that the landlords preferred to live as social parasites? Or could it be argued that the objective economic conditions in Bengal were not favourable for the development of capitalism in agriculture? At the outset it may be mentioned that at the present stage of our knowledge about the economic history of Bengal it will be extremely difficult to offer any definite answers to these questions. In any case, the problem is too complex to be satisfactorily dealt with in one chapter. Therefore, our purpose will be only to suggest some possible lines of investigation. However, we are not concerned only with the zamindars, but the whole body of landlords which, according to the tenancy laws, included, as well as the zamindars, tenure-holders of all grades. If the land possessed by a raiyat was 33 acres or more, he was presumed to be a tenure-holder and, therefore, a landlord.

Our investigation proceeds on two assumptions usually made about the zamindari system in Bengal. Firstly, the business class invested their capital in buying up or taking leases on land. Secondly, the landlords did not take the desired initiative in agricultural development. It is likely that the transfer of commercial capital was not as marked as has been generally assumed. It is also likely that there were many landlords who did play some role in augmenting agricultural production. But in spite of these possibilities we are proceeding on the basis of these two assumptions, because sufficient evidence has not yet been presented to question their validity.[1]

To begin with, let us raise two questions: (a) What role was played by English landlords in bringing about the Agricultural Revolution in England? (b) What stimulated them to play such a role? In England, where a landlord–tenant relationship existed in agriculture the landlords did take initiative in agricultural development. It is therefore useful to examine the nature of and the causal factors behind the economic role of the English landlords.

On the first question the traditional view is that the landlords played the key role in bringing about the transformation of English agriculture. They

---

Rai Sitanath Ray Bahadur in *Minutes of Evidence taken before the Indian Industrial Commission, 1916–18*, Vol. 2 (UK Parliamentary Papers, 1919, XVIII).

[1] The possibility that the transfer of commercial capital was not all that considerable is suggested by the findings of Dr M. S. Islam. For details see his, *The Permanent Settlement and the Landed Interests in Bengal* (Unpublished PhD thesis, University of London, 1972), Ch. 4; see also B. B. Chaudhuri, 'Land Markets in Eastern India, 1793–1940. Part II: The Changing Composition of Landed Society', *The Indian Economic and Social History Review*, Vol. XII, No. 2.

experimented with new methods on their own farms, supported agricultural societies and thus helped the wide use of the new technology in English agriculture. As to the representativeness of such landlords the students of English agricultural history are now less confident than they were in the past.[1] However, it is not denied that there were many landlords who made use of new technology in their farms. Secondly it is generally agreed that in at least one respect the English landlords did make a decisive contribution. This was in making provision for permanent capital – enclosure, drainage and farm buildings. Of these the most important was the enclosure of scattered fields into compact production units. This affected so many complicated property rights that it could not perhaps have been carried through without the compulsion exercised by the landlords. Provision for permanent capital, together with the recognition of the fixity of tenure and the practice of some landlords to share the tenants' losses in bad years, provided enterprising tenants with a favourable physical and psychological environment for making innovations in agriculture.

With regard to the second question it has to be emphasised that the interest of the landlords in making provision for permanent capital or introducing new technology in their own farms was financial return rather than agricultural development. Firstly, as the growth of population and increasing urbanisation as a result of the Industrial Revolution pushed up the price of agricultural produce, the rate of return on investment in agriculture increased. It has been estimated that the landlords' gross return on their investment was between 15 to 20 per cent as against a return of only 5 or 6 per cent from land purchase or investment in 'funds'. Thus, enclosure became by far the most profitable use of capital in connection with land and this explains the great popularity of the enclosure movement in the late eighteenth and nineteenth centuries.[2] Secondly, it is believed that without the requisite investment in land it was difficult for landlords to attract the substantial capitalist tenants.[3] This pressure from the side of the tenants underlines the importance of the absorption of an increasing volume of manpower in the industrial sector in inducing the landlords to invest in land improvement. Thus, on the whole, it seems that it was the Industrial Revolution which,

---

[1] H. J. Habakkuk, 'Economic Function of the English Landlords in the Eighteenth Century', in W. E. Minchinton (ed.), *Essays in Agrarian History* (London, 1968), Vol. 1; G. E. Mingay, *English Landed Society in the Eighteenth Century* (London, 1963). For the traditional view about the role of the English landlords see, for example, Paul Mantoux, *The Industrial Revolution in the Eighteenth Century* (London, 1964), pp. 163–5.

[2] J. D. Chambers and G. E. Mingay, *The Agricultural Revolution 1750–1880* (London, 1966), p. 84.

[3] Habakkuk, *op. cit.*, p. 199.

through its impact on the product market and the labour market, created favourable conditions for the land-lords to make productive investment in agriculture.[1]

Now let us return to our original question as to why the Bengal land-lords failed to imitate their English counterparts. The basic question is whether there was a sufficient inducement for the Bengal landlords to invest for agricultural development. The fundamental requirement from the angle of capitalistic development is that the potential investor must believe that investment will be more profitable to him than consumption. Secondly, the opportunity cost must not be higher than the rate of return.

In the agricultural sector capital may be invested for the extension of cultivation to new areas and/or to increase the productive power of the land already under cultivation. Such (productive) investment does not only increase the income of the capitalist farmer, but it also leads to an expansion of agricultural output. Secondly, capital may be invested only for purchasing the proprietary rights in land or for money lending or trade in agricultural produce (unproductive investment). In such a case there is only a distributive effect.[2] From the above account, capital will be invested for productive or unproductive purposes depending on the relative rate of estimated return. The Industrial Revolution in England created a favourable environment for productive investment in agriculture and landlords took advantage of the opportunities. Were the objective economic conditions in Bengal so favourable for productive investment?

Two main features characterised the changes which took place in the economic life of Bengal after the establishment of foreign rule. Firstly, in spite of the rapid growth of population under more stable conditions, the size of the domestic market for agricultural production remained limited. As the rate of industrialisation remained insignificant, Bengal's economy continued to be characterised by its heavy dependence on agriculture. Thus, whereas in England rapid progress in industrialisation was pushing up the demand for agricultural produce, under the particular conditions of Bengal growth of population was increasing the pressure on the available land for cultivation.[3] In England the percentage of the population in agriculture declined from about 60–80 per cent at the end of the seventeenth century to 36 per

---

[1] As mentioned in Chapter one this is not, however, to suggest that the basic relationship between agriculture and industry was one of unidirectional causation.

[2] Leibenstein calls the first type of investment 'zero-sum enterprise' and the second type 'positive-sum enterprise'. For details, see H. Leibenstein, *Economic Backwardness and Economic Growth* (New York, 1957), pp. 112–119.

[3] If we believe that in the eighteenth and nineteenth centuries the foreign rulers followed a policy of 'deindustrialisation' or 'ruralisation', this would mean that the pressure of population on land did not increase only in absolute terms, but also in relative terms.

cent at the beginning of the nineteenth and 7 per cent in 1921.[1] On the other hand, the percentage of total population dependent on agriculture in Bengal was as high as 77.3 per cent in 1921.[2] Once again, whereas the average size of a holding was 111 acres in England,[3] it was only six acres in Bengal.[4] In these circumstances, it is clear that the level of rent in Bengal was going to be 'determined not by the fertility of land, but by the fertility of human beings'.[5] Thus, as land was the scarce factor of production it would have commanded a high price in terms of rent under any system of land tenure. But the institutional monopoly granted to the landlords in 1793 would seem to have given them a better opportunity to take advantage of the scramble for land.

Secondly, the scheme of economic development based on international specialisation pursued by the foreign rulers under the policy of selective intervention led to an expansion of the foreign demand for agricultural produce. The improvement of the means of transport and communication, the increase of both the volume and value of export and the development of certain industrial and commercial centres within the country made the agricultural sector of Bengal more market-oriented than in the past. To this extent the establishment of foreign rule must be said to have created conditions for productive investment in agriculture. At the time of the introduction of permanent settlement vast areas of Bengal were yet to be brought under cultivation[6] and the revenue-demand of the government on the landlords was fixed. It may be argued that under such circumstances the Bengal landlords, like many of their counterparts in England, could have invested capital in large-scale farming.

Thus, to summarise this part of the discussion, it would seem that the establishment of foreign rule created conditions both for productive and nonproductive investment in Bengal agriculture. But it is clear that the Bengal landlords preferred the latter type of investment; they invested their capital for the purchase of proprietary rights in land without trying to improve its

[1] P. Deane and W. A. Cole, *British Economic Growth, 1688–1959* (Cambridge, 1967), pp. 137, 142.

[2] *Census of India, 1921, Bengal*, Part I (Calcutta, 1923), p. 377.

[3] This was the estimated average in England and Wales in 1851. The position at the turn of the nineteenth century is not believed to have been much different. For details see, J. H. Clapham, *An Economic History of Modern Britain* (Cambridge, 1932), pp. 264, 451.

[4] *LRC*, p. 84.

[5] D. Warriner, 'Land Reform and Economic Development', in C. K. Eicher and L. W. Witt (eds.), *Agriculture and Economic Development* (New York, 1964), pp. 272–98.

[6] It has been estimated that 1/3 to 2/3 of the total area in Bengal was cultivable waste. See, *LRC*, Vol. II, p. 211.

productive quality. As a tentative generalisation it may be suggested that this tendency of the landlords was due to the fact that the expected rate of return on non-productive investment appeared to be higher than that on the productive investment. This assumption is based upon the following considerations.

Returns on capital invested in agricultural production tend to materialise slowly. This, together with the fact that there are usually large fluctuations in the price level and yield per acre, discourages large-scale investment even when production is meant for the domestic market. It is natural that such a tendency would be stronger when the production was oriented towards meeting the demands of the foreign buyers. Firstly there are the difficulties of foreseeing accurately such factors as the nature of current demand in the world market and the prices to be obtained in competition with other countries. Secondly, the export trade in agricultural produce was monopolised by foreigners. This may have had the effect of depressing the share of domestic producers in the benefits which would have otherwise accrued to them from the expansion of foreign demand. Such risk and uncertainties would seem to have had the effect of making the rate of return on the socially productive investment of capital appear lower.

Thus, the Bengal landlords' preference for non-productive investment would seem to have been due to the fact that their monopoly control of land enabled them, under conditions of the adverse land–man ratio, to gain a rate of return higher than that on productive investment in agriculture. The preference of the landlords in making investment in land purchase, money lending and trade in agricultural produce to those fields which would have led to a net gain in agricultural output may appear irrational or traditional. But, as pointed out by Aubrey, this kind of thinking implies a welfare judgement which does not conform to the profit-oriented investment criterion of the investing individual.[1]

It is true that the landlords did not always enjoy unrestricted control over land. Beginning from the Tenancy Act of 1859 the area held by the occupancy raiyats increased as the number of cultivators belonging to this class increased and the freedom of the landlords to let land at whatever rate they could charge was curtailed in respect of these tenants. Such interference with the rental market represented a significant shift from the policy of *laissez-faire* implicit in the plan of 1793. But the landlords were still left with considerable power to increase the rate of rent without taking initiative in

---

[1] H. G. Aubrey, 'Investment Decisions in Underdeveloped Countries', in National Bureau of Economic Research, *Capital Formation and Economic Growth* (Princeton, 1955).

agricultural development. Thus, under the Tenancy Acts the money-rent payable by the occupancy raiyats could be increased on the following grounds:

(a) the rate was below the prevailing rate in the village or neighbouring village,
(b) rise in the average price of food crops,
(c) improvement of the productive quality of land by the action of the landlords,
(d) improvement effected by fluvial action.

Moreover, the landlords were entitled to a fee of 20 per cent of the value of land transferred or leasehold created by a raiyat.[1] Thus, the tenancy laws left sufficient scope for the landlords to increase the rate of rent payable by raiyats. It may be safely assumed that, under conditions of growing pressure of population on land, the landlords took the advantage to increase rent per unit of land.

It is difficult to estimate the extent to which rent per acre of land increased in the nineteenth century. Gross rental of the landlords estimated on the basis of Road Cess was published by the government beginning from 1871. But it was not shown to what extent the increase in the gross rental was due to (a) the extension of cultivation to new areas and (b) enhancement of the rate of rent per acre. However, some idea may be made from the figures relating to the period after the first decade of the present century when the extension of cultivation seems to have come to a virtual end (Table 7.1).

It seems that during the quarter century following 1914 the rent paid by the raiyats increased by nearly 40 per cent. It should be noted that in 1936/37 five per cent of the legal rental was paid by the raiyats with fixed rent and some lands were held by rent-free raiyats. Secondly, this increase in the

TABLE 7.1 *Gross rental (in thousand Rs)*

Year	Total legal rental	Index
1914/15–1918/19	122 388	100
1919/20–1923/24	139 556	113
1924/25–1928/29	148 842	120
1929/30–1933/34	161 466	131
1934/35–1938/39	169 996	138

Source: Report on *Land Revenue Administration of the Bengal Presidency*.

[1] For details see, L . Kabir, *The Rights and Liabilities of the Bengal Raiyots Under Tenancy Legislation from 1885 to 1947* (PhD Thesis, University of London, 1965).

rate of rent does not show the increase in the collection of illegal cesses which is likely to have taken place during the same period.[1] Thirdly, these figures on gross rental do not include the income from the transfer fee paid by the raiyats. It is possible that the income from this source increased in view of the increased transfer of land. Fourthly, though population increased at a high rate during this period total agricultural production remained more or less stagnant. However, it is quite clear that the landlords were making substantial gains from their monopoly control of land. The opportunity of making profit from the proprietary rights in land was hardly conducive to the productive investment of capital by the landlords.

Market conditions in Japan were far more favourable than in Bengal, but even then the concentration of land in the hands of the landlords did not lead to large-scale farming by them. This was mainly due to the high rent which characterised Japanese agriculture after 1873. So long as the landlords could sit back and collect 50 to 60 per cent of the produce as rent, there was little incentive for them to become capitalist farmers.[2] From the available statistics it does not seem that the rate of rent collected by the Bengal landlords from the raiyats was as high as in Japan. But in the light of this experience it does not seem to be difficult to explain why the Bengal landlords, instead of undertaking large scale farming, remained satisfied only with the legal proprietorship of land (i.e. unproductive investment of capital).[3]

It may, however, be argued that the landlords could have helped agricultural development by undertaking such measures as the dissemination of the use of fertiliser, manures, improved seeds and breeds among the cultivators. Capital requirements for such intensive farming methods are usually modest and this takes mainly the form of working capital which yields a quick return by way of increased output. If the landlords had invested their capital for such purpose, they could have increased the rate of rent per acre of land. The usual explanation which has been given for the lack of initiative in this direction was the existence of different grades of subinfeuda-

---

[1] Illegal cess was estimated by some members of the Provincial Legislative Council as ranging between 60 and 120 million rupees. Cited by R. K. Mukherjee, *Dynamics of a Rural Society: A Study of the Economic Structure in Bengal Villages* (Berlin, 1957).

[2] Nobutaka Ike, 'Taxation and Land-ownership in the Westernisation of Japan', *The Journal of Economic History*, Vol. VII, No. 1 (1947).

[3] The Royal Commission on Agriculture felt that one of the greatest drawbacks in the way of agricultural development in India was the absence of large farms. (See Report, p. 425). But considered in the context of the problems discussed here it would seem that the absence of large farms was not the cause, but the result of the failure of Bengal landlords to become capitalist farmers. In this study it is not being suggested that large-scale farming was a condition of success. We are only trying to explain why the Bengal landlords, unlike their English counterparts, did not start large-scale farming.

tion between the actual cultivators and the original tenure-holders or proprietors. Thus, according to the Land Revenue Commission this growth of intermediaries prevented the 'Zamindars from fulfilling the functions which provide the economic justification for a landlord and tenant system because with few exceptions the tenure-holders above the raiyots have neither the incentive nor the capital to effect agricultural improvement. The Zamindar to-day cannot obtain an enhancement of rent even for any improvement which he makes and he feels that he is no longer responsible for improvement'.[1] The Minority Report which mainly reflected the opinion of the different Landholder's Associations and the British India Association also took the same view.[2]

At first sight it seems that this thesis of the Land Revenue Commission offers a satisfactory explanation of the problem under investigation. But a closer scrutiny suggests that this view is somewhat superficial. Firstly, why should it be assumed that all the tenure-holders immediately above the raiyats did not have either the capital or the incentive to effect agricultural development? Is it not true that many of these landlords invested capital in money-lending business and other profitable alternatives? Under the tenancy legislation the landlords were allowed to increase the rate of rent for any improvement effected by them in the productive power of land. Moreover, from the District Settlement Reports it is clear that in most cases the rent payable by the tenure-holders to the superior landlords was fixed. Thus it is not correct to argue that these tenure-holders did not have the incentive or the capital to improve the productive power of land.

Secondly, it is true that the original landlords did not have an incentive to invest capital in the land in the case of which there were intermediaries between them and the raiyats. But the important question that has to be asked in this connection is what portion of land was affected by the creation of intermediaries? It is difficult to obtain detailed evidence on this question. However, if the situation in three districts is regarded as significant, it would appear that the Land Revenue Commission grossly exaggerated the difficulties arising out of the creation of tenure-holders. Thus, while in Dacca and Mymensingh the landlords had direct relationship with the raiyats in respect of respectively 64 and 66 per cent of the total land in their zamindari, in Faridpur it was 34 per cent.[3] This evidence suggests that a sizable portion

[1] *LRC*, p. 34.
[2] *Ibid.*, p. 215.
[3] For the evidence on Dacca see *Final Report on the Survey and Settlement Operations in the District of Dacca, 1910–1917* (Calcutta, 1917), p. 69; for Faridpur see *Final Report on the Survey and Settlement Operations in the Faridpur District, 1910–1914* (Calcutta, 1916), p. 25; for Mymensingh see, *Final Report on the Survey and Settlement Operations in the District of Mymensingh, 1908–1919* (Calcutta, 1920). Calculated from appendix 9 and 10. The following

of the zamindari land remained unaffected by the growth of intermediaries. But the superior landlords did not invest capital to improve the productive power of the land in respect of which they had direct dealings with the raiyats. Thus, it seems that the thesis of the Land Revenue Commission does not really explain why the landlords did not invest through the raiyats.

The real explanation seems to lie in the considerations mentioned earlier. With regard to the question of productive investment of capital directly by the landlords it has been argued that such investment involved so many risks and uncertainties that the rate of return appeared to be lower than the rate of return on land purchase. It is but natural that such a rate of return would appear to be lower if the landlords were going to invest capital through the agency of the tenants who were so numerous, for two reasons: with the standard of living of most of the tenants so low the landlords would have found it very difficult to raise the additional rent on improved (e.g. irrigated) land; secondly, as in many cases the landlords were sure to be involved in litigation with the tenants, the cost of collection of rent would have been high. From this it would follow that even if there were no intermediaries between the Zamindars and the cultivators, the former would have hardly taken the initiative in productive investment in agriculture.

At this stage it would be quite legitimate to ask: if monopoly control of land had created an opportunity for the landlords to claim a high price for land, why were the different grades of tenure-holders created? Secondly, if there was any need to create intermediaries, why in most cases were the rates of rent per acre paid by them fixed? Clearly such an arrangement went against the interests of the original landlords or tenure-holders. Thus, for example, it was shown in the Settlement Report on the Mymensingh district that the average rent paid by the tenure-holders of the first grade was less than 12 annas per acre. But the average rate of rent paid by the raiyats under the original landlords was just under Rs 2/12. Again, whereas the average rate of rent paid by the tenure-holders of the second grade was less than one rupee, the average rate paid by the raiyats under the first grade tenure-holders was nearly Rs 3. This meant that both the original landlords and the first-grade tenure-holders were incurring a loss of nearly Rs 2 per acre by the creation of intermediaries. It was calculated that as a result of the creation of intermediaries the superior landlords in Dacca, Faridpur, Bakerganj and Mymensingh lost respectively Rs 60, 63, 200 and 102 per 100 acres.

information is available from the Settlement Reports regarding the number of the grades of intermediaries: Dacca (9), Jessore (6 or 7), Khulna (8), Bogra (10), Bakerganj (12), and Mymensingh (3). These show that the opinion of the *Indian Statutory Commission* (cited by *Bengal Land Revenue Commission*, p. 37) that there were 35 to 50 grades of tenure holders is grossly exaggerated.

As pointed out earlier, it seems that both the number of the grades of tenure-holders and the proportion of land in which such interests were created have been exaggerated. However the fact that such interests were created contradicts our contention that the purchase of land was so profitable and/or the landlords were really aware of such profit-making possibilities. Nothing definite can be said on this score unless we know to what extent the creation of intermediaries was due to (a) the rigidity in the collection of rent by the government, particularly in the decades immediately following 1793, (b) the fact that the lands of the landlords were scattered in different districts and (c) the acceptance of other occupations by landlords which took them permanently to the urban areas. The landlords constituted the dominant class in the society. Therefore, it is but natural that many among the landlords who had taken up other occupations would like to maintain their legal rights in land and, thus, have the satisfaction of being known as a landlord.

By the time the Agricultural Revolution started in England the tradition of the landlords' engaging in large-scale farming and providing permanent capital to the tenants was well established, as this was the practice in the preceding two centuries when the entire economy was undergoing gradual changes. The contribution of the Industrial Revolution of the late eighteenth century was essentially to widen the scale of this practice by creating greater opportunities for productive investment in agriculture. Against this the economy of Bengal (as that of any other part of India) had a long history of relative stagnation during which the landlords had hardly looked upon land as an avenue of productive investment. One important factor in this respect was the fact that since they were not the owners of land, there was uncertainty about the enjoyment of the fruits of investment by the landlords. Considered against this background it seems that the declaration of the proprietary rights in land was a necessary step in transforming the traditional attitude of the landlords, but this was not a sufficient condition. Such a condition could be created in an environment in which returns on productive investment would appear to be greater than the profit from the alternative sources – monopoly control of land, money-lending and trade in agricultural produce. Economic development on the basis of international specialisation does not seem to have created such an economic environment in Bengal.

As pointed out earlier the experience of the years after 1793 when the landlords did not show the desired initiative in agricultural development seems to have had considerable influence on the policy of the foreign rulers in favour of establishing direct relationship with the peasant and the village communities.[1] In Bengal, however, the government followed a policy of com-

---

[1] Eric Stokes, *The English Utilitarians and India* (Oxford, 1959), Ch. II.

promise i.e. a policy of keeping intact the institutional monopoly of the landlords and at the same time giving relief to the raiyats. The protective legislation by which such an objective was sought was not, however, passed till the question of the landlord–tenant relationship had assumed political significance. Thus, as pointed out by Mr Ilbert while introducing the Rent Bill of 1885, the efforts of the landlords to obtain higher rents and the opposition of the tenant to what they considered as unjust was creating a serious state of affairs.[1] In these circumstances the government could neither restore the raiyats to their status in 1793 nor 'attack the vested interest of the landlords in any degree'.[2] Therefore, the protective laws which were being passed had to 'contain much that is in the nature of expedients, adjustments and compromises'.[3] The result was that though the landlords were not fulfilling their economic role they were allowed to obtain, as mentioned earlier, enhancement of rent on many grounds.

This is not, however, to suggest that the landlords would not have claimed rent at an enhanced rate if there were legal sanctions against it.[4] Similarly, it cannot be expected that the additional income earned by the government from the abolition of landlordism would have been spent in a co-ordinated plan for agricultural development. In the raiyatwary areas the government were the landlords as the recipient of economic rent, but under the prevailing doctrine of *laissez-faire* its role in agricultural development remained limited. Thus, the protective laws were quite close to the realities of economic life of British India. But such a policy of compromise could at best create conditions for the perpetuation of economic stagnation. It is interesting that even in the 1920s when the government had abandoned the policy of *laissez-faire* it sought to maintain the compromise by asking the Royal Commission on Agriculture not to make any recommendation regarding the 'existing system of land-ownership or tenancy or of assessment of revenue'.[5]

It has, however, to be mentioned that the attitude of the nationalist leaders and newspapers to the question of landlordism was not different either. In the last quarter of the nineteenth century they gave full support to the protective legislation against the powerful opposition from landlords. There were differences of opinion in matters of detail and some of the leaders even took

[1] *Abstracts of the Proceedings of the Council of the Governor General of India Assembled for the Purpose of Making Laws and Regulations, 1883*, pp. 77, 277.
[2] Statement of the Lt. Governor of Bengal, *Ibid.*, p. 440.
[3] Ilbert's Statement in the Council of the Governor General of India. See, *Proceedings*, 1885, p. 191.
[4] This is suggested by the failure of the Bombay Tenancy Act which fixed a ceiling on rental demand. Cited by G. Myrdal, *Asian Drama: An Enquiry into the Poverty of Nations* (London, 1968), Vol. II, pp. 1328–9.
[5] Cited by R. P. Dutt, *India To-day* (Bombay, 1949), p. 182.

the side of the landlords, but the main body of opinion was that such legislation was essential for the well-being of the peasantry.[1] It is interesting that
though many of these leaders demanded the reduction or fixing of revenue
in other provinces as an incentive for greater productive efforts by the
cultivators and as a safeguard against famines, they do not seem to have
opposed either the restricted or the unrestricted rights given to the landlords
to increase the rental paid respectively by the cash-paying occupancy raiyats
and other categories of raiyats and under-raiyats. It is difficult to accept the
prevailing view that such measures would have really offered a solution to the
basic problems of the agrarian economy of these provinces. However, the
fact that the nationalist leaders took such a different line in Bengal seems to
bring out some of the inherent complications arising from the concentration
of interest in landed property.

These complications were more sharply focused in the 1920s and 1930s.
The first occasion came in 1923 when Sir John Keir proposed, in his amendment to the Tenancy Act of 1885, the extension of occupancy rights to the
share croppers and other measures generally unfavourable to the landlords.
This drew such strong protests from both within and outside the Bengal
Legislative Council that the Bill had to be abandoned.[2] The Act of 1885 was
at last amended in 1928, but with the support of the Congress and Swaraj
members the landlords successfully resisted a move by a section of the
members to deprive them of their right to collect transfer fee and pre-
emption and even to giving a legal status to the share croppers. Thus, even
in the 1920s the policy of the nationalist leaders remained essentially one
of compromise, i.e. to grant greater security to the raiyats and at the same
time to safeguard the interest of the landlords. Again, there were differences
of opinion as to the extent of rights to be granted to the different grades of
the raiyats, but there was as yet no proposal for a radical change in the existing system. The first serious proposal for the abolition of the zamindari
system was made in 1932 at a conference of the Bengal Provincial Praja
Samity formed in 1929 and later renamed as the Krishak Praja Party.[3] This
party contested the provincial elections of 1937 on the basis of its programme
for the abolition of landlordism without compensation. The coalition
ministry which was formed under the Premiership of A. K. Fazlul Huq, the
leader of the Krishak Praja Party, appointed a Commission to devise ways

[1] For details see, B. Chandra, *The Rise and Growth of Economic Nationalism in India* (New Delhi,
1966), Chs. IX and X.
[2] See *LRC*, p. 28.
[3] For details of the background of the formation of this party and the various other demands
made at this conference relating to the agrarian economy, see A. M. Ahmed, *Amar Dekha
Rajnitir Panchash Basar* (Dacca, 1968), Chs. IV–XII.

and means to replace the Permanent Settlement 'by a more equitable system and laws suitable to the needs and requirements of the people' as, it was argued, it had 'arrested the economic growth and development of the province and had adversely affected the national outlook of the people'.[1] The Commission recommended the abolition of landlordism with compensation, but this was not implemented.

However, the fact that there was such a move compelled the other political parties to define their policy with regard to the Permanent Settlement more categorically than they had done before. In the late 1920s the 'nationalists had reached a turning point. Their increasing sense of political power combined with the catastrophic economic events brought sharply into focus the fact that the long preparation for political education must be accompanied by a definite programme of economic policy'.[2] This was particularly true with regard to the Congress. The increased emphasis on the problems of rural life which the changed circumstances called for and the argument of the Krishak Praja Party that these were due to the prevailing system of landownership and should, therefore, be abolished must have created a dilemma for the Congress. For it could neither alienate the support of the landlords nor overlook the problems of the rural masses who were now empowered to vote. So, on the one hand, the party openly opposed the abolition of the Permanent Settlement[3] and, on the other, championed the cause of the reconstruction of the rural economy. The policies which were formulated remained, however, vague, impractical and inadequate as a solution to the basic problems of poverty.[4]

The Muslim League also opposed the idea of the abolition of landlordism. This was in spite of the fact that the landlords mostly belonged to the Hindu community and thus offered the League leaders a great opportunity to enlist the support of the Muslim masses. It is true that subsequently this party abandoned its opposition when it entered into a coalition with the Krishak

[1] *The Indian Annual Register* (1938), Vol. II, p. 219.
[2] K. N. Chaudhuri, 'Economic Problems and Indian Independence', in C. H. Philips and M. D. Wainwright (eds.), *The Partition of India: Policies and Perspectives, 1935–47* (London, 1970), pp. 294–315. This work discusses in detail the policies of the different parties with regard to the economic problems of the time.
[3] Thus, in 1931 the working committee of the Congress passed a resolution assuring the zamindars that there was no design on interests legitimately acquired and appealing to the landed and monied class for financial help. See *Indian Annual Register* (1931), Vol. II, p. 86. The dilemma faced by Congress is further shown by the evidence cited earlier that in 1926 a zamindar asked his tenants to raise Rs3000 for the payment of his contribution to the Congress. For details see, *Proceedings of the Bengal Legislative Council*, 1927, Vol. XXV, No. 2, pp. 98–9.
[4] See, for example, the resolutions passed at Karachi in 1931. Quoted by Chaudhuri, *op. cit.*, p. 301.

Praja Party,[1] but it would seem that this change of attitude was more apparent than real.

The reaction of the landlords was predictably very strong. They had always zealously tried to safeguard all the benefits which could be obtained from their monopoly control of land. The result was that the provisions of the Tenancy Act of 1885 and its amendment in 1928 were less favourable to the tenants than they were originally intended to be.[2] The usual landlords' defence was that the protective legislation was a violation of the declaration of proprietary rights made in 1793. Now when they were threatened with the total abolition of their rights, they made the further claim that they were a minority community and as such were entitled to special protection by the Provincial Governor under the Act of 1935.[3] Some of the more determined landlords went to the extent of declaring their support for the continuation of foreign rule.[4]

The replacement of the Permanent Settlement by the establishment of a direct relationship between the government and the cultivators was a necessary condition for the modernisation of Bengal agriculture. But clearly, in itself, this was not going to be sufficient. Such a condition could be fulfilled if the surplus extracted from the agricultural sector in the form of rent was spent by the government for experimenting with and the diffusion of new techniques of production. The fact that neither Congress nor the government recognised the necessity of abolishing landlordism made their plans for agricultural development somewhat contradictory. On the other hand, from the resolution quoted earlier it would seem that the plan of the Krishak Praja Party was not conceived in a spirit of facilitating official efforts for modernising the agricultural sector. In other words, abolition of the Permanent Settlement was identified with the solution of the manifold problems of the rural economy of Bengal.[5] But whatever might have been the

[1] *Indian Annual Register* (1935), Vol. II, p. 219.

[2] For a discussion of how some of the important concessions proposed to the tenants by the Rent Law Commission (1880) were dropped see Chandra, *op. cit.*

[3] LRC (Minority Report), Vol. I.

[4] Thus, in 1938 the Chairman of the All-India Landlords' Association declared, 'If we are to exist as a class, it is our duty to strengthen the hold of the government.' Cited by S. G. Madim, *Need for Institutional Changes and Regional Planning for Optimal Development of the Agricultural Resources of India* (Wisconsin, 1949), p. 33.

[5] This argument that the change of tenurial arrangements does not automatically solve the problem of low productivity is clearly borne out by the experience in Bangladesh. Here superior landlordism was abolished in 1950, but till the middle of the 1960s productivity remained as low as it was before the abolition of the Permanent Settlement. The proximate economic effect of the abolition of the Permanent Settlement remained confined to an enhancement of government revenue. For details see Abu Abdullah, *Land Reform and Agrarian Change in Bangladesh* (Dacca, 1973), pp. 25–37.

motive of the Krishak Praja Party it is clear that their call to do away with landlordism pointed the way in which the tenurial system had to be changed sooner or later.

As mentioned earlier, in the present stage of our knowledge about the different aspects of landlordism in Bengal it is not possible to form a clear idea about the question why the landlords did not fulfil their economic role. But the points which have been raised in this chapter would suggest that the main problem was the absence of a sufficiently favourable economic environment to encourage private agencies such as landlords to improve agriculture, either directly through their own efforts or through their tenants. The chief factor which accounted for the absence of such a favourable environment was the very slow pace of industrialisation and the consequent restricted nature of the market and the high demand for land by the peasant producers. In these circumstances, the abolition of the zamindari system had to be the first step towards the modernisation of the agricultural sector. But such an idea was not favoured either by the foreign government or the major political parties of India, though there was increasing awareness of the problems of the rural areas. The only move which was made came in the changed circumstances of the 1930s, but it did not succeed. Evidently political and ideological evolution in India had not yet reached the stage when a drastic change in the land system could be carried out.

CONCLUSION

In this work an attempt has been made to present a quantitative picture of the performance of the agriculture of Bengal during the period from 1920/21 to 1945/46. The main emphasis has been on the trends in crop output and its two determinants – acreage under cultivation and yield. In the light of the available data from independent sources, we have seen that the officially published data on acreage were mostly underestimated and those on yield overestimated, but at least in the case of the former the pattern was not uniform over the entire period. The acreage data have accordingly been revised and it has been contended that the trends estimated from the revised series can be expected to provide a more reliable picture of the agrarian economy of Bengal. The picture which thus emerges has four important features.

During the quarter century from 1920 there was hardly any improvement in yield at the aggregate level and only a marginal expansion of the acreage under cultivation. The obvious result was that there was a marked disparity between population growth and crop production. However, there were considerable differences in the trends of the two crop groups – food crops and cash crops. Thus, in the case of the former a small expansion of acreage was accompanied by a corresponding decline in yield. This was due mainly to the stagnation of the acreage and yield of winter rice. Acreage and yield of minor crops like wheat, barley and gram increased, but their combined weight was so small that this increase could hardly improve the aggregate picture in this group of crops. The rate of expansion of the acreage under cash crops was even smaller, but the yield per acre increased considerably. The rate of improvement of the yield of jute, the largest single crop in this group, was very low, but the improvement in the case of other crops, particularly sugarcane, was very marked; overall, the yield and acreage of the major crops declined or remained more or less stagnant, and those of the minor ones increased. The example of acreage under the minor crops suggests the direction in which the expansion of acreage is likely to take place in a long settled country – through an increase in double-cropping; most of these minor crops are raised as secondary crops.

Secondly, it is significant that though the trends in the revised series are more adverse than in the official series they are much better than those estimated by Blyn. This would substantiate the belief that the inclusion of Bihar and Orissa considerably depressed the trend rates for Bengal proper. It is also significant that the trends in our revised series are more in conformity with the experience in other parts of India during this period than shown either in the officially published data or by Blyn.

Thirdly, agricultural trends in the five regional units of Bengal varied considerably both with regard to area under cultivation and yield per acre. In some cases these dissimilarities seem to reflect the differences in geophysical conditions or the change in intensity of cultivation which took place during these years.

It is not difficult to appreciate why there was virtual stagnation in the all-crop acreage since the scope for the extension of cultivation to new areas was limited. But why was there no significant improvement in yield per acre despite the relative abundance of labour? Could it be argued that this was due to the lack of efficiency on the part of the cultivators in the allocation of the factors of production? It has not been possible, for lack of data, to investigate this specific problem. Instead as an alternative test we have examined whether the cultivators were responsive to changes in the price level using data on individual crops and aggregated crops. No significant elasticity of all-crop acreage has been found with regard to changes in the terms of trade with the non-agricultural sector. But a closer look at specific considerations affecting production during a period of falling prices, and given limited scope for increasing production during a period of rising prices, does not suggest any 'perversity' or 'survival-mindedness' in the production behaviour of the cultivators. Greater insight into the 'rationality' of production decisions by the peasantry is provided by findings on the elasticity of individual crop acreage with regard to changes in relative prices and yields. For these show that, though the inelastic supply of the most important production input – land – did not allow the Bengal cultivators to increase the total acreage under cultivation, they were still maximising their proceeds from the given resources by crops that were more profitable either as a result of rise in relative price or yield. As indicated by the findings on the price elasticity of the acreage under autumn rice it is also clear that such response was not confined to cash crops. Cultivation of food crops was responsive to changes in price where there was adequate scope for substitution with alternative crops. In spite of the obvious limitations of the available data and the method of estimation it would, therefore, seem that cultivators were taking 'rational' production decisions such as were desirable within the given technological and institutional constraints.

The real explanation for the low productivity and the near-zero trend during the period under review would thus seem to be due to the low level of capital formation. It could be argued that capital formation was adversely affected by the low and declining per capita income in the agricultural sector. It has not been possible to estimate either the trends in capital formation or its proportion in total income in the rural areas. Instead estimates have been presented on the trends of the four items of physical capital involved in Bengal agriculture – land, animal labour, occupied houses and ploughs. Land has been included as an index of the investment of money and effort in expanding productive acreage as opposed to that which may have increased or prevented the fall in the productivity of land already under cultivation. The findings substantiate our assumption that in an agricultural system characterised by relative abundance of labour supply and stagnant technology most of the increase in capital formation is likely to take a form which would expand the productive acreage. There was a considerable increase in the number of houses but it is not known if this was at the cost of changes in size and type. On the other hand the number of ploughs and animal labour declined from the beginning of the 1930s. In view of the nature of the crop statistics it is difficult to say anything definite as to whether this decline adversely affected the productivity per unit of land. But if estimated trends are considered reliable, it would seem that yield per acre was not significantly affected. This would indicate either the presence of surplus capacity at the beginning of the period or a shift towards other categories of investment. The possibility of surplus capacity during the initial years which appears to be more likely would strengthen the belief that the scope for obtaining increased output from the additional use of the traditional factors of production was limited or even negligible. It would therefore follow that the basic problem was not the inadequacy of investment in the traditional factors of production as such but the absence of technological innovations.

Closely connected with the problem of investment made by the cultivators is the availability of credit. For a long time the only source of credit in the rural areas was the money-lenders. But the finances drawn from them became a burden on the borrowers instead of contributing to their prosperity. The solution offered to the problems of high rates of interest and indebtedness by the inauguration of the Co-operative Credit Movement and the statutory regulation of money lending had two important limitations. Firstly, there was inadequate realisation of the need for making provision for credit as part of a wider plan for economic development; provision for cheap credit was not accompanied by the development and diffusion of such new inputs as would result in a sustained increase in output. Secondly, some of the underlying assumptions behind the Credit Movement and the statutory restriction on the rate of interest to be charged by the money-lenders were unrealistic in that they did not take note of the specific forces which pushed up the price of credit and gave the money-lenders a hold in the rural economy. The result was that the progress of the Credit Movement remained very slow and the problem of rural indebtedness was far from being solved. Thus, even at the height of the Co-operative Movement only 10 per cent of the borrowers in the agricultural sector were covered by the Primary Societies and only 24 per cent of their credit needs were met. And most important of all, in the 1940s nine tenths of the outstanding loans were overdue. Thus, evidently there remained a wide gap between the expectations and the actual performance of the Co-operative Movement.

Finally we have raised some questions about the reasons why the expectations that the landlords would take initiatives in agricultural development were not fulfilled in spite of the flow of capital to agriculture. The discussion suggested that under the prevailing circumstances the landlords found it more profitable to take advantage of the high demand for land than to make productive investment. The greatest disincentive to making productive investment in large-scale farming was that the market for produce was uncertain and inelastic. As against this disincentive was the opportunity to demand a high rent for land. Such an environment made private agencies such as landlords unsuitable for the purpose of improving agriculture either through their direct efforts or indirectly through the peasant cultivators. Under these circumstances what was needed was the abolition of the monopoly control of land by the landlords and the use of the surplus generated in agriculture for its modernisation. But political considerations made such a move unacceptable either to the foreign government or to the major political parties of India. Instead a policy of compromise was pursued. This is noticed in the attempts to regulate the profit which the landlords made from their monopoly control of land and to grant security to increasing number of raiyats and under-raiyats. In the interests of agricultural development the government maintained an Agricultural Department and experimental centres, but since most of the surplus in agriculture was being expropriated by the landlords the official efforts remained nominal.

Thus, the government could not do much because it was financially handicapped, the landlords did not take the initiative because they did not find it profitable and the raiyats could not improve their productive techniques because they could not develop new inputs, and the inputs which were developed at the experimental centres were not available on the market.

To summarise, the picture of the agrarian economy of Bengal which thus emerges is clear enough – it had reached an equilibrium at a low level of production. This is shown by the near-constancy of cultivated area and a near-zero trend in yield per acre; this equilibrium at a low level of productivity reflected the efficiency of the known techniques of production. The price of credit remained high as the money lenders were still virtually the only source; and the finances drawn from them, to the extent that these were used for directly productive purposes, continued to be invested in the traditional factors of production. The result was that agricultural indebtedness was still very acute. The solution to these problems would have meant action to an extent not forthcoming either from the landlords, or from the government.

APPENDIX: STATISTICAL TABLES

1.1 WINTER RICE

Year	Official acreage (in '000s)	Output ('000 tons)	Revised acreage (in '000s)	Revised output ('000 tons)	Yield per acre (in lbs)
			All-Bengal		
1920	15344	6187	20714	8353	903
1921	15850	7069	21397	9544	999
1922	16240	7246	21924	9782	999
1923	14954	5467	20188	7381	819
1924	15589	6124	21045	8268	880
1925	15619	6622	21086	8940	950
1926	14290	5576	19292	7528	874
1927	13211	4689	17835	6330	795
1928	15363	6921	20741	9344	1009
1929	14794	5918	19971	7989	896
1930	15120	6069	20412	8194	899
1931	15571	6418	21021	8664	923
1932	15580	6457	21032	8717	928
1933	15500	6255	20924	8445	904
1934	14759	6235	19924	8417	946
1935	14837	4988	20030	6734	753
1936	15803	8271	21334	11166	1172
1937	15921	6878	21493	9286	968
1938	15836	5970	21378	8059	844
1939	16096	6565	21729	8863	914
1940	14916	4844	20137	6539	727
1941	16914	7427	20804	9135	984
1942	16211	5007	20750	6408	692
1943	18195	8533	20742	9727	1050
1944	20798	7540	20798	7540	812
1945	18933	7013	19470	7013	830
			Rajshahi		
1920	3581	1226	5479	1875	767
1921	3733	1689	5711	2584	1013

I.I   **WINTER RICE** (*cont.*)

Year	Official acreage (in '000s)	Output ('000 tons)	Revised acreage (in '000s)	Revised output ('000 tons)	Yield per acre (in lbs)
1922	3940	1468	6028	2246	835
1923	3057	844	4676	1291	619
1924	3715	1593	5684	2437	960
1925	3964	1688	6065	2583	954
1926	3375	1166	5164	1784	774
1927	2733	865	4181	1324	709
1928	3644	1691	5576	2587	1039
1929	3255	1212	4980	1854	834
1930	3326	1253	5089	1918	844
1931	3491	1508	5341	2308	968
1932	3553	1523	5437	2330	960
1933	3624	1644	5545	2515	1016
1934	3531	1566	5402	2396	994
1935	3651	1434	5586	2195	880
1936	3695	1797	5653	2750	1090
1937	3619	1421	5538	2174	879
1938	3543	1369	5421	2095	866
1939	3624	1515	5545	2318	936
1940	2992	830	4577	1270	621
1941	3923	1707	5256	2287	975
1942	3329	925	5260	1461	622
1943	4340	2056	5252	2488	1061
1944	5240	1728	5240	1728	739
1945	4767	1600	5164	1600	752
			Dacca		
1920	3726	1709	4211	1932	1028
1921	4236	2039	4787	2304	1078
1922	4207	1759	4754	1988	937
1923	4082	1703	4612	1925	935
1924	4092	1445	4624	1633	791
1925	4166	2129	4707	2406	1145
1926	3786	1380	4278	1559	817
1927	3958	1682	4473	1901	952
1928	4089	1850	4620	2090	1014
1929	4036	1789	4561	2022	993
1930	3900	1511	4407	1707	868
1931	4159	1759	4699	1987	947
1932	4159	1751	4699	1979	943
1933	4171	1480	4713	1672	795
1934	4204	1973	4750	2230	1052
1935	4311	1688	4868	1907	878
1936	4311	2150	4871	2430	1117

1937	4388	1847	4959	2087	943
1938	4327	1669	4889	1886	864
1939	4381	1845	4950	2085	943
1940	4278	1538	4834	1738	805
1941	4485	1976	4889	2154	987
1942	4521	1577	4928	1719	781
1943	4667	2185	4947	2316	1049
1944	4954	1738	4954	1738	786
1945	4509	1609	5107	1609	799

Chittagong

1920	1883	804	2166	925	956
1921	1894	992	2178	1141	1173
1922	1912	1017	2199	1169	1191
1923	1898	824	2183	947	972
1924	1929	733	2219	842	851
1925	1936	829	2227	954	959
1926	1714	731	1971	841	955
1927	1822	763	2096	877	938
1928	1809	822	2080	945	1018
1929	1912	741	2199	852	868
1930	1987	783	2285	901	883
1931	2030	813	2335	935	897
1932	2024	808	2328	930	894
1933	2017	750	2319	863	833
1934	1995	840	2295	967	944
1935	1977	698	2274	803	791
1936	1887	921	2170	1060	1094
1937	1978	801	2275	922	908
1938	1965	723	2260	831	824
1939	1921	777	2209	894	906
1940	1904	693	2189	796	815
1941	1874	757	2286	924	905
1942	1968	749	2283	869	852
1943	2064	941	2290	1044	1021
1944	2295	816	2295	816	797
1945	2089	759	2371	759	814

Presidency Division

1920	2441	912	3368	1259	837
1921	2433	959	3357	1323	883
1922	2512	1062	3466	1466	947
1923	2384	870	3290	1201	817
1924	2374	963	3276	1329	909
1925	2357	921	3252	1271	876
1926	2331	960	3217	1324	922
1927	1989	608	2745	840	685
1928	2231	981	3079	1354	985
1929	2190	901	3022	1243	921

1.1 WINTER RICE (*cont.*)

Year	Official acreage (in '000s)	Output ('000 tons)	Revised acreage (in '000s)	Revised output ('000 tons)	Yield per acre (in lbs)
1930	2388	996	3296	1375	934
1931	2474	1031	3414	1423	934
1932	2459	1037	3393	1431	945
1933	2382	927	3287	1279	871
1934	2206	892	3044	1231	906
1935	2284	575	3152	794	564
1936	2547	1352	3515	1866	1189
1937	2650	1150	3657	1587	972
1938	2835	988	3912	1363	780
1939	2851	1048	3934	1446	823
1940	2892	904	3991	1247	700
1941	3048	1424	3658	1708	1046
1942	3039	1052	3707	1283	775
1943	3487	1673	3731	1790	1074
1944	3744	1515	3744	1515	906
1945	3413	1425	3318	1425	935

Burdwan

Year	Official acreage (in '000s)	Output ('000 tons)	Revised acreage (in '000s)	Revised output ('000 tons)	Yield per acre (in lbs)
1920	3712	1536	5791	2397	927
1921	3554	1390	5545	2169	876
1922	3669	1940	5724	3026	1184
1923	3534	1226	5513	1913	777
1924	3478	1391	5426	2169	896
1925	3197	1055	4987	1646	739
1926	3084	1339	4812	2089	973
1927	2709	770	4226	1201	637
1928	3590	1578	5601	2462	985
1929	3401	1275	5305	1989	840
1930	3520	1526	5491	2380	971
1931	3418	1307	5332	2039	857
1932	3384	1337	5279	2086	885
1933	3306	1454	5157	2269	986
1934	2823	963	4404	1502	764
1935	2617	592	4082	924	507
1936	3364	2050	5247	3198	1365
1937	3285	1659	5125	2588	1131
1938	3166	1221	4939	1905	864
1939	3319	1380	5177	2152	931
1940	2850	880	4447	1373	692
1941	3584	1563	4695	2048	977
1942	3355	704	4629	972	470

1943	3637	1679	4619	2132	1034
1944	4564	1742	4564	1742	855
1945	4155	1620	3511	1620	873

Note: As explained in chapter 1, section 1.6 the figures in the revised series up to 1940/41 are obtained by using the same Revision Factor, i.e., the margin of error during these years is assumed to be uniform. Separate Revision Factors are used for 1941/42 to 1943/44 and 1945/46.

In the case of all the crops the year 1920 stands for the agricultural year 1920/21.

1.2   AUTUMN RICE

All-Bengal

1920	5114	1714	5676	1903	751
1921	5608	1855	6225	2059	741
1922	5160	1598	5728	1774	694
1923	4984	1521	5532	1689	684
1924	4857	1403	5391	1557	647
1925	5139	1486	5705	1649	648
1926	5015	1566	5567	1738	699
1927	5072	1438	5630	1597	635
1928	5649	1840	6270	2043	730
1929	5031	1506	5585	1672	671
1930	5082	1641	5641	1821	723
1931	6163	1986	6841	2205	722
1932	5788	2069	6424	2296	801
1933	5775	2076	6411	2305	805
1934	5572	1804	6185	2002	725
1935	5851	2013	6495	2235	771
1936	5757	2130	6390	2365	829
1937	5865	1962	6510	2178	749
1938	5727	1393	6357	1546	545
1939	5742	1752	6373	1945	684
1940	5416	1529	6012	1697	632
1941	6479	2235	6479	2235	773
1942	6507	1809	6507	1809	623
1943	7922	3023	6496	2479	855
1944	8084	2644	6629	2168	733
1945	7357	2449	6672	2449	746

Rajshahi

1920	1213	387	1735	554	715
1921	1428	465	2042	665	730
1922	1272	387	1819	554	682
1923	1175	317	1680	453	604
1924	1180	404	1687	578	767
1925	1231	377	1760	539	686

1.2 AUTUMN RICE (*cont.*)

Year	Official acreage (in 'ooos)	Output ('ooo tons)	Revised acreage (in 'ooos)	Revised output ('ooo tons)	Yield per acre (in lbs)
1926	1230	375	1758	536	683
1927	1250	403	1787	577	723
1928	1311	448	1875	640	765
1929	1282	399	1833	571	698
1930	1285	409	1838	586	714
1931	1389	429	1987	614	692
1932	1417	542	2026	776	857
1933	1392	550	1991	787	885
1934	1395	539	1994	770	865
1935	1460	549	2088	786	843
1936	1344	485	1922	693	808
1937	1395	464	1995	663	744
1938	1316	311	1881	445	529
1939	1344	449	1922	642	748
1940	1153	326	1649	466	633
1941	1691	668	1691	668	885
1942	1664	459	1664	459	618
1943	2172	838	1976	762	864
1944	2177	721	1981	656	742
1945	1982	669	1972	669	756
			Dacca		
1920	1306	456	1097	383	782
1921	1604	532	1348	447	743
1922	1480	439	1243	369	664
1923	1427	476	1198	400	748
1924	1413	328	1187	275	520
1925	1353	373	1137	313	617
1926	1269	346	1066	291	611
1927	1290	353	1083	297	613
1928	1316	469	1105	394	799
1929	1318	339	1107	285	576
1930	1316	434	1106	364	738
1931	2017	620	1695	521	688
1932	1804	666	1516	559	827
1933	1740	552	1462	464	711
1934	1735	563	1457	473	727
1935	1907	696	1602	584	817
1936	1869	721	1570	605	864
1937	1890	635	1587	533	753
1938	1848	487	1552	409	590
1939	1873	562	1573	472	672
1940	1836	543	1542	456	663

1941	2138	675	2138	675	707
1942	2104	591	2104	591	629
1943	2678	1032	1687	650	864
1944	2699	780	1700	491	647
1945	2456	720	1709	720	656

Chittagong

1920	924	310	1349	453	752
1921	978	348	1428	508	797
1922	968	369	1413	538	854
1923	958	323	1399	471	754
1924	956	273	1395	398	639
1925	952	279	1390	407	655
1926	882	270	1287	394	686
1927	928	266	1354	388	642
1928	944	307	1379	448	728
1929	728	221	1063	323	681
1930	759	227	1108	331	669
1931	887	278	1294	406	703
1932	787	236	1149	344	671
1933	792	277	1156	405	784
1934	785	229	1145	335	655
1935	819	261	1195	381	714
1936	782	305	1141	445	873
1937	790	259	1153	378	735
1938	763	211	1114	307	618
1939	772	236	1127	344	684
1940	743	239	1085	349	720
1941	830	211	830	211	570
1942	891	296	891	296	745
1943	1001	362	911	330	810
1944	1105	392	1005	357	795
1945	1005	364	1029	364	810

Presidency Division

1920	1146	405	1421	502	792
1921	1079	330	1338	409	685
1922	1033	248	1281	308	538
1923	1031	285	1279	353	618
1924	997	291	1236	361	655
1925	1044	301	1295	374	646
1926	1069	348	1325	432	730
1927	1079	275	1338	341	570
1928	1381	334	1713	414	541
1929	1098	337	1361	418	687
1930	1103	345	1368	427	700
1931	1213	441	1504	546	814
1932	1164	404	1443	500	777

1.2   AUTUMN RICE (*cont.*)

Year	Official acreage (in '000s)	Output ('000 tons)	Revised acreage (in '000s)	Revised output ('000 tons)	Yield per acre (in lbs)
1933	1156	429	1434	532	830
1934	1136	326	1409	404	643
1935	1168	361	1448	448	692
1936	1190	371	1476	460	699
1937	1248	406	1547	503	728
1938	1269	198	1574	245	349
1939	1237	332	1533	412	602
1940	1209	309	1499	384	574
1941	1266	469	1266	469	830
1942	1278	317	1278	317	556
1943	1496	580	1540	598	869
1944	1532	573	1578	590	837
1945	1393	532	1581	532	855

Burdwan

Year	Official acreage (in '000s)	Output ('000 tons)	Revised acreage (in '000s)	Revised output ('000 tons)	Yield per acre (in lbs)
1920	525	156	336	100	664
1921	519	179	332	115	775
1922	407	155	261	99	851
1923	393	121	252	78	691
1924	312	107	200	68	768
1925	559	156	358	100	625
1926	567	227	363	145	896
1927	526	141	337	90	601
1928	697	282	446	181	907
1929	606	210	388	134	775
1930	619	226	396	145	818
1931	657	219	420	140	746
1932	616	221	394	142	804
1933	695	268	445	172	864
1934	522	147	334	94	629
1935	498	146	318	94	659
1936	572	249	366	159	975
1937	542	199	347	127	822
1938	531	187	340	120	788
1939	516	173	330	111	752
1940	475	112	304	71	526
1941	554	211	554	211	854
1942	571	145	571	145	570
1943	576	211	380	139	819
1944	572	178	377	118	698
1945	520	165	380	165	709

Note: A single Revision Factor is used to obtain the figures in the revised series up to
   1940/41. No adjustment is made in the case of the figures for 1941/42 and 1942/
   43. Separate Revision Factors are used for the subsequent years.

1.3   SUMMER RICE

All-Bengal

1920	426	199	563	263	1048
1921	375	152	495	201	908
1922	403	166	532	219	923
1923	408	157	538	207	862
1924	422	165	557	218	876
1925	375	139	495	183	830
1926	408	151	539	199	829
1927	400	160	528	211	896
1928	398	161	525	213	908
1929	400	160	528	211	896
1930	380	156	501	206	922
1931	394	152	521	201	864
1932	394	198	520	261	1126
1933	399	200	526	264	1126
1934	408	209	538	276	1148
1935	404	189	533	249	1048
1936	432	203	571	269	1054
1937	414	198	546	261	1073
1938	425	207	561	273	1090
1939	418	194	551	255	1038
1940	437	203	577	268	1038
1941	443	206	584	272	1041
1942	580	266	557	256	1029
1943	508	238	554	260	1052
1944	557	242	557	242	974
1945	508	214	543	214	945

Rajshahi

1920	51	24	54	25	1048
1921	55	22	58	24	908
1922	51	21	54	22	923
1923	59	23	62	24	862
1924	58	23	61	24	876
1925	57	21	61	23	830
1926	57	21	60	22	829
1927	51	21	54	22	896
1928	52	21	55	22	908
1929	53	21	56	22	896
1930	47	19	50	21	922
1931	51	20	54	21	864
1932	50	25	53	27	1126
1933	51	25	54	27	1126
1934	53	27	56	29	1148
1935	45	21	48	23	1048
1936	62	29	66	31	1054
1937	62	30	66	32	1073
1938	60	29	64	31	1090

1.3   SUMMER RICE *(cont.)*

Year	Official acreage (in '000s)	Output ('000 tons)	Revised acreage (in '000s)	Revised output ('000 tons)	Yield per acre (in lbs)
1939	59	27	63	29	1038
1940	62	29	66	31	1038
1941	63	29	66	31	1041
1942	196	90	63	29	1029
1943	79	37	62	29	1052
1944	63	27	63	27	974
1945	57	13	32	13	945
Dacca					
1920	272	127	340	159	1048
1921	229	93	286	116	908
1922	248	102	310	128	923
1923	248	95	310	119	862
1924	272	106	340	133	876
1925	257	95	321	119	830
1926	258	95	322	119	829
1927	261	104	326	130	896
1928	263	107	329	133	908
1929	264	106	330	132	896
1930	266	109	332	137	922
1931	279	108	349	134	864
1932	279	140	349	175	1126
1933	282	142	352	177	1126
1934	294	151	367	188	1148
1935	302	141	378	177	1048
1936	304	143	380	179	1054
1937	284	136	355	170	1073
1938	284	138	355	173	1090
1939	280	130	349	162	1038
1940	286	133	358	166	1038
1941	289	134	361	168	1041
1942	280	129	373	171	1029
1943	300	141	378	178	1052
1944	379	165	379	165	974
1945	345	152	384	152	945
Chittagong					
1920	59	27	93	44	1048
1921	60	24	95	38	908
1922	60	25	95	39	923
1923	60	23	95	37	862
1924	55	21	87	34	876
1925	31	12	50	18	830

1926	32	12	51	19	829
1927	31	12	50	20	896
1928	29	12	45	18	908
1929	29	11	46	18	896
1930	38	16	60	25	922
1931	36	14	57	22	864
1932	36	18	57	29	1126
1933	36	18	56	28	1126
1934	34	17	53	27	1148
1935	34	16	54	25	1048
1936	35	16	55	26	1054
1937	35	17	55	27	1073
1938	33	16	53	26	1090
1939	34	16	55	25	1038
1940	44	20	70	32	1038
1941	46	21	73	34	1041
1942	47	22	48	22	1029
1943	49	23	47	22	1052
1944	45	20	45	20	974
1945	41	19	49	19	1038

Presidency Division

1920	17	8	24	11	1048
1921	19	8	27	11	908
1922	17	7	25	10	923
1923	17	7	25	9	862
1924	16	6	23	9	876
1925	17	6	24	9	830
1926	47	17	66	25	829
1927	46	18	65	26	896
1928	43	18	61	25	908
1929	43	17	61	24	896
1930	15	6	21	9	922
1931	16	6	23	9	864
1932	16	8	23	11	1126
1933	17	9	24	12	1126
1934	17	9	24	12	1148
1935	16	7	22	10	1048
1936	26	12	36	17	1054
1937	27	13	38	18	1073
1938	41	20	58	28	1090
1939	30	14	42	20	1038
1940	28	13	40	18	1038
1941	29	13	41	19	1041
1942	33	15	41	19	1029
1943	57	27	41	19	1052
1944	42	18	42	18	974
1945	38	3	8	3	180

1.3   SUMMER RICE (*cont.*)

Year	Official acreage (in 'ooos)	Output ('ooo tons)	Revised acreage (in 'ooos)	Revised output ('ooo tons)	Yield per acre (in lbs)
			Burdwan		
1920	28	13	120	56	1048
1921	12	5	52	21	908
1922	28	11	117	48	923
1923	25	9	105	40	862
1924	22	8	92	36	876
1925	13	5	54	20	830
1926	14	5	61	23	829
1927	11	4	45	18	896
1928	10	4	44	18	908
1929	11	4	47	19	896
1930	14	6	58	24	922
1931	13	5	55	21	864
1932	13	7	56	28	1126
1933	13	7	57	29	1126
1934	11	5	45	23	1148
1935	6	3	26	12	1048
1936	6	3	26	12	1054
1937	5	3	23	11	1073
1938	6	3	25	12	1090
1939	15	7	64	29	1038
1940	17	8	73	34	1038
1941	17	8	71	33	1041
1942	24	11	33	15	1029
1943	24	11	30	14	1052
1944	28	12	28	12	974
1945	26	28	71	28	2428

Note: As the condition factors at the district level were not available yield per acre is assumed to be the same in all the regions. The figures in the revised series up to 1941/42 are obtained by using the same adjustment factor. Separate Revision Factors are used for the subsequent years.

1.4   GRAM

			All-Bengal		
1920	162	45	299	82	618
1921	142	32	262	60	510
1922	141	34	260	62	535
1923	130	29	241	54	498
1924	130	33	241	62	576
1925	136	30	251	55	489

1926	126	32	233	59	563
1927	92	18	170	33	431
1928	143	38	264	71	602
1929	154	42	285	78	613
1930	152	44	280	81	648
1931	180	50	332	92	619
1932	177	57	327	105	720
1933	175	52	324	96	665
1934	207	70	383	130	760
1935	183	48	338	88	583
1936	242	76	448	141	705
1937	280	71	517	132	572
1938	342	96	632	178	630
1939	310	84	573	156	611
1940	319	76	591	141	533
1941	316	92	584	170	652
1942	428	132	565	174	689
1943	429	113	584	153	589
1944	600	149	600	149	557
1945	496	110	493	110	498

Rajshahi

1920	27	9	69	22	713
1921	26	7	66	19	636
1922	26	6	66	16	557
1923	24	5	60	14	514
1924	23	6	58	15	567
1925	23	5	57	14	533
1926	23	7	58	17	656
1927	24	6	59	15	571
1928	26	8	66	20	663
1929	28	8	72	20	623
1930	33	9	83	23	621
1931	34	9	86	24	623
1932	33	10	83	26	693
1933	34	9	85	23	613
1934	39	13	99	34	774
1935	42	13	105	33	696
1936	43	14	109	37	754
1937	43	12	108	31	652
1938	45	12	114	31	616
1939	37	10	95	25	583
1940	49	11	125	27	479
1941	49	13	123	32	588
1942	79	22	120	33	617
1943	62	17	123	33	603
1944	126	33	126	33	586
1945	104	24	96	24	509

1.4 GRAM (*cont.*)

Year	Official acreage (in '000s)	Output ('000 tons)	Revised acreage (in '000s)	Revised output ('000 tons)	Yield per acre (in lbs)
		Dacca			
1920	7	2	24	8	764
1921	8	2	27	8	670
1922	8	2	29	8	587
1923	9	2	31	8	575
1924	9	2	32	9	619
1925	9	2	31	8	583
1926	9	2	31	8	586
1927	9	2	31	8	595
1928	9	3	31	9	632
1929	9	3	31	9	638
1930	9	3	31	10	696
1931	10	3	35	11	679
1932	9	3	32	12	843
1933	8	3	28	9	747
1934	10	4	35	13	831
1935	10	3	36	12	751
1936	12	4	42	14	775
1937	11	3	39	11	619
1938	10	3	35	10	656
1939	10	3	36	10	647
1940	11	3	37	10	628
1941	10	3	36	11	677
1942	14	4	38	10	591
1943	14	4	39	10	589
1944	40	10	40	10	579
1945	33	8	21	8	519
		Presidency Division			
1920	109	28	175	44	569
1921	92	18	147	29	437
1922	90	20	144	32	501
1923	84	18	134	28	472
1924	85	21	135	34	556
1925	91	19	146	30	456
1926	78	18	124	29	521
1927	46	6	73	10	296
1928	92	24	147	38	576
1929	101	27	162	43	600
1930	92	27	147	43	647
1931	120	33	192	52	607
1932	119	37	190	59	699

1933	118	35	189	55	656
1934	142	47	227	76	747
1935	118	28	188	44	525
1936	170	51	271	81	672
1937	208	50	332	80	542
1938	267	75	428	120	629
1939	243	65	389	105	603
1940	243	59	388	94	540
1941	237	70	379	112	664
1942	309	99	367	118	717
1943	326	84	379	98	580
1944	392	95	392	95	544
1945	324	71	346	71	490

Burdwan

1920	18	6	39	13	714
1921	16	5	35	10	656
1922	16	5	35	10	663
1923	13	3	30	8	572
1924	13	4	30	9	689
1925	13	3	28	7	583
1926	16	4	36	10	626
1927	13	3	29	7	537
1928	16	4	35	10	638
1929	15	5	34	10	669
1930	18	5	39	12	683
1931	15	5	34	10	676
1932	16	6	35	13	827
1933	15	5	33	12	813
1934	16	6	35	13	805
1935	13	4	29	8	623
1936	17	7	38	15	869
1937	18	6	40	12	705
1938	19	6	42	12	664
1939	18	6	41	14	760
1940	17	4	37	9	525
1941	19	6	43	13	658
1942	27	8	39	11	634
1943	26	8	39	12	667
1944	40	10	40	10	574
1945	33	8	28	8	518

Note: Revised figures on acreage and output for the period up to 1941/42 are calculated on the basis of the assumption that the margin of error was uniform. Separate adjustment factors are used for the subsequent years.

Year	Official acreage (in '000s)	Output ('000 tons)	Revised acreage (in '000s)	Revised output ('000 tons)	Yield per acre (in lbs)
		1.5 WHEAT			
		All-Bengal			
1920	117	31	132	35	600
1921	124	26	140	30	475
1922	125	29	141	32	516
1923	120	23	136	26	430
1924	126	31	143	35	543
1925	131	28	147	31	475
1926	129	32	146	36	556
1927	107	22	120	25	468
1928	123	31	139	35	561
1929	126	34	143	39	606
1930	143	35	161	39	542
1931	145	35	164	39	533
1932	143	41	161	46	641
1933	146	40	164	45	617
1934	155	51	175	57	735
1935	127	32	144	37	572
1936	150	46	169	52	688
1937	161	45	182	51	633
1938	174	44	197	50	565
1939	177	45	200	51	573
1940	169	34	191	38	446
1941	170	41	192	47	546
1942	179	53	191	57	670
1943	191	50	195	51	588
1944	198	46	198	46	523
1945	198	42	202	42	474
		Rajshahi			
1920	63	19	63	19	661
1921	72	17	72	17	526
1922	73	17	73	17	512
1923	70	14	70	14	451
1924	69	18	69	18	575
1925	70	16	70	16	496
1926	68	18	68	18	590
1927	63	15	63	15	539
1928	56	13	56	13	534
1929	66	18	66	18	609
1930	78	19	78	19	546
1931	79	19	79	19	541
1932	80	22	80	22	612

1933	81	22	81	22	599
1934	81	27	81	27	750
1935	75	20	75	20	598
1936	73	23	73	23	706
1937	75	19	75	19	579
1938	73	18	73	18	552
1939	78	20	78	20	568
1940	78	15	78	15	422
1941	78	18	78	18	527
1942	82	28	82	28	756
1943	85	23	85	23	601
1944	81	19	81	19	531
1945	81	18	90	18	492

Dacca

1920	7	1	9	2	454
1921	7	1	8	1	362
1922	7	2	9	2	500
1923	7	1	9	2	401
1924	7	2	9	2	565
1925	7	2	9	2	502
1926	7	2	9	2	499
1927	7	2	9	2	523
1928	7	2	8	2	579
1929	7	2	8	2	573
1930	7	2	8	3	686
1931	12	3	15	4	646
1932	12	3	15	4	635
1933	12	3	14	3	502
1934	13	4	16	5	690
1935	10	3	13	4	657
1936	10	3	12	4	679
1937	10	3	12	4	648
1938	9	3	12	3	669
1939	8	3	10	3	693
1940	7	2	9	3	635
1941	7	2	9	3	705
1942	8	2	13	3	543
1943	15	5	13	4	686
1944	13	3	13	3	568
1945	13	3	14	3	506

Presidency Division

1920	36	9	34	8	537
1921	36	6	34	6	400
1922	34	8	33	7	495
1923	34	6	33	6	379
1924	41	8	39	8	460

1.5   WHEAT *(cont.)*

Year	Official acreage (in 'ooos)	Output ('ooo tons)	Revised acreage (in 'ooos)	Revised output ('ooo tons)	Yield per acre (in lbs)
1925	43	8	41	7	398
1926	44	10	42	9	496
1927	29	4	28	4	295
1928	49	12	47	12	567
1929	43	11	41	11	583
1930	46	10	44	10	483
1931	41	8	40	8	439
1932	39	11	37	11	657
1933	40	11	39	11	636
1934	48	15	46	14	712
1935	31	7	30	6	489
1936	55	16	53	15	651
1937	64	19	62	19	678
1938	80	19	77	19	543
1939	80	20	77	19	546
1940	75	15	72	14	441
1941	76	18	73	18	541
1942	77	21	67	18	605
1943	79	20	69	17	557
1944	71	16	71	16	493
1945	71	14	77	14	441
Burdwan					
1920	11	3	30	7	547
1921	10	2	28	6	450
1922	11	3	29	8	625
1923	9	2	25	5	472
1924	10	3	27	8	648
1925	11	3	29	8	625
1926	10	3	28	8	625
1927	8	2	22	5	482
1928	12	3	32	9	661
1929	11	3	30	9	704
1930	13	4	34	10	658
1931	13	4	35	11	682
1932	13	4	35	12	773
1933	13	5	35	12	776
1934	13	5	36	12	767
1935	11	3	30	7	547
1936	12	4	32	11	761
1937	12	4	32	10	712
1938	12	4	32	10	711

1939	11	4	31	10	707
1940	9	2	25	6	541
1941	10	3	26	7	641
1942	12	3	32	8	591
1943	12	3	32	8	579
1944	32	8	32	8	548
1945	32	7	21	7	489

Note: Official acreage and output data for the period up to 1941/42 are uniformly deflated. Data for the subsequent years are revised by different factors.

1.6 BARLEY

All-Bengal

1920	96	29	200	60	677
1921	83	25	173	52	675
1922	84	24	174	50	648
1923	82	23	170	48	628
1924	79	22	164	46	624
1925	86	22	180	46	573
1926	75	23	156	48	687
1927	67	18	138	38	611
1928	82	26	170	54	710
1929	84	27	175	56	720
1930	86	28	179	58	729
1931	88	27	182	56	695
1932	86	27	179	56	703
1933	85	24	176	50	632
1934	91	30	190	63	738
1935	90	26	187	54	647
1936	95	31	198	65	731
1937	95	30	198	62	707
1938	101	32	211	67	710
1939	98	31	205	65	709
1940	102	29	213	60	637
1941	103	33	213	68	718
1942	136	45	206	68	741
1943	135	41	208	63	680
1944	210	66	210	66	706
1945	166	44	166	44	594

Rajshahi

1920	47	14	176	53	677
1921	36	11	137	41	675
1922	37	11	137	40	648
1923	36	10	134	38	628
1924	35	10	129	36	624
1925	34	9	129	33	573

1.6   BARLEY *(cont.)*

Year	Official acreage (in '000s)	Output ('000 tons)	Revised acreage (in '000s)	Revised output ('000 tons)	Yield per acre (in lbs)
1926	22	7	84	26	687
1927	20	6	76	21	611
1928	23	7	85	27	710
1929	25	8	93	30	720
1930	26	8	97	31	729
1931	26	8	99	31	695
1932	27	8	100	31	703
1933	26	7	98	28	632
1934	30	10	114	37	738
1935	32	9	118	34	647
1936	33	11	123	40	731
1937	32	10	121	38	707
1938	37	12	137	43	710
1939	35	11	129	41	709
1940	38	11	142	40	637
1941	38	12	144	46	718
1942	63	21	117	39	741
1943	58	18	117	35	680
1944	117	37	117	37	706
1945	84	22	84	22	594

Dacca

Year	Official acreage (in '000s)	Output ('000 tons)	Revised acreage (in '000s)	Revised output ('000 tons)	Yield per acre (in lbs)
1920	28	8	40	12	677
1921	27	8	39	12	675
1922	27	8	39	11	648
1923	27	8	39	11	628
1924	27	7	39	11	624
1925	32	8	46	12	573
1926	33	10	47	14	687
1927	33	9	47	13	611
1928	32	10	47	15	710
1929	32	10	45	15	720
1930	32	10	46	15	729
1931	32	10	47	14	695
1932	31	10	44	14	703
1933	31	9	45	13	632
1934	32	11	47	15	738
1935	33	10	48	14	647
1936	32	11	47	15	731
1937	32	10	46	14	707
1938	31	10	44	14	710
1939	31	10	44	14	709

1940	31	9	45	13	637
1941	31	10	44	14	718
1942	36	12	47	16	741
1943	34	10	47	14	680
1944	47	15	47	15	706
1945	42	11	42	11	594

Presidency Division

1920	14	4	18	5	677
1921	13	4	17	5	675
1922	13	4	17	5	648
1923	12	3	15	4	628
1924	12	3	15	4	624
1925	14	4	18	5	573
1926	15	4	18	6	687
1927	10	3	12	3	611
1928	22	7	27	9	710
1929	22	7	28	9	720
1930	23	7	29	9	729
1931	24	7	30	9	695
1932	24	7	30	9	703
1933	23	6	28	8	632
1934	24	8	30	10	738
1935	22	6	28	8	647
1936	26	9	33	11	731
1937	27	8	34	11	707
1938	30	10	38	12	710
1939	29	9	37	12	709
1940	30	8	38	11	637
1941	30	10	38	12	718
1942	33	11	40	13	741
1943	39	12	41	13	680
1944	43	13	43	13	706
1945	35	9	35	9	594

Burdwan

1920	7	2	8	2	677
1921	6	2	7	2	675
1922	7	2	8	2	648
1923	7	2	8	2	628
1924	5	1	6	2	624
1925	6	1	6	2	573
1926	5	2	6	2	687
1927	4	1	5	1	611
1928	5	2	6	2	710
1929	5	2	6	2	720
1930	6	2	7	2	729
1931	5	2	6	2	695
1932	5	2	6	2	703

1.6   BARLEY *(cont.)*

Year	Official acreage (in 'ooos)	Output ('ooo tons)	Revised acreage (in 'ooos)	Revised output ('ooo tons)	Yield per acre (in lbs)
1933	5	I	6	2	632
1934	5	2	6	2	738
1935	4	I	4	I	647
1936	4	I	5	2	731
1937	4	I	5	2	707
1938	4	I	5	2	710
1939	4	I	5	2	709
1940	3	I	4	I	637
1941	4	I	4	I	718
1942	4	I	4	~ I	741
1943	4	I	4	I	680
1944	4	I	4	I	706
1945	3	I	3	I	594

Note: No data either on condition factor or standard yield were published. Therefore, yield is assumed to have been the same in all the districts. Official acreage and output data for the period upto 1941/42 are revised by the same factor. Different factors are used for the later years. Data on output were published in the *Estimates*.

1.7   JUTE

All-Bengal

1920	2168	5304	2602	6364	978
1921	1316	3586	1579	4304	1090
1922	1197	3533	1436	4240	1181
1923	2412	7471	2895	8965	1239
1924	2360	7173	2832	8608	1216
1925	2680	7332	2867	7845	1095
1926	3314	10626	3546	11370	1283
1927	2929	8989	3134	9618	1228
1928	2667	8502	2854	9098	1275
1929	2983	9136	3192	9775	1225
1930	3028	9877	2756	8989	1305
1931	1597	4981	1868	5827	1248
1932	1821	5747	2131	6724	1262
1933	2142	7055	2506	8254	1317
1934	2321	7644	2716	8944	1317
1935	1898	6475	2221	7576	1364
1936	2220	7940	2575	9210	1431
1937	2161	6976	2507	8092	1291
1938	2475	5842	2870	6777	944
1939	2504	8248	2904	9567	1318

1940	4938	14680	3604	10717	1189
1941	1533	4246	1655	4585	1108
1942	2704	8173	2920	8827	1209
1943	2146	6077	2318	6563	1133
1944	1694	5525	1830	5967	1305
1945	2033	6771	2195	7313	1333

Rajshahi

1920	635	1573	762	1887	990
1921	381	917	457	1101	964
1922	398	1189	477	1427	1196
1923	676	1937	811	2325	1147
1924	685	2317	822	2781	1353
1925	759	2083	812	2228	1098
1926	951	3038	1017	3250	1278
1927	843	2481	902	2654	1177
1928	759	2343	812	2507	1235
1929	844	2564	903	2744	1216
1930	820	2526	746	2299	1232
1931	438	1397	513	1634	1274
1932	515	1575	603	1842	1223
1933	631	2041	738	2388	1294
1934	639	2147	748	2512	1344
1935	505	1680	591	1965	1330
1936	584	2071	677	2402	1420
1937	597	1926	693	2235	1290
1938	692	1428	802	1656	826
1939	686	2069	796	2399	1206
1940	1613	4831	1178	3527	1198
1941	521	1422	562	1536	1092
1942	891	2649	962	2861	1190
1943	720	1872	778	2022	1039
1944	589	1920	636	2073	1304
1945	706	2347	763	2534	1329

Dacca

1920	1039	2629	1247	3155	1012
1921	635	1892	762	2270	1192
1922	526	1620	631	1944	1233
1923	1178	3883	1413	4659	1319
1924	1122	3411	1347	4093	1216
1925	1201	3268	1285	3496	1089
1926	1482	5145	1586	5505	1389
1927	1334	4235	1427	4531	1270
1928	1262	4099	1350	4386	1299
1929	1418	4363	1517	4669	1231
1930	1493	5121	1359	4660	1372
1931	804	2460	941	2878	1224
1932	901	2907	1054	3401	1291

1.7   JUTE *(cont.)*

Year	Official acreage (in '000s)	Output ('000 tons)	Revised acreage (in '000s)	Revised output ('000 tons)	Yield per acre (in lbs)
1933	1013	3398	1185	3976	1342
1934	1134	3876	1327	4535	1367
1935	916	3350	1072	3920	1463
1936	1075	4046	1247	4693	1506
1937	1021	3289	1184	3815	1289
1938	1231	3124	1428	3624	1015
1939	1264	4403	1466	5107	1394
1940	1947	5913	1421	4316	1215
1941	599	1638	647	1769	1093
1942	1142	3490	1233	3769	1223
1943	888	2629	959	2839	1184
1944	669	2188	723	2364	1308
1945	803	2708	867	2925	1349

Chittagong

Year	Official acreage (in '000s)	Output ('000 tons)	Revised acreage (in '000s)	Revised output ('000 tons)	Yield per acre (in lbs)
1920	255	470	306	564	739
1921	158	426	189	511	1082
1922	159	479	190	575	1208
1923	317	1007	381	1209	1270
1924	302	746	363	895	987
1925	374	1014	400	1085	1084
1926	422	1296	452	1387	1228
1927	375	1137	401	1217	1212
1928	318	1114	341	1192	1400
1929	371	1113	397	1191	1199
1930	372	1212	339	1103	1302
1931	168	523	197	612	1244
1932	215	739	251	865	1377
1933	233	794	273	929	1362
1934	303	887	355	1038	1170
1935	236	708	276	829	1199
1936	270	1000	314	1160	1480
1937	255	905	296	1050	1418
1938	278	718	323	832	1031
1939	292	1106	338	1283	1516
1940	567	1831	414	1337	1293
1941	157	426	169	460	1086
1942	278	924	301	998	1327
1943	197	611	212	660	1244
1944	158	570	171	616	1442
1945	190	686	205	740	1446

Appendix: statistical tables

Presidency Division

1920	190	489	228	587	1029
1921	113	275	135	329	975
1922	96	206	115	248	862
1923	212	575	254	690	1088
1924	230	660	276	792	1146
1925	302	840	323	899	1113
1926	394	1004	422	1074	1019
1927	320	949	342	1015	1186
1928	279	802	299	858	1150
1929	304	950	325	1017	1250
1930	296	875	269	796	1182
1931	156	500	183	585	1282
1932	160	427	187	500	1069
1933	219	659	256	771	1204
1934	206	612	241	717	1189
1935	216	661	253	773	1224
1936	259	719	300	834	1111
1937	257	760	298	882	1183
1938	243	477	282	553	786
1939	238	604	276	700	1014
1940	688	1741	502	1271	1012
1941	218	651	236	703	1192
1942	337	954	364	1030	1133
1943	295	845	319	912	1145
1944	238	721	257	779	1211
1945	286	877	309	947	1227

Burdwan

1920	50	142	60	170	1143
1921	31	76	37	92	1001
1922	19	39	23	47	826
1923	30	69	36	83	910
1924	20	40	24	48	790
1925	44	128	47	137	1160
1926	65	143	70	153	879
1927	57	187	61	200	1314
1928	49	144	52	154	1178
1929	46	145	49	155	1263
1930	47	143	43	130	1219
1931	30	101	35	118	1343
1932	31	99	36	116	1288
1933	46	162	54	190	1411
1934	39	122	46	143	1255
1935	25	76	29	89	1219
1936	32	104	37	120	1297

1.7   JUTE *(cont.)*

Year	Official acreage (in '000s)	Output ('000 tons)	Revised acreage (in '000s)	Revised output ('000 tons)	Yield per acre (in lbs)
1937	30	95	35	110	1268
1938	31	96	36	111	1233
1939	24	·66	28	77	1098
1940	122	364	89	265	1191
1941	38	110	41	119	1159
1942	56	156	61	168	1112
1943	46	120	50	130	1043
1944	40	125	43	135	1261
1945	48	155	52	167	1295

Note: As shown in chapter 1, Table 1.12, the margin of error was not the same during the whole period. Therefore, the figures in the revised series are calculated by using separate Revision Factors for the five quinquennial periods. Data on acreage and output were often revised by the Director of Agriculture and published in the Calcutta Gazette. These figures have been used in preparing the official series. Output figures are in thousand bales.

1.8   MUSTARD

All-Bengal

1920	882	150	679	115	380
1921	895	145	689	111	362
1922	753	127	580	98	378
1923	733	116	564	89	355
1924	737	118	567	91	357
1925	731	98	563	75	299
1926	757	129	583	99	382
1927	741	126	570	97	382
1928	700	120	539	92	383
1929	705	130	543	100	415
1930	769	137	592	105	399
1931	770	136	593	105	396
1932	716	153	551	118	479
1933	693	165	534	127	532
1934	724	180	557	139	557
1935	711	157	547	121	496
1936	740	179	570	138	542
1937	771	156	593	120	454
1938	771	149	594	115	433
1939	764	140	589	108	410
1940	753	129	580	99	384
1941	741	145	571	112	438

1942	885	163	558	103	412
1943	809	145	550	98	400
1944	549	92	549	92	375
1945	549	92	551	92	375

Rajshahi

1920	361	63	296	52	393
1921	325	56	267	46	385
1922	302	51	247	42	380
1923	312	49	256	40	354
1924	300	51	246	42	378
1925	303	48	248	40	356
1926	308	52	252	42	376
1927	308	49	253	40	352
1928	295	50	242	41	378
1929	289	49	237	41	383
1930	325	58	267	47	398
1931	339	64	278	52	422
1932	316	70	259	57	492
1933	297	71	244	58	532
1934	320	79	262	65	552
1935	323	70	265	58	489
1936	327	74	268	61	507
1937	358	69	294	57	431
1938	354	70	290	57	441
1939	341	61	280	50	402
1940	343	55	281	45	362
1941	335	65	275	53	432
1942	453	77	277	47	382
1943	349	56	279	45	362
1944	280	43	280	43	341
1945	280	43	253	43	341

Dacca

1920	399	68	283	49	384
1921	451	73	320	52	362
1922	332	55	236	39	371
1923	305	48	217	34	352
1924	305	48	217	34	351
1925	296	30	210	21	224
1926	308	57	219	40	414
1927	300	59	213	42	442
1928	283	49	201	35	390
1929	309	62	219	44	449
1930	318	57	226	40	399
1931	314	51	223	37	367
1932	281	57	199	40	453
1933	278	69	197	49	555

1.8   MUSTARD *(cont.)*

Year	Official acreage (in '000s)	Output ('000 tons)	Revised acreage (in '000s)	Revised output ('000 tons)	Yield per acre (in lbs)
1934	280	75	199	53	596
1935	283	69	201	49	543
1936	282	76	200	54	604
1037	283	59	201	42	464
1938	278	53	197	38	428
1939	281	49	199	35	395
1940	272	49	193	35	401
1941	275	53	195	38	431
1942	279	53	178	34	423
1943	294	56	177	33	424
1944	172	32	172	32	416
1945	172	32	185	32	416
Chittagong					
1920	40	6	35	5	328
1921	40	6	35	5	325
1922	41	9	36	8	478
1923	40	8	35	7	451
1924	53	7	46	6	307
1925	54	7	47	6	301
1926	64	8	55	7	293
1927	61	9	53	8	347
1928	43	8	37	7	408
1929	32	6	27	5	397
1930	50	9	43	7	384
1931	39	7	34	6	393
1932	41	9	35	8	476
1933	39	8	34	7	487
1934	39	8	34	7	477
1935	39	8	34	7	462
1936	40	9	35	8	499
1937	40	9	35	8	515
1938	39	7	34	6	393
1939	37	7	32	6	429
1940	32	7	28	6	506
1941	34	7	30	6	454
1942	37	9	31	7	530
1943	40	10	30	7	540
1944	30	6	30	6	451
1945	30	6	37	6	451
Presidency Division					
1920	59	9	42	6	327
1921	58	7	42	5	263

1922	58	8	42	6	327
1923	51	7	37	5	291
1924	52	7	37	5	318
1925	52	8	37	6	350
1926	53	8	38	6	337
1927	52	6	38	5	273
1928	57	9	41	6	348
1929	51	9	37	6	389
1930	51	9	37	7	408
1931	55	9	39	7	385
1932	56	13	40	9	503
1933	57	11	41	8	441
1934	61	13	44	9	472
1935	46	7	33	5	323
1936	63	13	45	9	459
1937	62	14	45	10	493
1938	79	15	57	11	433
1939	83	17	60	12	460
1940	84	13	60	10	360
1941	74	16	54	12	484
1942	92	19	52	11	472
1943	98	17	53	9	393
1944	54	9	54	9	370
1945	54	9	54	9	370

Burdwan

1920	24	4	14	2	334
1921	21	3	12	2	341
1922	20	4	11	2	415
1923	25	4	14	2	377
1924	27	5	15	3	380
1925	27	4	15	3	368
1926	24	4	14	2	397
1927	18	3	11	2	322
1928	22	4	13	2	410
1929	25	5	15	3	421
1930	25	5	14	3	434
1931	24	5	14	3	448
1932	23	6	13	3	578
1933	23	6	13	3	562
1934	24	6	14	3	535
1935	19	3	11	2	396
1936	28	7	16	4	580
1937	28	6	16	3	489
1938	23	5	13	3	452
1939	23	5	13	3	478
1940	22	4	13	2	412
1941	22	4	13	2	430
1942	24	5	14	3	445

1.8   MUSTARD *(cont.)*

Year	Official acreage (in 'ooos)	Output ('ooo tons)	Revised acreage (in 'ooos)	Revised output ('ooo tons)	Yield per acre (in lbs)
1943	28	6	14	3	445
1944	14	3	14	3	410
1945	14	3	22	3	410

Note: Officially published data for the period up to 1941/42 are revised by the same factor to obtain the figures in the revised series. Separate adjustment factors are used for the later years.

1.9   TOBACCO

All-Bengal

1920	258	78	132	40	680
1921	298	90	152	46	680
1922	299	91	152	46	680
1923	288	87	147	45	680
1924	280	85	143	43	680
1925	293	92	150	47	700
1926	295	123	151	63	931
1927	290	120	148	61	926
1928	291	121	149	62	932
1929	295	123	151	63	936
1930	284	120	145	61	945
1931	293	123	149	63	939
1932	281	139	143	71	1109
1933	286	123	146	63	964
1934	308	144	157	73	1047
1935	307	129	157	66	938
1936	307	135	157	69	981
1937	313	127	160	65	907
1938	316	132	161	67	937
1939	316	128	161	65	905
1940	322	123	164	63	860
1941	321	135	164	69	940
1942	304	128	164	69	947
1943	300	120	165	66	894
1944	165	68	165	68	920
1945	174	69	176	69	883

Rajshahi

1920	200	61	80	24	680
1921	225	68	90	27	680
1922	225	68	90	27	680

1923	224	68	90	27	680
1924	223	68	89	27	680
1925	242	76	97	30	700
1926	238	99	95	40	936
1927	236	102	94	41	971
1928	235	103	94	41	977
1929	240	105	96	42	980
1930	229	100	92	40	976
1931	236	103	95	41	977
1932	224	114	89	46	1141
1933	230	98	92	39	959
1934	250	118	100	47	1053
1935	251	105	100	42	940
1936	250	110	100	44	991
1937	250	99	100	40	889
1938	251	105	100	42	936
1939	250	100	100	40	893
1940	254	95	102	38	838
1941	253	105	101	42	927
1942	233	96	102	42	928
1v43	226	88	104	40	868
1944	104	41	104	41	890
1945	110	42	105	42	856

Dacca

1920	25	7	22	7	680
1921	42	13	38	11	680
1922	42	13	38	12	680
1923	37	11	33	10	680
1924	33	10	30	9	680
1925	27	8	24	8	700
1926	27	11	25	10	939
1927	26	9	24	8	753
1928	26	8	24	8	717
1929	26	8	24	8	720
1930	28	10	26	9	799
1931	29	10	27	9	739
1932	30	14	28	12	1007
1933	29	14	27	12	1037
1934	31	15	29	14	1091
1935	32	14	29	13	1009
1936	33	15	30	14	1008
1937	39	19	36	17	1090
1938	40	18	36	16	1001
1939	40	18	37	16	1002
1940	41	19	38	17	1028
1941	42	20	38	18	1063
1942	43	21	34	16	1073
1943	46	21	34	16	1018

1.9 TOBACCO *(cont.)*

Year	Official acreage (in '000s)	Output ('000 tons)	Revised acreage (in '000s)	Revised output ('000 tons)	Yield per acre (in lbs)
1944	34	15	34	15	1006
1945	36	16	44	16	962
			Chittagong		
1920	9	3	11	3	680
1921	9	3	11	3	680
1922	8	2	10	3	680
1923	10	3	12	4	680
1924	9	3	11	3	680
1925	10	3	12	4	700
1926	10	4	12	5	842
1927	9	3	12	4	829
1928	9	3	12	4	822
1929	9	3	12	4	844
1930	9	4	12	5	920
1931	10	4	12	5	862
1932	10	4	12	5	946
1933	10	4	13	5	939
1934	10	4	13	5	936
1935	10	5	13	6	1006
1936	10	4	13	5	850
1937	10	4	13	5	854
1938	10	4	13	5	855
1939	10	4	13	5	797
1940	10	4	13	5	817
1941	10	4	13	5	822
1942	11	4	13	5	899
1943	10	4	14	5	899
1944	14	6	14	6	937
1945	14	6	12	6	902
			Presidency Division		
1920	19	6	23	7	680
1921	18	5	21	7	680
1922	19	6	22	7	680
1923	12	4	15	5	680
1924	12	4	14	4	680
1925	11	4	14	4	700
1926	14	6	17	7	939
1927	12	3	15	4	576
1928	13	4	16	5	715
1929	13	4	16	5	703

Appendix: statistical tables

1930	10	3	12	4	722
1931	10	4	13	4	762
1932	10	4	12	5	893
1933	11	4	13	5	842
1934	11	5	14	5	901
1935	10	3	12	3	623
1936	10	4	12	4	788
1937	10	3	12	4	723
1938	11	4	14	5	852
1939	12	5	14	6	888
1940	12	4	15	5	769
1941	13	5	16	7	902
1942	15	6	12	5	956
1943	15	6	11	5	914
1944	11	4	11	4	911
1945	12	5	13	5	877

Burdwan

1920	6	2	3	1	680
1921	5	2	3	1	680
1922	5	2	3	1	680
1923	5	1	2	1	680
1924	4	1	2	1	680
1925	4	1	2	1	700
1926	7	2	3	1	816
1927	7	2	3	1	787
1928	7	3	4	1	796
1929	7	3	4	1	806
1930	7	3	4	1	877
1931	7	3	4	1	865
1932	7	3	4	2	1063
1933	7	3	3	1	1012
1934	5	2	2	1	993
1935	4	1	2	1	797
1936	4	2	2	1	936
1937	4	2	2	1	870
1938	4	1	2	1	795
1939	4	2	2	1	947
1940	4	2	2	1	899
1941	3	1	2	1	923
1942	3	1	2	1	774
1943	3	1	2	1	840
1944	2	1	2	1	916
1945	2	1	3	1	880

Note: Figures in the revised series up to 1941/42 are obtained by using the same Revision Factors. Different Revision Factors are used for the subsequent years.

Year	Official acreage (in '000s)	Output ('000 tons)	Revised acreage (in '000s)	Revised output ('000 tons)	Yield per acre (in lbs)
		I.10 SUGARCANE			
		All-Bengal			
1920	218	255	124	145	2621
1921	220	240	125	137	2446
1922	200	213	114	121	2390
1923	207	224	118	128	2424
1924	205	210	117	120	2295
1925	214	246	122	140	2571
1926	200	214	114	122	2403
1927	208	235	118	134	2535
1928	195	217	111	124	2497
1929	197	222	112	126	2528
1930	197	249	113	142	2827
1931	232	273	132	156	2633
1932	232	454	132	259	4381
1933	256	457	146	261	4007
1934	275	494	157	281	4018
1935	324	557	185	318	3848
1936	354	651	202	371	4123
1937	289	485	165	276	3760
1938	298	437	170	249	3289
1939	315	525	179	299	3738
1940	330	530	188	302	3595
1941	313	477	178	272	3417
1942	302	419	172	239	3115
1943	337	475	192	271	3153
1944	308	421	176	240	3058
1945	321	489	184	278	3412
		Rajshahi			
1920	66	76	40	46	2569
1921	69	78	42	47	2528
1922	61	68	37	41	2485
1923	69	75	42	46	2464
1924	71	79	44	48	2473
1925	74	73	45	45	2234
1926	68	71	42	43	2328
1927	72	82	44	50	2571
1928	72	84	44	51	2621
1929	72	80	44	49	2512
1930	72	96	44	59	2987
1931	92	115	56	70	2782
1932	88	158	53	96	4041

1933	93	172	57	105	4122
1934	102	188	62	115	4141
1935	118	215	72	131	4081
1936	132	262	81	160	4429
1937	106	188	64	115	3991
1938	109	165	66	101	3398
1939	131	219	80	134	3761
1940	139	221	85	135	3554
1941	119	175	73	107	3290
1942	114	134	70	82	2635
1943	119	138	73	84	2588
1944	100	116	61	71	2579
1945	104	133	69	81	2855

Dacca

1920	67	86	24	30	2872
1921	68	77	24	27	2514
1922	64	64	22	22	2254
1923	63	69	22	24	2440
1924	73	71	26	25	2183
1925	75	98	26	34	2924
1926	67	69	23	24	2332
1927	72	85	25	30	2650
1928	68	78	24	27	2542
1929	69	79	24	28	2550
1930	68	84	24	29	2751
1931	86	91	30	32	2366
1932	88	187	31	65	4759
1933	104	174	36	61	3771
1934	112	197	39	69	3931
1935	139	235	49	82	3797
1936	153	264	54	92	3849
1937	117	179	41	63	3430
1938	121	167	42	58	3078
1939	113	183	40	64	3623
1940	112	183	39	64	3638
1941	123	190	43	67	3478
1942	121	192	42	67	3551
1943	146	224	51	78	3432
1944	135	187	47	65	3108
1945	140	217	45	76	3474

Chittagong

1920	13	16	13	16	2799
1921	13	16	13	16	2743
1922	13	18	13	18	3124
1923	13	17	13	17	2997
1924	11	13	11	13	2531

1.10   SUGARCANE *(cont.)*

Year	Official acreage (in '000s)	Output ('000 tons)	Revised acreage (in '000s)	Revised output ('000 tons)	Yield per acre (in lbs)
1925	12	14	12	14	2749
1926	11	14	11	14	3010
1927	10	13	10	13	2932
1928	9	12	9	12	2985
1929	8	11	8	11	3011
1930	9	11	9	11	2952
1931	8	11	8	11	2975
1932	9	17	9	17	4543
1933	9	19	9	19	4657
1934	9	16	9	16	4062
1935	10	18	10	18	4091
1936	10	22	10	22	4697
1937	10	20	10	20	4302
1938	10	18	10	18	4069
1939	10	19	10	19	4231
1940	10	19	10	19	4122
1941	10	18	10	18	3977
1942	10	18	10	18	4106
1943	10	18	10	18	4136
1944	10	19	10	19	4201
1945	10	22	11	22	4698

Presidency Division

Year	Official acreage (in '000s)	Output ('000 tons)	Revised acreage (in '000s)	Revised output ('000 tons)	Yield per acre (in lbs)
1920	18	18	15	16	2326
1921	19	19	17	16	2196
1922	15	14	13	12	2078
1923	14	12	12	10	1925
1924	14	13	12	11	2081
1925	14	14	12	12	2241
1926	15	15	13	13	2152
1927	15	12	13	11	1802
1928	13	12	11	10	2018
1929	14	13	12	11	2123
1930	13	15	11	13	2482
1931	16	19	14	17	2676
1932	17	31	15	27	4077
1933	18	32	16	27	3866
1934	22	37	19	32	3743
1935	29	43	25	37	3304
1936	29	49	25	42	3789
1937	26	45	22	38	3838
1938	27	32	23	28	2703
1939	29	48	25	41	3664

1940	35	55	30	47	3509
1941	32	51	27	44	3571
1942	32	47	27	40	3285
1943	35	53	30	46	3431
1944	35	52	30	45	3332
1945	36	61	35	52	3756

Burdwan

1920	53	58	53	58	2423
1921	50	51	50	51	2258
1922	47	49	47	49	2342
1923	48	50	48	50	2341
1924	35	34	35	34	2174
1925	40	46	40	46	2591
1926	39	45	39	45	2592
1927	39	42	39	42	2442
1928	33	32	33	32	2188
1929	34	39	34	39	2563
1930	36	44	36	44	2748
1931	29	37	29	37	2830
1932	31	60	31	60	4395
1933	31	61	31	61	4340
1934	30	55	30	55	4119
1935	29	46	29	46	3605
1936	29	55	29	55	4310
1937	30	53	30	53	3977
1938	31	55	31	55	3988
1939	32	57	32	57	3966
1940	33	53	33	53	3548
1941	29	43	29	43	3319
1942	25	28	25	28	2576
1943	28	42	28	42	3424
1944	29	48	29	48	3769
1945	30	56	30	56	4209

Note: The same Revision Factor is used to obtain the figures in the revised series for the entire period.

1.11   SESAMUM

All-Bengal

1920	199	33	113	19	376
1921	207	34	118	19	367
1922	156	24	89	14	347
1923	157	25	90	14	359
1924	159	24	90	14	338
1925	153	25	87	14	368
1926	160	25	91	14	353

1.11 SESAMUM *(cont.)*

Year	Official acreage (in '000s)	Output ('000 tons)	Revised acreage (in '000s)	Revised output ('000 tons)	Yield per acre (in lbs)
1927	150	26	85	15	382
1928	153	23	87	13	336
1929	157	26	89	15	366
1930	153	26	87	15	387
1931	161	26	92	15	365
1932	161	36	92	20	500
1933	158	35	90	20	502
1934	159	35	90	20	492
1935	166	36	95	21	487
1936	184	41	105	23	501
1937	210	46	120	26	494
1938	188	32	107	18	375
1939	180	33	103	19	414
1940	174	33	99	19	428
1941	179	32	102	19	408
1942	172	33	98	19	434
1943	187	38	106	22	458
1944	189	39	103	22	464
1945	164	32	89	19	445
Rajshahi					
1920	39	6	11	2	354
1921	39	6	11	2	322
1922	35	4	9	1	286
1923	34	5	9	1	300
1924	32	4	9	1	296
1925	33	4	9	1	303
1926	42	6	11	2	347
1927	41	6	11	2	335
1928	41	6	11	2	338
1929	42	8	11	2	404
1930	43	7	12	2	388
1931	44	7	12	2	348
1932	41	8	11	2	429
1933	38	9	10	2	518
1934	42	9	11	3	504
1935	44	9	12	3	473
1936	43	9	12	3	485
1937	49	11	13	3	498
1938	40	6	11	2	362
1939	41	7	11	2	371
1940	40	9	11	2	479
1941	41	8	11	2	464

1942	37	6	10	2	397
1943	36	8	10	2	464
1944	35	7	10	2	433
1945	30	6	8	2	416

Dacca

1920	112	20	47	9	405
1921	117	21	49	9	400
1922	73	11	31	5	349
1923	80	13	34	6	369
1924	82	13	34	5	349
1925	76	12	32	5	357
1926	75	10	32	4	304
1927	66	12	28	5	413
1928	70	9	30	4	302
1929	72	10	30	4	319
1930	72	12	30	5	372
1931	75	12	31	5	349
1932	76	18	32	8	535
1933	76	16	32	7	488
1934	74	16	31	7	472
1935	82	18	34	8	504
1936	97	22	41	9	506
1937	115	26	48	11	513
1938	102	16	43	7	351
1939	92	17	39	7	419
1940	86	15	36	6	386
1941	90	14	38	6	357
1942	87	17	37	7	430
1943	99	19	42	8	440
1944	86	18	36	7	456
1945	73	14	31	6	437

Chittagong

1920	22	3	22	3	277
1921	22	3	22	3	305
1922	23	4	23	4	430
1923	20	4	20	4	420
1924	25	4	25	4	345
1925	24	5	24	5	475
1926	24	5	24	5	480
1927	24	4	24	4	391
1928	22	4	22	4	395
1929	25	5	25	5	413
1930	21	4	21	4	428
1931	25	5	25	5	417
1932	25	6	25	6	513
1933	25	6	25	6	513
1934	25	6	25	6	535

1.11   SESAMUM *(cont.)*

Year	Official acreage (in '000s)	Output ('000 tons)	Revised acreage (in '000s)	Revised output ('000 tons)	Yield per acre (in lbs)
1935	27	6	27	6	514
1936	27	6	27	6	519
1937	27	5	27	5	408
1938	27	5	27	5	454
1939	28	5	28	5	436
1940	28	6	28	6	469
1941	28	6	28	6	439
1942	28	6	28	6	470
1943	29	6	29	6	491
1944	36	9	36	9	534
1945	31	7	30	7	513
Presidency division					
1920	8	1	12	2	365
1921	7	1	11	2	379
1922	7	1	10	2	332
1923	7	1	10	1	276
1924	6	1	10	1	297
1925	8	1	12	2	352
1926	7	1	11	2	340
1927	8	1	12	2	303
1928	8	1	12	2	321
1929	7	1	10	2	322
1930	6	1	10	1	324
1931	7	1	11	2	325
1932	7	1	11	2	415
1933	7	1	11	2	429
1934	7	1	10	2	419
1935	4	1	7	1	339
1936	8	1	12	2	429
1937	8	2	12	2	457
1938	7	1	10	2	328
1939	8	2	12	2	448
1940	8	2	13	3	507
1941	9	2	14	3	485
1942	9	2	14	3	491
1943	10	2	16	3	502
1944	19	4	17	6	427
1945	17	3	15	5	409
Burdwan					
1920	18	3	9	2	371
1921	21	3	11	2	326

1922	18	3	9	1	349
1923	17	3	9	2	400
1924	14	2	7	1	376
1925	12	2	6	1	420
1926	12	2	6	1	428
1927	11	2	6	1	414
1928	12	2	6	1	428
1929	11	2	6	1	453
1930	11	2	6	1	434
1931	11	2	6	1	453
1932	11	3	6	1	548
1933	12	3	6	1	557
1934	11	3	6	1	528
1935	10	2	5	1	393
1936	9	2	5	1	542
1937	11	3	6	1	530
1938	13	3	7	1	463
1939	11	2	6	1	449
1940	10	2	5	1	404
1941	11	2	6	1	470
1942	11	2	6	1	445
1943	12	3	6	1	481
1944	13	3	7	1	460
1945	13	2	7	1	444

Note: Data on acreage and output are deflated by the same Revision Factor to calculate the figures in the revised series for the whole period.

1.12   TEA

All-Bengal

Year	Acreage (in 000s)	Output (000 lbs)	Yield per acre (in lbs)
1920	172	76187	444
1921	177	58753	332
1922	180	71663	398
1923	181	64579	358
1924	182	87062	479
1925	188	84623	451
1926	189	94942	503
1927	190	97014	511
1928	194	94924	490
1929	195	109950	564
1930	199	97003	487
1931	199	88464	445
1932	198	108847	550
1933	200	96684	484

I.12 TEA *(cont.)*

All-Bengal

Year	Acreage (in 000s)	Output (000 lbs)	Yield per acre (in lbs)
1934	200	97860	490
1935	201	96112	478
1936	203	99453	490
1937	202	108658	538
1938	201	106319	530
1939	201	112290	559
1940	201	115686	576
1941	201	121597	604
1942	201	149182	742
1943	198	159593	805
1944	200	130819	653
1945	200	154491	772

Rajshahi

Year	Acreage (in 000s)	Output (000 lbs)	Yield per acre (in lbs)
1920	167	74002	444
1921	172	57378	334
1922	175	70010	401
1923	176	62702	357
1924	176	85404	484
1925	182	82984	456
1926	183	93334	510
1927	184	95258	518
1928	188	93439	497
1929	189	108454	573
1930	193	95663	495
1931	193	86948	450
1932	193	107243	557
1933	194	95172	492
1934	194	96372	498
1935	195	94665	487
1936	195	97689	500
1937	196	106923	547
1938	194	104335	537
1939	194	110229	567
1940	195	113677	584
1941	195	119470	613
1942	195	146758	753
1943	194	158107	813
1944	194	128434	662
1945	194	152106	785

Chittagong

Year	Acreage (in 000s)	Output (000 lbs)	Yield per acre (in lbs)
1920	5	2185	437
1921	6	1375	250

1922	5	1654	312
1923	5	1877	368
1924	5	1658	307
1925	6	1639	298
1926	6	1607	282
1927	6	1756	308
1928	6	1485	256
1929	6	1496	258
1930	6	1339	227
1931	6	1516	266
1932	5	1604	297
1933	6	1512	252
1934	6	1488	240
1935	7	1447	216
1936	8	1763	232
1937	6	1734	271
1938	6	1984	315
1939	6	2061	322
1940	6	2009	324
1941	6	2127	343
1942	6	2424	391
1943	4	1486	391
1944	6	2385	391
1945	6	2385	391

Note: Only the officially published data are used to estimate trend rates.

1.13   LINSEED

All-Bengal

1920	126	16	126	16	288
1921	133	17	133	17	280
1922	127	20	127	20	357
1923	122	17	122	17	306
1924	121	19	121	19	352
1925	134	18	134	18	307
1926	136	20	136	20	328
1927	119	13	119	13	250
1928	132	20	132	20	337
1929	114	19	114	19	370
1930	116	19	116	19	364
1931	126	20	126	20	357
1932	125	25	125	25	448
1933	124	24	124	24	438
1934	126	27	126	27	474
1935	98	16	98	16	365
1936	131	25	131	25	437
1937	137	28	137	28	452
1938	156	29	156	29	415
1939	157	30	157	30	430

1.13   LINSEED *(cont.)*

Year	Official acreage (in 'ooos)	Output ('ooo tons)	Revised acreage (in 'ooos)	Revised output ('ooo tons)	Yield per acre (in lbs)
1940	155	22	155	22	322
1941	159	32	159	32	444
1942	157	32	157	32	453
1943	163	28	163	28	379
1944	150	22	150	22	324
1945	134	21	132	21	351

Rajshahi

Year	Official acreage (in 'ooos)	Output ('ooo tons)	Revised acreage (in 'ooos)	Revised output ('ooo tons)	Yield per acre (in lbs)
1920	30	4	30	4	292
1921	28	4	28	4	291
1922	30	4	30	4	294
1923	27	3	27	3	268
1924	26	4	26	4	355
1925	27	4	27	4	316
1926	27	4	27	4	339
1927	24	3	24	3	294
1928	24	4	24	4	348
1929	20	3	20	3	340
1930	21	3	21	3	326
1931	29	5	29	5	352
1932	27	5	27	5	427
1933	27	5	27	5	432
1934	28	6	28	6	478
1935	28	5	28	5	399
1936	28	6	28	6	469
1937	24	5	24	5	430
1938	23	4	23	4	391
1939	21	4	21	4	404
1940	23	3	23	3	303
1941	23	4	23	4	425
1942	22	5	22	5	461
1943	22	4	22	4	373
1944	24	3	24	3	328
1945	21	3	22	3	352

Dacca

Year	Official acreage (in 'ooos)	Output ('ooo tons)	Revised acreage (in 'ooos)	Revised output ('ooo tons)	Yield per acre (in lbs)
1920	15	3	15	3	393
1921	29	5	29	5	363
1922	18	3	18	3	379
1923	17	3	17	3	334
1924	16	2	16	2	349
1925	17	2	17	2	286
1926	17	2	17	2	313
1927	17	3	17	3	355

1928	16	3	16	3	376
1929	15	3	15	3	388
1930	14	3	14	3	433
1931	13	2	13	2	375
1932	13	3	13	3	447
1933	13	3	13	3	486
1934	13	3	13	3	467
1935	13	3	13	3	484
1936	13	3	13	3	494
1937	13	3	13	3	434
1938	12	2	12	2	404
1939	12	2	12	2	432
1940	11	2	11	2	382
1941	11	2	11	2	463
1942	11	2	11	2	449
1943	11	2	11	2	430
1944	10	2	10	2	380
1945	10	2	16	2	428

Chittagong

1920	10	2	10	2	398
1921	11	2	11	2	355
1922	11	2	11	2	466
1923	11	2	11	2	438
1924	10	2	10	2	420
1925	11	2	11	—	2	392
1926	11	2	11	2	345
1927	10	2	10	2	346
1928	9	2	9	2	394
1929	8	1	8	1	343
1930	8	1	8	1	250
1931	8	1	8	1	257
1932	7	1	7	1	316
1933	8	1	8	1	340
1934	9	2	9	2	457
1935	10	2	10	2	422
1936	13	3	13	3	463
1937	13	3	13	3	494
1938	13	3	13	3	446
1939	13	2	13	2	346
1940	13	2	13	2	375
1941	13	2	13	2	400
1942	13	2	13	2	396
1943	14	3	14	3	421
1944	9	2	9	2	418
1945	8	2	9	2	452

Presidency Division

1920	61	7	61	7	244
1921	55	5	55	5	220

1.13   LINSEED *(cont.)*

Year	Official acreage (in 'ooos)	Output ('ooo tons)	Revised acreage (in 'ooos)	Revised output ('ooo tons)	Yield per acre (in lbs)
1922	59	9	59	9	354
1923	58	7	58	7	284
1924	59	9	59	9	338
1925	67	9	67	9	286
1926	65	9	65	9	312
1927	54	4	54	4	163
1928	69	10	69	10	310
1929	57	10	57	10	374
1930	59	10	59	10	367
1931	62	10	62	10	355
1932	62	13	62	13	454
1933	62	12	62	12	428
1934	64	13	64	13	468
1935	36	4	36	4	267
1936	64	11	64	11	376
1937	75	15	75	15	457
1938	98	18	98	18	422
1939	102	20	102	20	446
1940	100	14	100	14	305
1941	102	21	102	21	454
1942	102	21	102	21	461
1943	107	18	107	18	368
1944	102	14	102	14	305
1945	90	13	80	13	329
Burdwan					
1920	10	1	10	1	269
1921	10	1	10	1	258
1922	10	2	10	2	407
1923	10	1	10	1	348
1924	9	2	9	2	369
1925	13	2	13	2	352
1926	17	3	17	3	377
1927	13	2	13	2	323
1928	14	2	14	2	368
1929	15	3	15	3	391
1930	14	3	14	3	409
1931	14	3	14	3	413
1932	15	3	15	3	528
1933	13	3	13	3	514
1934	12	3	12	3	516
1935	11	2	11	2	404
1936	13	3	13	3	585

1937	12	2	12	2	433
1938	11	2	11	2	377
1939	10	2	10	2	432
1940	9	2	9	2	398
1941	10	2	10	2	428
1942	8	2	8	2	425
1943	9	2	9	2	402
1944	5	1	5	1	394
1945	4	1	5	1	434

Note: Acreage data on linseed were not published in the Ishaque Report. So no revision is attempted.

1.14 REVISION FACTORS

Crops	Divisions and All-Bengal	From 1920/21 to 1940/41	1941/42	1942/43	1943/44	1944/45
	Presidency	1.38	1.20	1.22	1.07	n.r.
	Burdwan	1.56	1.31	1.38	1.27	n.r.
Winter rice	Rajshahi	1.53	1.34	1.58	1.21	n.r.
	Dacca	1.13	1.09	1.09	1.06	n.r.
	Chittagong	1.15	1.22	1.16	1.11	n.r.
	All-Bengal	1.35	1.23	1.28	1.14	n.r.
	Presidency	1.24	n.r.	n.r.	1.03	1.03
	Burdwan	0.64	n.r.	n.r.	0.66	0.66
Autumn rice	Rajshahi	1.43	n.r.	n.r.	0.91	0.91
	Dacca	0.84	n.r.	n.r.	0.63	0.63
	Chittagong	1.46	n.r.	n.r.	0.91	0.91
	All-Bengal	1.11	n.r.	n.r.	0.82	0.82
	Presidency	1.41	1.41	1.26	0.73	n.r.
	Burdwan	4.27	4.27	1.41	1.28	n.r.
Summer rice	Rajshahi	1.06	1.06	0.33	0.79	n.r.
	Dacca	1.25	1.25	1.33	1.26	n.r.
	Chittagong	1.59	1.59	1.02	0.96	n.r.
	All-Bengal	1.32	1.32	0.96	1.09	n.r.
	Presidency	0.96	0.96	0.87	0.88	n.r.
	Burdwan	2.73	2.73	2.76	2.62	n.r.
Wheat	Rajshahi	1.00	1.00	1.00	1.00	n.r.
	Dacca	1.26	1.26	1.55	0.83	n.r.
	Chittagong	–	–	–	–	–
	All-Bengal	1.13	1.13	1.07	1.02	n.r.
	Presidency	1.26	1.26	1.20	1.06	n.r.
	Burdwan	1.17	1.17	1.01	0.98	n.r.

1.14   REVISION FACTORS *(cont.)*

Crops	Divisions and All-Bengal	From 1920/21 to 1940/41	1941/42	1942/43	1943/44	1944/45
Barley	Rajshahi	3.75	3.75	1.86	2.01	n.r.
	Dacca	1.44	1.44	1.32	1.37	n.r.
	Chittagong	–	–	–	–	–
	All-Bengal	2.08	2.08	1.53	1.54	n.r.
	Presidency		1.60	1.19	1.16	n.r.
	Burdwan		2.23	1.46	1.50	n.r.
Gram	Rajshahi		2.53	1.53	1.99	n.r.
	Dacca		3.50	2.83	2.72	n.r.
	Chittagong		5.50	4.40	4.40	n.r.
	All-Bengal		1.85	1.32	1.36	n.r.
	Presidency		0.72	0.57	0.54	n.r.
	Burdwan		0.58	0.57	0.49	n.r.
Mustard	Rajshahi		0.82	0.61	0.80	n.r.
	Dacca		0.71	0.64	0.60	n.r.
	Chittagong		0.87	0.83	0.75	n.r.
	All-Bengal		0.77	0.63	0.68	n.r.
	Presidency		1.21	0.78	0.76	n.r.
	Burdwan		0.50	0.72	0.70	n.r.
Tobacco	Rajshahi		0.40	0.44	0.46	n.r.
	Dacca		0.91	0.79	0.75	n.r.
	Chittagong		1.28	1.28	1.32	n.r.
	All-Bengal		0.51	0.54	0.55	n.r.
	Presidency		1.54	same over entire period.		
	Burdwan		0.52	same over entire period.		
Sesamum	Rajshahi		0.28	same over entire period.		
	Dacca		0.42	same over entire period.		
	Chittagong		1.00	same over entire period.		
	All-Bengal		0.57	same over entire period.		
	Presidency		0.86	same over entire period.		
	Burdwan		1.00	same over entire period.		
Sugarcane	Rajshahi		0.61	same over entire period.		
	Dacca		0.35	same over entire period.		
	Chittagong		1.00	same over entire period.		
	All-Bengal		0.57	same over entire period.		

Note: The mode of the calculation of the Revision Factors is explained in Chapter 1, Section 1.6.
n.r. stands for no revision.

2.1 DESCRIPTION OF LAND USE: OFFICAL SERIES

(All figures are in 'ooo acres)

Year	Net cropped area	Double cropped area	Current fallow	Cultivable waste
		All-Bengal		
1920	23959	4281	5040	6060
1921	23701	4460	5027	5817
1922	23642	4108	4331	5944
1923	22806	4120	4813	6263
1924	23528	4219	4683	6207
1925	23841	4463	4657	5825
1926	23388	4082	5076	5808
1927	21902	4159	5960	6437
1928	23827	4875	4708	5935
1929	23369	4462	5387	6018
1930	23460	4939	5574	5974
1931	23568	5108	5301	5916
1932	23349	4826	5223	6235
1933	24002	4573	4764	6255
1934	23357	4564	5424	6626
1935	22674	5021	5670	6658
1936	24466	4937	4691	5950
1937	24728	4992	4926	5754
1938	24730	5293	5013	6634
1939	24916	5312	4742	6631
1940	24715	5317	5349	6034
1941	25488	5567	4618	5751
1942	26363	6040	4663	6125
1943	28059	6977	2957	6126
1944	29448	7770	2590	5079
1945	27976	6683	2694	5131
		Rajshahi		
1920	6479	863	1867	1361
1921	6646	625	1750	1361
1922	6631	663	1615	1406
1923	5742	698	2323	1590
1924	6603	620	1762	1340
1925	6796	795	1619	1296
1926	6436	738	2019	1256
1927	5739	740	2551	1421
1928	6601	764	1891	1220
1929	6225	804	2084	1451
1930	6227	955	2119	1441
1931	6293	878	2109	1436
1932	6252	964	2118	1470

2.1   DESCRIPTION OF LAND USE: OFFICIAL SERIES *(cont.)*

(All figures are in '000 acres)

Year	Net cropped area	Double cropped area	Current fallow	Cultivable waste
1933	6526	858	1884	1429
1934	6562	838	2076	1339
1935	6481	903	2111	1355
1936	6797	741	1867	1266
1937	6826	697	1839	1265
1938	6771	718	1961	1270
1939	6823	717	1834	1263
1940	6524	783	2132	1262
1941	6939	1177	1718	1159
1942	7218	1182	1439	1432
1943	8000	1363	656	1431
1944	8206	1843	375	1109
1945	7796	1585	390	1119
		Dacca		
1920	6508	1500	230	753
1921	6395	2075	328	753
1922	6261	1795	188	682
1923	6400	1869	221	633
1924	6461	1925	412	686
1925	6498	1969	417	593
1926	6383	1896	218	710
1927	6470	1930	182	721
1928	6601	1846	136	727
1929	6744	1850	179	615
1930	6754	1802	323	490
1931	6824	2045	287	561
1932	6819	1747	244	528
1933	6899	1867	169	528
1934	6945	1953	152	495
1935	6711	2314	147	472
1936	6842	2370	106	409
1937	6883	2411	116	408
1938	6959	2408	168	442
1939	7071	2397	164	305
1940	7261	2428	84	182
1941	6843	2382	498	182
1942	6868	2971	180	533
1943	6998	3413	50	533
1944	6917	3543	290	627
1945	6571	3047	302	633

Chittagong

1920	2747	790	540	1296
1921	2745	773	396	1296
1922	2679	857	459	1320
1923	2786	826	203	1330
1924	2807	869	149	1322
1925	2809	899	232	1249
1926	2795	669	246	1249
1927	2817	778	263	1210
1928	2858	658	219	1217
1929	2699	738	343	1221
1930	2760	834	322	1337
1931	2768	808	461	1317
1932	2742	750	370	1492
1933	2742	785	490	1384
1934	2728	827	476	1383
1935	2721	843	559	1232
1936	2730	747	563	1221
1937	2740	821	554	1193
1938	2780	744	388	1403
1939	2766	733	419	1401
1940	2900	733	438	1381
1941	2835	585	433	1428
1942	2938	772	533	1191
1943	2958	873	505	1195
1944	2902	1263	464	1342
1945	2757	1086	482	1355

Presidency Division

1920	3798	746	1377	1032
1921	3693	611	1355	1109
1922	3683	616	1425	1089
1923	3703	519	1330	1086
1924	3609	629	1415	1156
1925	3645	695	1351	1121
1926	3779	679	1420	1064
1927	3337	625	1529	1335
1928	3611	1055	1348	1317
1929	3443	905	1652	1234
1930	3514	981	1583	1215
1931	3531	1065	1338	1017
1932	3412	1087	1465	1015
1933	3629	866	1240	1189
1934	3529	795	1515	1415
1935	3451	841	1432	1536
1936	4002	860	1050	1479
1937	4290	824	1171	1356
1938	4476	1102	872	1801
1939	4402	1119	934	1816

2.1   DESCRIPTION OF LAND USE: OFFICIAL SERIES (*cont.*)

(All figures are in '000 acres)

Year	Net cropped area	Double cropped area	Current fallow	Cultivable waste
1940	4562	1081	891	1699
1941	4609	1119	880	1562
1942	5126	952	473	1357
1943	5659	1132	475	1357
1944	6038	925	475	995
1945	5736	795	494	1005

Burdwan

1920	4427	381	1027	1618
1921	4221	376	1198	1297
1922	4389	177	645	1447
1923	4174	207	736	1625
1924	4049	177	945	1703
1925	4093	105	1038	1566
1926	3995	99	1173	1530
1927	3538	86	1436	1750
1928	4157	553	1115	1454
1929	4259	166	1129	1496
1930	4206	367	1228	1493
1931	4152	312	1106	1585
1932	4124	278	1027	1731
1933	4207	197	981	1726
1934	3593	151	1206	1995
1935	3310	121	1421	2063
1936	4095	220	1105	1576
1937	3989	238	1246	1532
1938	3745	321	1624	1718
1939	3856	347	1391	1847
1940	3467	292	1804	1510
1941	4261	305	1089	1421
1942	4212	164	1341	1611
1943	4445	196	961	1610
1944	5385	198	987	1007
1945	5115	170	1026	1017

2.2   DESCRIPTION OF LAND USE: REVISED SERIES

(All figures are in '000 acres)

All-Bengal

1920	30189	6464	1209	4909
1921	29863	6735	1207	4711

1922	29789	6202	1040	4815
1923	28735	6221	1155	5073
1924	29646	6371	1124	5028
1925	30040	6739	1118	4718
1926	29468	6163	1218	4705
1927	27596	6280	1430	5214
1928	30022	7362	1130	4807
1929	29445	6738	1293	4874
1930	29560	7457	1338	4839
1931	29696	7712	1272	4792
1932	29420	7287	1254	5050
1933	30243	6906	1143	5067
1934	29430	6892	1302	5367
1935	28569	7582	1361	5393
1936	30828	7455	1126	4819
1937	31157	7537	1182	4661
1938	31160	7992	1203	5373
1939	31395	8021	1138	5371
1940	31140	8029	1284	4888
1941	30585	8017	1108	4658
1942	30845	8093	1119	4961
1943	30865	8163	1212	4962
1944	30920	8236	1217	5079
1945	27976	7083	1266	5131

Rajshahi

1920	8033	2468	317	1157
1921	8241	1787	297	1157
1922	8223	1897	275	1195
1923	7120	1197	395	1351
1924	8188	1773	299	1139
1925	8427	2273	275	1101
1926	7981	2110	343	1068
1927	7116	2116	434	1208
1928	8185	2184	321	1037
1929	7718	2299	354	1234
1930	7721	2731	360	1224
1931	7803	2512	359	1220
1932	7752	2758	360	1249
1933	8092	2455	320	1215
1934	8137	2396	353	1138
1935	8037	2583	359	1152
1936	8429	2118	317	1076
1937	8465	1992	313	1075
1938	8396	2053	333	1080
1939	8460	2050	312	1074
1940	8090	2240	362	1073
1941	8257	2354	292	985
1942	8301	2363	245	1218
1943	8319	2372	322	1217

2.2 DESCRIPTION OF LAND USE: REVISED SERIES *(cont.)*

(All figures are in 'ooo acres)

Year	Net cropped area	Double cropped area	Current fallow	Cultivable waste
1944	8288	2377	322	1109
1945	7796	2044	335	1119

Dacca

Year	Net cropped area	Double cropped area	Current fallow	Cultivable waste
1920	6508	1635	195	1544
1921	6395	2262	278	1544
1922	6261	1956	160	1399
1923	6400	2038	187	1297
1924	6461	2098	350	1406
1925	6498	2146	354	1216
1926	6383	2067	185	1455
1927	6470	2104	154	1479
1928	6601	2012	116	1491
1929	6744	2017	152	1261
1930	6754	1964	274	1004
1931	6824	2229	244	1150
1932	6819	1904	207	1082
1933	6899	2035	143	1082
1934	6945	2129	129	1014
1935	6711	2522	125	967
1936	6842	2583	90	837
1937	6883	2628	99	837
1938	6959	2625	143	905
1939	7071	2612	139	625
1940	7261	2646	71	373
1941	7117	2597	423	373
1942	7143	2644	153	1093
1943	7208	2662	145	1092
1944	7263	2728	142	627
1945	6571	2346	148	633

Chittagong

Year	Net cropped area	Double cropped area	Current fallow	Cultivable waste
1920	2967	1391	324	1296
1921	2965	1361	238	1296
1922	2893	1508	275	1320
1923	3009	1454	122	1330
1924	3031	1530	90	1322
1925	3034	1582	139	1249
1926	3018	1178	148	1249
1927	3043	1368	158	1210
1928	3086	1158	131	1217
1929	2915	1298	206	1221

1930	2981	1467	193	1337
1931	2990	1422	277	1317
1932	2961	1320	222	1492
1933	2961	1382	294	1384
1934	2946	1456	286	1383
1935	2939	1484	335	1232
1936	2948	1314	338	1221
1937	2959	1445	332	1193
1938	3003	1310	233	1403
1939	2987	1289	251	1401
1940	3132	1289	263	1381
1941	3005	1333	260	1428
1942	2997	1328	320	1191
1943	2988	1328	303	1195
1944	2989	1326	306	1342
1945	2757	1140	318	1355

Presidency Division

1920	5622	895	248	630
1921	5466	733	244	676
1922	5450	739	256	664
1923	5481	623	239	663
1924	5341	755	255	705
1925	5395	834	243	684
1926	5593	815	256	649
1927	4939	750	275	815
1928	5345	1266	243	803
1929	5095	1086	297	753
1930	5201	1177	285	741
1931	5226	1278	241	621
1932	5050	1304	264	619
1933	5370	1039	223	725
1934	5222	954	273	863
1935	5107	1009	258	937
1936	5923	1032	189	902
1937	6349	989	211	827
1938	6624	1322	157	1099
1939	6514	1343	168	1108
1940	6751	1298	160	1036
1941	6131	1309	158	953
1942	6151	1332	85	828
1943	6225	1358	180	828
1944	6280	1387	176	995
1945	5736	1193	183	1005

Burdwan

1920	7482	656	185	954
1921	7133	646	216	765

2.2   DESCRIPTION OF LAND USE: REVISED SERIES *(cont.)*

(All figures are in '000 acres)

Year	Net cropped area	Double cropped area	Current fallow	Cultivable waste
1922	7418	304	116	854
1923	7054	356	132	959
1924	6843	304	170	1005
1925	6916	181	187	924
1926	6751	170	211	902
1927	5979	148	258	1032
1928	7025	950	201	858
1929	7198	285	203	883
1930	7107	632	221	881
1931	7017	536	199	935
1932	6969	478	185	1021
1933	7110	339	177	1018
1934	6073	260	217	1177
1935	5594	207	256	1217
1936	6921	378	199	930
1937	6742	410	224	904
1938	6328	552	292	1013
1939	6516	596	250	1089
1940	5859	503	325	891
1941	6221	442	196	838
1942	6150	443	241	950
1943	6089	445	202	950
1944	6031	447	266	1007
1945	5115	384	277	1017

Note: The same Revision Factor is used to revise the official figures for the period up to 1941/42. Separate Revision Factors are used for the later years.

3.1   DATA ON PHYSICAL CAPITAL

(All figures in '000s)

Year	Occupied houses	Draught animals	Ploughs
	All-Bengal		
1920	8461	18351	4458
1926	8704	18937	4689
1930	8904	18703	4599

1935	9370	18208	4391
1940	9918	17728	4193
1945	10497	17097	4350

Rajshahi

1920	1891	5284	1325
1926	1922	5487	1376
1930	1947	5223	1321
1935	2037	5058	1283
1940	2147	4898	1247
1945	2262	4724	1293

Dacca

1920	2281	4522	1135
1926	2362	4268	1185
1930	2448	4621	1200
1935	2571	4494	1182
1940	2738	4370	1163
1945	2925	4215	1293

Chittagong

1920	1086	1726	497
1925	1139	1000	517
1930	1220	1677	491
1935	1321	1646	495
1940	1434	1617	499
1945	1557	1559	518

Presidency Division

1920	1690	3360	760
1926	1710	3635	823
1930	1725	3483	800
1935	1676	3505	726
1940	1806	3527	658
1945	1851	3401	683

Bundwan

1920	1515	3460	741
1926	1551	3747	788
1930	1582	3700	787
1935	1676	3503	702
1940	1792	3316	626
1945	1915	3198	649

Note: As explained in chapter 5, no cattle census was held in 1935. Therefore, figures for this year on livestock labour, and agricultural implements have been interpolated on the basis of the growth rate between 1930 and 1940. Livestock labour includes bullocks, cows and buffaloes (both male and female).

4.1 DATA ON PRIMARY CREDIT SOCIETIES

(All figures are in '000s)

Year	Societies	Members	Working capital (Rs)	Loans granted (Rs)	Loans paid (Rs)	Loans due (Rs)
			All-Bengal			
1920	5.8	161.9	12262	4967	2857	10077
1921	6.1	169.6	13081	3797	2902	10653
1922	7.1	186.6	14862	5275	3613	12132
1923	8.4	216.2	17933	7031	3852	14835
1924	9.9	246.1	21382	9066	6271	17345
1925	11.2	279.5	25654	11953	7986	21118
1926	13.4	328.5	32084	13791	7993	26452
1927	15.7	380.9	37784	14522	9350	31268
1928	16.9	407.6	42119	15427	11777	34317
1929	19.2	456.2	49034	16008	10050	40180
1930	20.2	475.7	53818	9269	5680	43245
1931	20.2	469.5	55626	5019	4688	43309
1932	20.0	464.1	56900	3584	3656	42843
1933	19.9	455.8	57311	3285	3637	42501
1934	19.8	450.9	58400	2448	2979	41529
1935	19.8	445.1	58922	2240	3043	40183
1936	19.9	445.6	59160	2194	3083	39539
1937	20.0	437.2	58860	1583	2539	38313
1938	26.1	529.3	59703	2284	1977	38305
1939	32.7	678.8	59547	4012	4518	37265
1940	35.3	774.3	58915	4704	5449	36178
1941	35.0	880.7	58555	4885	5625	35204
1942	36.2	866.2	57380	3138	3702	34094
1943	35.8	872.2	56067	2600	4739	32540
			Rajshahi			
1920	1.5	39.8	3872	1258	749	3220
1921	1.6	40.7	3987	785	651	3242
1922	1.8	46.4	4618	1387	851	3756
1923	2.0	51.6	4965	1335	855	4157
1924	2.2	54.0	5514	1662	1295	4250
1925	2.5	61.6	6291	2121	1434	5063
1926	2.9	66.8	7440	2396	1367	6041
1927	3.2	75.8	8450	2666	1684	6847
1928	3.3	76.8	8911	2618	2040	6972
1929	3.6	84.2	9947	2944	1887	8041
1930	3.9	88.3	10854	1884	1330	8591
1931	3.9	87.0	11107	904	862	8615
1932	3.9	85.5	11411	543	574	8568
1933	3.9	84.9	11278	621	654	8621

1934	3.9	83.6	11828	505	608	8426
1935	3.9	83.2	11947	425	614	8029
1936	3.9	82.0	11871	242	492	7872
1937	3.9	79.3	11777	158	400	7756
1938	6.1	115.6	12098	521	270	7938
1939	8.0	148.2	12051	1038	1085	7793
1940	8.8	163.7	11683	956	1178	7396
1941	9.2	186.2	11611	993	1216	7197
1942	9.0	201.7	11212	1192	1071	7033
1943	9.0	200.7	11001	965	1358	6758

Dacca

1920	1.7	47.2	4235	1797	866	3398
1921	1.8	49.7	4489	1093	867	3547
1922	2.0	51.3	4820	1508	1175	3800
1923	2.3	57.1	6134	2436	1306	4857
1924	2.7	67.1	7180	2912	2170	5737
1925	3.0	75.4	8635	4212	2814	6997
1926	3.5	87.3	10411	4415	2758	8452
1927	4.2	99.0	12193	4812	3288	9985
1928	4.6	107.0	13973	5676	4133	11401
1929	5.5	123.1	16731	5288	3156	13538
1930	5.9	130.7	18718	2378	962	14837
1931	5.9	127.7	19586	956	825	14870
1932	5.8	126.6	20172	782	778	14795
1933	5.8	124.9	20532	634	753	14634
1934	5.8	124.1	20728	426	574	14434
1935	5.7	121.4	20984	295	652	13942
1936	5.7	120.9	21025	539	898	13553
1937	5.8	120.1	20852	328	645	13177
1938	7.9	152.0	21314	615	413	13312
1939	9.6	203.2	21385	1297	1441	12921
1940	10.3	233.1	21038	1396	1799	12383
1941	10.5	265.1	20909	1449	1857	12050
1942	10.4	269.6	21082	854	856	12036
1943	10.0	259.8	20597	612	1229	11462

Chiltagong

1920	.8	18.6	1567	735	419	1362
1921	.8	20.0	1758	737	499	1529
1922	1.0	22.0	2051	813	533	1786
1923	1.2	26.3	2638	1190	536	2288
1924	1.5	33.0	3554	1927	1011	3098
1925	1.7	37.7	4364	2115	1330	3778
1926	2.0	45.0	5677	2540	1428	4882
1927	2.2	50.4	6261	2243	1745	5354
1928	2.3	55.1	6982	2732	2243	5921
1929	2.9	67.8	8701	3384	1927	7355
1930	3.0	70.2	9284	1875	1227	7699

4.1   DATA ON PRIMARY CREDIT SOCIETIES *(cont.)*

(All figures are in '000s)

Year	Societies	Members	Working capital (Rs)	Loans granted (Rs)	Loans paid (Rs)	Loans due (Rs)
1931	3.0	69.8	9767	1035	1005	7775
1932	2.9	68.6	9953	703	772	7590
1933	2.9	67.2	10200	754	815	7457
1934	2.9	66.1	10389	461	583	7263
1935	2.9	65.6	10378	543	711	6995
1936	2.9	65.9	10260	504	754	6711
1937	2.9	64.2	10259	400	585	6471
1938	3.6	71.9	10221	467	461	6338
1939	4.5	100.2	10063	620	780	6091
1940	4.8	118.6	9867	866	1047	5887
1941	5.2	134.9	9807	899	1081	5728
1942	5.2	121.4	9426	105	548	5577
1943	5.1	137.3	9273	33	529	4998
		Presidency Division				
1920	1.1	30.9	1604	622	436	1019
1921	1.2	33.1	1696	639	531	1096
1922	1.5	37.6	2014	862	568	1355
1923	1.8	46.8	2479	1159	680	1769
1924	2.2	52.3	3086	1580	1029	2254
1925	2.5	59.6	3836	2214	1539	2802
1926	3.1	73.4	5118	2633	1444	3901
1927	3.5	83.4	6162	2783	1754	4903
1928	3.6	85.8	6958	2451	1869	5465
1929	3.7	89.9	7512	2327	1815	6027
1930	3.8	91.2	8217	1646	1100	6529
1931	3.8	89.8	8438	1255	1062	6467
1932	3.7	89.2	8573	915	809	6445
1933	3.7	87.2	8744	814	767	6514
1934	3.7	87.1	8981	566	578	6315
1935	3.7	85.3	9065	459	549	6221
1936	3.7	85.3	9222	364	405	6223
1937	3.7	83.3	9249	307	446	6017
1938	4.3	93.6	9342	362	378	5978
1939	5.7	120.7	9363	610	626	5839
1940	6.3	146.3	9586	953	875	5866
1941	6.5	166.5	9527	989	903	5708
1942	6.5	155.8	9260	435	578	5258
1943	6.4	153.9	9070	452	733	5472
		Burdwan				
1920	.9	25.6	986	555	388	1079
1921	.9	26.2	1151	543	354	1238

1922	1.1	29.5	1359	704	486	1434
1923	1.3	34.7	1717	912	475	1763
1924	1.6	39.9	2049	985	767	2006
1925	1.7	45.3	2529	1291	869	2478
1926	2.0	56.2	3439	1807	996	3176
1927	2.8	72.5	4719	2019	879	4179
1928	3.3	83.1	5295	1950	1492	4559
1929	3.6	91.5	6144	2067	1266	5220
1930	3.9	95.5	6745	1487	1061	5588
1931	3.9	95.5	6728	870	934	5581
1932	3.9	94.3	6792	640	723	5444
1933	3.8	91.9	6558	462	647	5275
1934	3.8	90.1	6474	490	636	5091
1935	3.8	89.9	6548	518	518	4997
1936	3.9	91.7	6781	546	536	5179
1937	3.9	90.4	6723	391	463	4891
1938	4.5	96.4	6728	320	454	4740
1939	5.0	106.6	6684	446	585	4621
1940	5.3	112.8	6742	534	550	4646
1941	3.9	128.3	6700	554	568	4521
1942	5.4	117.9	6400	552	649	4190
1943	5.4	120.7	6126	539	891	3850

4.2 DATA ON PRIMARY CREDIT SOCIETIES

(All figures in 000 Rs)

Year	Loans overdue	Share capital	Reserve Fund	Members Deposits	Central Bank	Non-members deposits
			All-Bengal			
1920	2773	302	1573	627	9098	557
1921	4004	469	1833	639	9430	608
1922	4471	704	2164	698	10494	695
1923	5178	1028	2571	783	12478	807
1924	4927	1472	3072	933	14975	851
1925	5111	1998	3534	1121	17876	1024
1926	6746	2602	4349	1277	22564	1228
1927	9213	3283	5348	1491	26237	1360
1928	11829	4015	6552	1667	28294	1525
1929	16004	4790	7949	1883	32855	1500
1930	24389	5252	9676	2196	35144	1465
1931	29381	5429	11587	2005	34812	1697
1932	34659	5528	13364	1983	34225	1709
1933	34000	5589	15046	1979	32872	1730

4.2 DATA ON PRIMARY CREDIT SOCIETIES *(cont.)*

(All figures in 000 Rs)

Year	Loans overdue	Share capital	Reserve Fund	Members Deposits	Central Bank	Non-members deposits
1934	31048	5539	16550	1862	32828	1534
1935	32632	5419	17757	1974	32153	1497
1936	34581	5328	18739	1932	31540	1449
1937	34372	5214	19308	1919	30966	1374
1938	34270	5228	19944	1841	31345	1355
1939	32794	5252	20231	1758	30942	1218
1940	33156	5386	20444	1710	29973	1205
1941	32852	5501	20642	1623	29446	1209
1942	30797	5512	20269	1640	28882	1007
1943	29033	5450	20719	1626	27203	1018
			Rajshahi			
1920	901	110	522	154	2981	81
1921	1161	153	601	161	2958	88
1922	1408	227	688	179	3393	87
1923	1661	299	806	195	3519	99
1924	1484	404	927	222	3819	104
1925	1859	512	1011	243	4340	122
1926	1956	627	1250	260	5149	143
1927	2087	747	1463	292	5778	158
1928	2883	877	1683	320	5823	195
1929	3415	1013	1955	333	6491	147
1930	4661	1150	2305	327	6894	163
1931	5922	1122	2691	324	6783	155
1932	6636	1141	3097	320	6690	152
1933	7092	1167	3475	324	6148	151
1934	7208	1147	3749	320	6473	126
1935	7201	1119	3986	325	6340	135
1936	7321	1110	4163	313	6143	129
1937	7310	1088	4286	308	5956	119
1938	7138	1105	4308	308	6271	121
1939	6714	1121	4339	292	6170	108
1940	6842	1166	4273	280	5810	106
1941	6779	1191	4315	266	5708	106
1942	6115	1234	3924	242	5653	97
1943	5885	1274	3903	238	5468	90
			Dacca			
1920	739	80	552	177	3254	107
1921	1441	125	637	170	3374	121

1922	1651	181	750	185	3522	127
1923	1756	285	894	224	4342	143
1924	1680	412	1075	274	5243	152
1925	1545	577	1216	364	6296	165
1926	2018	750	1455	423	7554	199
1927	2653	976	1792	486	8691	215
1928	3316	1221	2193	542	9741	244
1929	4766	1482	2692	621	11651	259
1930	8746	1594	3312	856	12847	69
1931	9861	1647	4033	684	12942	251
1932	12850	1668	4639	695	12883	243
1933	11751	1664	5197	691	12674	263
1934	8713	1641	5716	660	12566	105
1935	10474	1605	6133	825	12276	106
1936	12126	1563	6504	821	11997	97
1937	11983	1513	6590	818	11830	67
1938	11732	1542	6818	787	12057	80
1939	11526	1564	7021	762	11859	76
1940	11555	1621	7117	740	11422	92
1941	11449	1656	7186	702	11221	92
1942	11186	1677	7250	756	11275	71
1943	10840	1628	7374	730	10751	73

Chiltagong

1920	276	34	129	76	1284	43
1921	343	65	162	92	1396	42
1922	301	100	213	108	1574	55
1923	407	151	275	137	1993	79
1924	414	223	352	187	2698	87
1925	422	305	453	250	3241	110
1926	607	410	604	312	4206	134
1927	1095	508	802	394	4386	162
1928	1439	630	1053	468	4649	173
1929	2019	779	1334	561	5835	182
1930	3422	851	1669	629	5911	211
1931	5011	905	2061	622	5921	244
1932	5820	934	2425	589	5723	268
1933	5662	950	2773	580	5589	295
1934	5517	944	3061	530	5525	315
1935	5454	915	3232	484	5412	318
1936	5252	882	3326	466	5269	309
1937	5294	861	3413	461	5203	310
1938	5469	849	3534	422	5163	301
1939	5038	830	3448	390	5118	273
1940	4969	826	3511	376	4915	258
1941	4923	844	3545	356	4829	259
1942	4949	835	3368	350	4745	176
1943	4340	805	3506	333	4400	209

4.2   DATA ON PRIMARY CREDIT SOCIETIES *(cont.)*

(All figures in 000 Rs)

Year	Loans overdue	Share capital	Reserve Fund	Members Deposits	Central Bank	Non-members deposits
Presidency Division						
1920	494	47	234	138	977	199
1921	535	74	275	129	999	212
1922	634	120	319	140	1196	235
1923	710	182	356	133	1536	271
1924	702	282	425	147	1931	298
1925	639	399	504	144	2426	354
1926	1262	541	616	156	3379	418
1927	1915	694	774	177	4039	470
1928	2480	830	974	176	4455	513
1929	3196	949	1197	208	4614	533
1930	4261	1013	1464	213	4931	583
1931	4736	1053	1720	202	4833	611
1932	5286	1049	1977	207	4719	601
1933	5193	1054	2238	211	4633	590
1934	5370	1048	2510	188	4662	562
1935	5302	1021	2738	191	4574	529
1936	5428	1006	2933	177	4576	515
1937	5527	984	3081	175	4498	497
1938	5748	974	3210	167	4473	500
1939	5423	982	3245	160	4526	438
1940	5688	1018	3320	166	4573	452
1941	5636	1040	3352	157	4492	454
1942	4984	1040	3338	144	4321	399
1943	4717	1021	3459	155	4002	417
Burdwan						
1920	364	31	136	82	601	128
1921	525	52	158	88	704	145
1922	477	76	195	87	809	191
1923	644	111	240	94	1089	216
1924	646	152	294	103	1284	210
1925	646	205	351	121	1573	272
1926	902	274	425	126	2276	334
1927	1463	358	518	141	3345	355
1928	1711	457	648	162	3626	401
1929	2608	566	772	160	4265	378
1930	3299	646	926	171	4562	439
1931	3852	702	1082	173	4333	436
1932	4068	737	1227	172	4210	444

1933	4302	753	1363	173	3829	432
1934	4239	760	1516	164	3602	426
1935	4201	760	1669	150	3551	410
1936	4453	767	1813	154	3555	398
1937	4259	768	1938	157	3478	382
1938	4183	757	2075	158	3381	354
1939	4093	755	2179	154	3269	324
1940	4103	754	2256	148	3253	297
1941	4065	770	2277	141	3196	298
1942	3564	727	2382	148	2888	264
1943	3252	722	2421	171	2581	230

Note: The Annual Report on the Working of the Co-operative Societies in Bengal, the source of these statistics, was available for the period up to 1943/44. Therefore, the figures for the last two years are not mentioned.

SELECT BIBLIOGRAPHY

I. PRINTED RECORDS
(i) *Government of undivided India*

Proceedings of the Board of Agriculture in India, 1913, 1916, 1919, 1922 and 1924.

Proceedings of the Meetings of the Crops and Soils Wing of the Board of Agriculture and Animal Husbandry in India, 1935, 1937, 1939.

Abstracts of the Proceedings of the Council of the Governor General of India Assembled for the Purpose of Making Laws and Regulations, 1881–85.

Proceedings of the Crop Planning Conference (Simla, 1934).

Proceedings of the Conference of the Registrars of Co-operative Societies, 9th (Bombay, 1926), 11th (New Delhi, 1934), 12th (New Delhi, 1936), 13th (New Delhi, 1939), 15th (Madras, 1947).

(ii) *Government of undivided Bengal*

Proceedings of the Bengal Legislative Council, 1920–39.

Proceedings in the Revenue Department (Agricultural Section).

2. PUBLICATIONS OF THE GOVERNMENT OF UNDIVIDED INDIA

(i) *Annual Publications by the Director General of Commercial Intelligence and Statistics*

Agricultural Statistics of India (2 vols.)

Annual Statement of the Sea-Borne Trade and Navigation of British India.

Estimates of Area and Yield of Principal Crops in India.

Indian Tea Statistics, 1920–39, 1941–42, 1943–44.

Statistical Abstracts of British India.

(ii) *Reports of miscellaneous committees and commissions*

Report of the Advisory Planning Board (New Delhi, 1947).

Report of the Agricultural Finance Sub-Committee (Delhi, 1945).

Report of the Indian Central Banking Enquiry Committee, Vol. 1 (Calcutta, 1931).

Report of the Committee on Co-operation in India (Calcutta, 1915).

Report of the Co-operative Planning Committee (Bombay, 1946).

Report of the Indian Economic Enquiry Committee, Vol. 1 (Calcutta, 1925).

Report of the Famine Enquiry Commission on Bengal (Delhi, 1945).

Report of the Foodgrain Policy Committee (Delhi, 1943).

Report of the Rent Law Commission (Calcutta, 1880).

(iii) *Other publications*

Agricultural Marketing Advisor, *Report On the Marketing of Gram in India* (Delhi, 1945).

Report on the Marketing of Linseed in India (Simla, 1938).
Report on the Marketing of Rice in India and Burma (Simla, 1941).
Report on the Marketing of Sugar in India and Burma (Delhi, 1941).
Report on the Marketing of Tobacco in India and Burma (Simla, 1939).
Census of India, 1921, *Bengal*, 2 Parts (Calcutta, 1923).
Census of India, 1931, Vol. V, Part I, *Bengal and Sikkim* (Calcutta, 1933).
Census of India, 1941, Vol. IV, *Bengal* (Simla, 1942).
Director General of Commercial Intelligence and Statistics, *Index Number of Indian Prices*, 1886–1931 (Delhi, 1933).
Livestock Census of India, 1st Report (1919) to 6th Report (1942).
Quinquennial Report on the Average Yield Per Acre of Principal Crops for the Period Ending 1936/37 (Calcutta, 1941).
Department of Food, *Foodgrain Shortage in India* (Delhi, 1944).
Food Statistics of India (New Delhi, 1946).
Imperial Council of Agricultural Research, *Review of Agricultural Operations*.
Reserve Bank of India, Agricultural Credit Department, *Bulletin* I (Bombay, 1937).
Report Submitted to the Government of India Under Section 55 (1) (B) of the Reserve Bank of India Act (Bombay, 1936).

3. PUBLICATIONS OF THE GOVERNMENT OF POST-1947 INDIA

Director of Economics and Statistics, *Abstracts of the Agricultural Statistics of India* 1936/37–1945/46 (Delhi, 1949).
Food Situation in India 1939–1953 (Delhi, 1954).
Rice Statistics (Delhi, 1948).
Economic and Statistical Adviser, *Studies in the Economics of Farm Management in West Bengal* (Delhi, 1963).
Reserve Bank of India, *All-India Rural Credit Survey*, 3 vols. (Bombay, 1954–56).
Census of India, 1951, Vol. I, Part I–B (Delhi, 1955).
Final Report of the National Income Committee (Delhi, 1954).

4. PUBLICATIONS OF THE GOVERNMENT OF BENGAL

(i) *Annual publications*

Annual Report of the Department of Agriculture.
Agricultural Statistics of Bengal.
Report on the Land Revenue Administration of the Presidency of Bengal.
Report on the Working of the Co-operative Societies in Bengal.
Season and Crop Report.

(ii) *Reports of miscellaneous committees and commissions*

Report of the Bengal Provincial Banking Enquiry Committee, 2 vols. (Calcutta, 1930).
Preliminary Report of the Board of Economic Enquiry on Rural Indebtedness (Calcutta Gazette, January 1935).
Report of the Foodgrains Procurement Committee (Calcutta, 1944).
Report of the Bengal Jute Enquiry Committee (Finlow Committee), Vol. I (Calcutta, 1934).
Report of the Bengal Jute Enquiry Committee (Fawcus Committee) (Calcutta, 1940).

Report of the Bengal Land Revenue Commission, Vols. I–IV (Calcutta, 1940), Vols. V–VI (Calcutta, 1941).
Report of the Bengal Paddy and Rice Enquiry Committee, 2 vols. (Calcutta, 1939).

(iii)   *District settlement reports* (arranged alphabetically)

Final Report on the Survey and Settlement Operations in the District of: Bakergunj 1900–1908 (Calcutta, 1915); *Bankura 1917–1924* (Calcutta, 1926); *Burdwan 1927–1934* (Calcutta, 1940); *Chittagong 1922–1933* (Calcutta, 1939); *Dacca 1910–1917* (Calcutta, 1917); *Faridpur 1904–1914* (Calcutta, 1916); *Dihi Bhadra Estate in the Khulna District 1905–1909* (Calcutta, 1911); *Howrah 1934–1939* (Calcutta, 1940); *Jessore 1920–1924* (Calcutta, 1925); *Malda 1928–1935* (Calcutta, 1939); *Murshidabad 1925–1932* (Calcutta, 1938); *Rajshahi 1912–1922* (Calcutta, 1922); *Rangpur 1931–1938* (Calcutta, 1940).

(iv)   *Other publications* (by the Department of Agriculture)

Agricultural Statistics by Plot to Plot Enumeration in Bengal 1944–45, 3 Parts (Calcutta, 1946).
Cattle Census Report, 1920, 1925, 1930.
Manual of Rules for the Preparation of Crop Reports and Agricultural Statistics in Bengal, 3rd Edition (Calcutta, 1908), 4th Edition (Calcutta, 1922).
Report on the Crop-Cutting Experiments During the Quinquennium from 1917/18 to 1921/22 (Calcutta, 1922).
Quinquennial Report on the Crop-Cutting Experiments for the Years 1922/23 to 1926/27 (Calcutta, 1927).
Quinquennial Report on the Crop-Cutting Experiments for the Years 1927/28 to 1931/32 (Calcutta, 1932).

5   GOVERNMENT OF THE UNITED KINGDOM

Report of the Royal Commission on Agriculture in India (London, 1928).
Report of the Royal Commission on Agriculture in India (Bombay, 1927).
   Vol. IV (Evidence taken in Bengal).

6   SECONDARY WORKS: BOOKS AND ARTICLES

Abhyankar, A. G., *Provincial Debt Legislation in Relation to Rural Credit* (New Delhi, 1940).
Agarwala, A. N. and Singh, S. P. (eds.), *The Economics of Underdevelopment* (New York, 1968).
Aitken, H. G. J. (ed.), *The State and Economic Growth* (New York, 1959).
Anstey, V., *The Economic Development of India* (London, 1957).
Archibald, G. C. and Lipsey, R. G., *An Introduction to a Mathematical Treatment of Economics* (London, 1967).
Aubrey, H. G., 'Investment Decision in Underdeveloped Countries', in National Bureau of Economic Research, *Capital Formation and Economic Growth* (Princeton, 1955).
Bagchi, A. K., *Private Investment in India 1900–1939* (Cambridge, 1972).
Baran, P., *The Political Economy of Growth* (New York, 1967).

Barker, S. G., *Report on the Scientific and Technical Development of the Jute Manufacturing Industry of Bengal* (Calcutta, 1935).

Bauer, P. T. and Yamey, B. S., *The Economics of Underdeveloped Countries* (Cambridge, 1957).

'A Case Study of Response to Price in an Underdeveloped Economy', *Economic Journal*, Vol. LIX (1959).

Behrman, J. R., *Supply Response in Underdeveloped Agriculture: A Case Study of Four Major Annual Crops in Thailand, 1937–1963* (Amsterdam, 1968).

Berg, E. J., 'Backward-Sloping Labour Supply Function in Dual Economics – The African Case', *Quarterly Journal of Economics*, Vol. LXXV (1961).

Bhattacharya, J. P. (ed.), *Studies in Indian Agricultural Economics* (Bombay, 1958).

Bhattacharya, S., 'Laissez Faire in India', *The Indian Economic and Social History Review*, Vol. II (1965).

Black, R. D. C., 'Economic Policy in Ireland and India in the Time of J. S. Mill', *Economic History Review*, 2nd Series, Vol. XXII (1969).

Blyn, G., *Agricultural Trends in India, 1891–1947: Output, Availability, and Productivity* (University of Pennsylvania Press, 1966).

Boeke, J. H., *Economics and Economic Policies of Dual Societies* (New York, 1953).

Boserup, E., *The Conditions of Agricultural Growth* (London, 1965).

Bottomley, A., *Factor Pricing in Underdeveloped Rural Areas* (London, 1970).

'The Structure of Interest Rates in Underdeveloped Rural Areas', *Journal of Farm Economics*, Vol. 46 (1964).

Bowley, A. L. and Robertson, D. H., *A Scheme for an Economic Census of India* (New Delhi, 1934).

Brandow, G. E., 'A Note on the Nerlovian Estimate of Supply Elasticity', *Journal of Farm Economics*, Vol. XL (1958).

Brenner, Y. S., *Theories of Economic Development and Growth* (London, 1966).

Broomfield, J. H., *Elite Conflict in a Plural Society* (Berkeley, 1968).

Burns, W., *Technological Possibilities of Agricultural Development in India* (Lahore, 1944).

Cairncross, A. K., 'The Stages of Economic Growth', *Economic History Review*, 2nd Series, Vol. XIII (1961).

Catanach, I. J., *Rural Credit in Western India, 1875–1930* (Berkeley, 1970).

Chambers, J. D. and Mingay, G. E., *The Agricultural Revolution 1750–1880* (London, 1966).

Chandra, B., *The Rise and Growth of Economic Nationalism in India* (New Delhi, 1966).

Chaudhuri, B., *Growth of Commercial Agriculture in Bengal (1757–1900)*, Vol. I (Calcutta, 1964).

'Growth of Commercial Agriculture in Bengal, 1859–1885', *Indian Economic and Social History Review*, Vol. 7 (1970).

'Growth of Commercial Agriculture and its Impact on Peasant Economy', *Indian Economic and Social History Review*, Vol. 7 (1970).

'Rural Credit Relations in Bengal 1859–1885', *Indian Economic and Social History Review*, Vol. VI (1969).

Chaudhuri, K. C., *The History and Economics of Land System in Bengal* (Calcutta, 1927).

Chaudhuri, K. N., 'Economic Problems and Indian Independence' in C. H. Philips and M. D. Wainwright (eds.), *The Partition of India: Policies and Perspectives 1935–47* (London, 1970).

Clairmonte, F. F., *Economic Liberalism and Underdevelopment* (Bombay, 1960).

Croxton, F. E. and Cowden, D. J., *Applied General Statistics* (London, 1962).

Dabasi-Schwing, L., 'The Problem of Transforming Traditional Agriculture', *World Politics*, Vol. XVII (1965).

Darling, M. L., *The Punjab Peasant in Prosperity and Debt* 4th edn. (London, 1947).

Dasgupta, N. R., 'Index Number of Money Income of the Agricultural Population of Bengal From 1911 to 1935', *Sankhya: Indian Journal of Statistics*, Vol. 5 (1941).

Datta, K. L., *Report on the Enquiry into the Rise of Prices in India* (Calcutta, 1914).

Davis, L., 'Professor Fogel and the New Economic History', *Economic History Review*, 2nd Series, Vol. XIX, (1966).

Dean, E., *The Supply Response of African Farmers: Theory and Measurement in Malawi* (Amsterdam, 1966).

Deane, P., *The First Industrial Revolution* (Cambridge, 1967).

Deane, P. and Cole, W. A., *British Economic Growth 1688–1959* (Cambridge, 1967).

Desai, M., 'Some Issues in Econometric History', *Economic History Review*, 2nd Series, Vol. XXI (1968).

Desai, R. C., *Standard of Living in India and Pakistan 1931/32 to 1940/41* (Bombay, 1953).

Dore, R. P., 'Agricultural Improvement in Japan' in E. L. Jones and S. J. Woolf (eds.), *Agrarian Change and Economic Development: The Historical Problems* (London, 1969).

'The Meji Landlord: Good or Bad?, *Journal of Asian Studies*, Vol. XVIII (1959).

Driver, P. N., *Problems of Zamindari and Land Tenure Reconstruction in India* (Bombay, 1949).

Dubey, V., 'The Marketed Agricultural Surplus and Economic Growth in Underdeveloped Countries', *Economic Journal*, Vol. LXXII (1963).

Dutt, R. C., *The Economic History of India in the Victorian Age* (London, 1956).

Dutt, R. P., *India Today* (Bombay, 1949).

Eicher, C. K. and Witt, L. W. (eds.), *Agriculture in Economic Development* (New York, 1964).

Falcon, W. P., 'Farmer Response to Price in a Subsistence Economy: The Case of West Pakistan', *Agricultural Economics Research*, Vol. LIV (1964).

Fei, J. C. H. and Ranis, G., 'Agrarianism, Dualism and Economic Development' in I. Adelman and E. Thorbeck (eds.), *The Theory and Design of Economic Development* (Baltimore, 1966).

Firth, R. and Yamey, B. S. (eds.), *Capital, Saving and Credit in Peasant Societies* (London, 1964).

Fisher, F. M., *A Priori Information and Time Series Analysis: Essays in Economic Theory and Measurement* (Amsterdam, 1962).

Fishlow, A., 'Empty Economic Stages', *Economic Journal*, Vol. LXXV (1965).

Fleming, M., *Introduction to Economic Analysis* (London, 1969).

Fogel, R. W., 'The New Economic History: Its Findings and Methods', *Economic History Review*, 2nd Series, Vol. XIX (1966).

Food and Agricultural Organisation (UN), *Agricultural Credit in Economically Backward Countries* (Rome, 1959).

Agricultural Credit Through Co-operatives and Other Institutions (Rome, 1965).

Freund, J. E. and Williams, F. J., *Modern Business Statistics* (London, 1967).

Frykenberg, R. E. (ed.), *Land Control and Social Structure in Indian History* (Wisconsin, 1969).

Gaitskell, A., 'Importance of Agriculture in Economic Development' in W. W. McPherson (ed.), *Economic Development of Tropical Agriculture* (University of Florida Press, 1968).

Galbraith, J. K. and Black, J. D., 'The Maintenance of Agricultural Production During Depression: The Explanations Reviewed', *Journal of Political Economy*, Vol. XLVI (1938).

Ganguli, B. N., *Trends of Agriculture and Population in the Ganges Valley* (London, 1938).

Readings in Indian Economic History (Bombay, 1964).

Geertz, C., *Agricultural Involution* (Berkeley, 1963).

Gerschenkron, A., *Economic Backwardness in Historical Perspective* (New York, 1962).

Ghate, B. G., *Changes in the Occupational Distribution of Population* (New Delhi, 1940).

Ghose, T. P. and Sinha, H. C., 'Agricultural Co-operation in Bengal and the Rest of British India (1918/19–1938/39)', *Sankhya: Indian Journal of Statistics*, Vol. 7, Part 2 (1945/46).

Gopal, S., *The Permanent Settlement in Bengal and its Results* (London, 1949).

Griliches, Z., 'Estimates of the Aggregate United States Farm Supply Function', *Journal of Farm Economics*, Vol. XLII (1960).

Guha, R., *A Rule of Property for Bengal* (Paris, 1963).

Habakkuk, H. J., *American and British Technology in the Nineteenth Century* (Cambridge, 1962).

'Economic Functions of the English Landlords in the Eighteenth Century' in W. E. Minchinton (ed.), *Essays in Agrarian History*, Vol. I (London, 1968).

Habib, Irfan, *Agrarian System of Mughal India* (London, 1963).

Hartwell, R. M. (ed.), *The Causes of the Industrial Revolution* (London, 1967).

Hartwell, R. M., *Industrial Revolution and Economic Growth* (London, 1971).

Hicks, Sir J. Richard, *A Theory of Economic History* (Oxford, 1969).

Higgins, B., *Economic Development* (New York, 1959).

'The Dualistic Theory of the Underdeveloped Countries', *Economic Development and Cultural Change*, Vol. IV (1956).

Hirschman, A., *The Strategy of Economic Development* (Yale, 1970).

Hopper, W. D., 'Allocation Efficiency in a Traditional Indian Agriculture', *Journal of Farm Economics*, Vol. XXXXVII (1965).

Hough, E. M., *The Co-operative Movement in India* (Bombay, 1959).

Hunter, G., *Modernising Peasant Agriculture* (Oxford, 1969).

Ishikawa, S., *Economic Development in Asian Perspective* (Tokyo, 1967).

Jack, J. C., *The Economic Life of a Bengal District* (Oxford, 1916).

John, P. V., *Some Aspects of the Structure of Indian Agricultural Economy 1947/48 to 1961/62* (Delhi, 1968).

Johnston, B. F. and Mellor, J. W., 'The Role of Agriculture in Economic Development', *American Economic Review*, Vol. LI (1961).

Johnston, B. F. and Nielsen, S. T., 'Agricultural and Structural Transformation in a Developing Society', *Economic Development and Cultural Change*, Vol. XIV (1966).

Johnston, B. F. and Tolley, G. S., 'Strategy For Agriculture in Development', *Journal of Farm Economics*, Vol. XLVII (1965).

Johnston, J., *Econometric Methods* (New York, 1963).

Jones, E. L., *Agriculture and Economic Growth 1650–1815* (London, 1967).

Kidron, M., *Foreign Investments in India* (London, 1965).

Krishna, R., 'Farm Supply Response in India–Pakistan: A Case Study of the Punjab Region', *Economic Journal*, Vol. LXXIII (1963).

'The Marketable Surplus Function For a Subsistence Crop', *Economic Weekly*, Vol. XVII (1965).

'A Note on the Elasticity of the Marketable Surplus of a Subsistence Crop', *Indian Journal of Agricultural Economics*, Vol. XVII (1962).

Kuznets, S., *Modern Economic Growth* (Yale, 1967).

'International Differences in Capital Formation and Financing' in National Bureau of Economic Research, *Capital Formation and Economic Growth* (Princeton, 1955).

Kuznets, S. and others (eds.), *Economic Growth: Brazil, India and Japan* (Durham, NC, 1955).

Lachmann, L. M., *Capital and its Structure* (London, 1956).

Leibenstein, H., *Economic Backwardness and Economic Growth* (New York, 1957).

Lewis, J. P., *Quiet Crises in India* (New York, 1964).

Lewis, W. A., *The Theory of Economic Growth* (London, 1955).

'Economic Development with Unlimited Supplies of Labour', *Manchester School*, Vol. XXII (1954).

Lipsey, R. G., *An Introduction to Positive Economics* (London, 1966).

Livingstone, I., *Economic Policy for Development* (London, 1971).

Madalgi, S. S., 'Prices and Production Trends in Indian Agriculture During 1900 to 1953', *Indian Journal of Agricultural Economics*, Vol. XVII (1954).

Mahalanobis, P. C., 'Recent Experiments in Statistical Sampling in the Indian Statistical Institute', *Journal of the Royal Statistical Society*, Vol. CIX, Part IV (1946).

'A Sample Survey of the After Effects of the Bengal Famine of 1943', *Sankhya: Indian Journal of Statistics*, Vol. 7 Part IV (1946).

Mahalanobis, P. C. and Sengupta, J. C., 'On the Size of Sample Cuts in Crop-Cutting Experiments', *Bulletin of the International Statistical Institute*, Vol. XXXIII, Part 2 (1951).

Majumder, S. C., *Rivers of the Bengal Delta* (Calcutta, 1942).

Martin, A., *Economics and Agriculture* (London, 1968).

Meier, G. M., *The International Economics of Development* (Tokyo, 1968).

Meier, G. M. and Baldwin, R. E., *Economic Development, Theory, History, Policy* (Cambridge, Mass., 1957).

Mellor, J. W., *The Economics of Agricultural Development* (Ithaca, 1966).

Mellor, J. W. and Stevens, R. D., 'The Average and Marginal Product of Farm Labour in Underdeveloped Countries', *Journal of Farm Economics*, Vol. XXXVIII (1956).

Mestor, Lord, 'Statistics in India', *Journal of the Royal Statistical Society*, Vol. XCVI (1933).

Metcalf, T. R., 'The Influence of the Mutiny of 1857 on Land Policy in India', *Historical Journal*, Vol. IV (1961).

'The British and Money-Lenders in Nineteenth Century India', *Journal of Modern History*, Vol. XXXIV (1962).

'The Struggle over Land Tenure in India 1860–1868', *Journal of Asian Studies*, Vol. XXI (1962).

Mingay, G. E., *English Landed Society in the Eighteenth Century* (London, 1963).

Montosh, S. R., *Concentration of Economic Power in India* (Allahabad, 1959).

Moore, B. (Jr.), *Social Origins of Dictatorship and Democracy* (London, 1967).

Moore, F. G., 'A Note on Rural Debt and Control of Ceremonial Expenditure in India', *Economic Development and Cultural Change*, Vol. II (1953/54).

Moore, R. J., *Charles Wood's India Policy, 1853–1866* (Manchester, 1966).

Morris, D. M., 'Values as Obstacles to Economic Growth in South Asia: An Historical Survey', *Journal of Economic History*, Vol. XXVII (1967).

Mukerjee, R. K., *Changing Face of Bengal: A Study in Riverine Economy* (Calcutta, 1938).

Food Planning for Four Hundred Millions (London, 1938).

Land Problems of India (London, 1933).

Mukerjee, R. K. and Dey, H. L. (eds.), *Economic Problems of Modern India*, Vol. II (London, 1941).

Mukerji, K., *Agriculture, Famine and Rehabilitation in South Asia* (Santiniketan, 1965).

The Problems of Land Transfer (Santiniketan, 1957).

Mukerji, K., *Levels of Economic Activity and Public Expenditure in India* (Poona, 1965).

Mukherjee, B., 'Economic Reconstruction and Agrarian Debt', *Indian Co-operative Review*, Vol. I (1935).

Mukherjee, P. K., *Economic Surveys in Underdeveloped Countries: A Study in Methodology* (Bombay, 1959).

Mukherjee, R., *The Rise and Fall of the East India Company* (Berlin, 1955).

Dynamics of a Rural Society, A Study of the Economic Structure in Bengal Villages (Berlin, 1957).

Myint, H., *The Economics of the Developing Countries* (London, 1964).

'The "Classical Theory of International Trade" and the Underdeveloped Countries', *Economic Journal*, Vol. LXVIII (1958).

Myrdal, G., *Asian Drama*, 3 vols. (London, 1968).

Economic Theory and Underdeveloped Regions (London, 1965).

Naidu, B. V. N., *Report of the Economist for Enquiry into Rural Indebtedness* (Madras, 1946).

'Relief of Rural Debt', *Indian Co-operative Review*, Vol. I (1935).

Naidu, V. T., *Farm Credit and Co-operation in India* (Bombay, 1968).

Nair, K., *Blossoms in the Dust: The Human Factor in Indian Development* (New York, 1965).

Nakamura, J. I., *Agricultural Production and the Economic Development of Japan* (Princeton, 1966).

'Meji Land Reform, Distributions of Income and Savings from Agriculture', *Economic Development and Cultural Change*, Vol. XIV (1966).

Nanavati, M. B., 'Rethinking on Rural Credit', *Indian Journal of Agricultural Economics*, Vol. XII (1957).

'Re-organisation of the Co-operative Movement', *Indian Journal of Agricultural Economics*, Vol. VII (1952).

Nanavati, M. B. and Anjara, J. J., *The Indian Rural Problem* (Bombay, 1947).

Narain, D., *Impact of Price Movements on Areas under Selected Crops in India, 1900–39* (Cambridge, 1965).

Neale, W. C., *Economic Change in Rural India: Land Tenure and Reform in Utter*

Pradesh, 1880–1955 (Yale University Press, 1962).

'Economic Accounting and Family Farming in India', *Economic Development and Cultural Change*, Vol. VII (1959).

Nerlove, M., 'Estimates of the Elasticities of Supply of Selected Agricultural Commodities', *Journal of Farm Economics*, XXXVII (1956).

'Distributed Lags and Estimation of Long-run Supply and Demand Elasticities: Theoretical Considerations', *Journal of Farm Economics*, Vol. XL (1958).

'Statistical Estimates of Long-run Elasticities of Supply and Demand', *Journal of Farm Economics*, XL (1958).

'The Analysis of Changes in Agricultural Supply: Problems and Approaches', *Journal of Farm Economics*, XLII (1960).

The Dynamics of Supply: Estimation of Farmers' Response to Price (Baltimore, 1958).

Nicholls, W. H., 'Industrialisation, Factor Market and Agricultural Development', *Journal of Political Economy*, LXIX (1961).

Niyogi, J. P., *The Co-operative Movement in Bengal* (London, 1940).

Nobutak, Ike, 'Taxation and Landownership in the Westernisation of Japan', *Journal of Economic History* Vol. VII (1947).

Nurkse, R., *Problems of Capital Formation in Underdeveloped Countries* (Oxford, 1966).

Lectures on Economic Development (Istanbul, 1958).

Ohkawa, K. and others (eds.), *Agriculture and Economic Growth: Japan's Experience* (Tokyo, 1969).

Ohkawa, K., 'Concurrent Growth of Agriculture and Industry: A Study of Japanese Case' in R. N. Dixey (ed.), *International Explorations of Agricultural Economics* (Ames, Iowa, 1964).

Olson, R. O., 'The Impact and Implications of Foreign Surplus Disposal on Underdeveloped Economies', *Journal of Farm Economics*, XLII (1960).

Panandikar, S. C., *Wealth and Welfare of Bengal Delta* (Calcutta, 1926).

Panse, V. G., 'Trends of Areas and Yields of Principal Crops in India', *Agricultural Situation in India*, Vol. VII (1952).

Parikh, A., 'Market Responsiveness of Peasant Cultivators: Some Evidence from pre-war India', *Journal of Development Studies*, Vol. 8 (1972).

Patel, S. J., *Agricultural Labourers in Modern India and Pakistan* (Bombay, 1952).

'Long-Term Changes in Output and Income in India: 1896–1960', *Indian Economic Journal* Vol. V (1958).

Qureshi, A. I., *The Future of Co-operative Movement in India* (Bombay, 1947).

Ranis, G., 'The Financing of Japanese Economic Development', *Economic History Review*, Vol. XI (1959).

Rao, M. R., 'Reserve Bank of India and Agricultural Credit', *Indian Co-operative Review*, Vol. I (1935).

'The State and Agricultural Credit', *Indian Co-operative Review*, Vol. II (1936).

Rao, V. K. R. V., *The National Income of British India 1931/32* (London, 1940).

'"Grow More Food Policy" in India', *Indian Journal of Agriculture Economics*, Vol. IV (1949).

Ray. P., *Agricultural Economics of Bengal*, Part I (Calcutta, 1947).

Roll, E., *A History of Economic Thought* (London, 1953).

Rostow, W. W., *The Stages of Economic Growth* (Cambridge, 1971).

Rostow, W. W. (ed.), *The Economics of Take-Off into Self-Sustained Growth* (London, 1965).

Rottenberg, S., 'Income and Leisure in an Underdeveloped Economy', *Journal of Political Economy*, Vol. LX (1952).

Rowney, D. K. and Graham, J. Q. (eds.), *Quantitative History* (Illinois, 1969).

Russell, Sir John, *Report on the Work of the Imperial Council of Agricultural Research in Applying Science to Crop Production in India* (Simla, 1937).

Saha, K. B., *The Economics of Rural Bengal* (Calcutta, 1930).

Schultz, T. W., *Agriculture in an Unstable Economy* (New York, 1945).

Economic Organisation of Agriculture (New York, 1953).

Transforming Traditional Agriculture (Yale, 1964).

'Reflections on Poverty Within Agriculture', *Journal of Political Economy*, Vol. LVIII (1950).

Sen, A. K., 'Peasants and Dualism With or Without Surplus Labour', *Journal of Political Economy*, Vol. LXXIV (1966).

Sen, A. K. (ed.), *Growth Economics* (London, 1970).

Sen, S. K., *Studies in Industrial Policy and Development of India, 1848–1926* (Calcutta, 1966).

Shanin, T., *Peasants and Peasant Societies* (London, 1971).

Shukla, T., *Capital Formation in Indian Agriculture* (Bombay, 1965).

Singh, T., *Poverty and Social Change: A Study in the Economic Reorganisation of Indian Rural Society* (London, 1945).

Singh, V. B. (ed.), *Economic History of India* (Bombay, 1965).

Sinha, A. R., 'Inter-relation Between Supply and Price of Raw Jute', *Sankhya: Indian Journal of Statistics*, Vol. 4 (1938/40).

'A Study of the Indian Official Jute Forecast', *Sankhya: Indian Journal of Statistics*, Vol. 3 (1938).

Sinha, H., 'Indian Agricultural Statistics', *Journal of the Royal Statistical Society*, Vol. XCVII (1934).

Sinha, N. K., *The Economic History of Bengal*, Vol. I (Calcutta, 1961); Vol. II (Calcutta, 1962).

Smith, F., 'Jute Experiments in Bengal', *Indian Journal of Agricultural Economics*, Vol. II (1907).

Southworth, H. M. and Johnston, B. F. (eds.), *Agricultural Development and Economic Growth* (New York, 1967).

Stern, R. M., 'The Price Responsiveness of Primary Producers', *Review of Economics and Statistics*, Vol. XLIV (1962).

Strauss, E., *Soviet Agriculture in Perspective* (London, 1969).

Sturt, D. W., 'Producer Response to Technological Change in West Pakistan', *Journal of Farm Economics*, Vol. XXXXVII (1965).

Subramaniam, S., 'Production and Prices', *Guide to Current Official Statistics*, Vol. I (1945).

Supple, B. S., *The Experience of Economic Growth: Case Studies in Economic History* (New York, 1963).

Szentes, T., *The Political Economy of Underdevelopment* (Budapest, 1971).

Tang, A. M., *Economic Development in the Southern Piedmont 1860–1950* (University of North Carolina Press, 1958).

'Research and Education in Japanese Agricultural Development', *Economic Studies Quarterly*, Vol. XIII (1963).

Tawney, R. H., *The Agrarian Problems of the Sixteenth Century* (London, 1912).

Thavaraj, M. J. K., 'Capital Formation in the Public Sector in India: A Historical

Survey 1898–1938' in V. K. R. V. Rao and others (eds.), *Papers on National Income and Allied Topics*, Vol. I (Bombay, 1960).

Thomas, P. J. and Shastry, N. S. R., *Indian Agricultural Statistics* (Madras, 1939).

Thorbecke, E. (ed.), *The Role of Agriculture in Economic Development* (New York, 1969).

Thorner, D., *The Agrarian Prospect in India* (Delhi, 1956).

Thorner, D. and A., *Land and Labour in India* (Bombay, 1962).

Tostlebe, A. S., *Capital in Agriculture: Its Formation and Financing* (Princeton, 1957).

Unakar, R. S. M. V., 'Correlation Between Weather and Crops with Special Reference to Punjab Wheat', *Memoirs of the Indian Meteorological Department*, Vol. XXV, Part IV.

Warriner, D., *Economics of Peasant Farming* (New York, 1965).

  Land Reform in Principle and Practice (Oxford, 1969).

Watts, H. W., 'Review of Nerlove, Distributed Lags and Demand Analysis for Agricultural and Other Commodities', *Journal of Farm Economics*, Vol. XLI (1959).

Wharton, C. R. (Jr.), 'The Economic Meaning of Subsistence', *Malayan Economic Review*, Vol. VIII (1963).

  (ed.), *Subsistence Agriculture and Economic Development* (Chicago, 1970).

Wickizer, V. D. and Bennet, N. K., *The Rice Economy of Monsoon Asia* (Stanford, 1941).

Wilson, T. and Andrews, P. W. S. (eds.), *Oxford Studies in the Price Mechanism* (Oxford, 1951).

Wittfogel, C. A., *Oriental Despotism: A Comparative Study of Total Power* (New Haven, 1957).

Works in Bengali

Ahmed, A. M., *Amar Dekha Rajnitir Panchash Basar* (Dacca, 1968).

Unpublished PhD theses

Ghatak, S., *Rural Money Markets in India* (University of London, 1972).

Ghosh, A. K., *An Analysis of the Indian Price Structure from 1861* (University of London, 1949).

Kabir, L., *The Rights and Liabilities of the Bengal Raiyats Under Tenancy Legislation from 1855 to 1947* (University of London, 1965).

Rabbani, A. K. M. G., *Jute in the World Economy: A Statistical Study* (University of London, 1964).

Ray, P., *Land Tenure as Related to Agricultural Efficiency and Rural Welfare in India* (University of London, 1964).

7.   ACTS (arranged chronologically)

The Bengal Tenancy (Amendment) Act, 1928.
The Bengal Tenancy (Amendment) Act, 1930.
The Bengal Money-lenders Act, 1933.
The Bengal Agricultural Debtors Act, 1935.
The Bengal Tenancy (Amendment) Act, 1938
The Bengal Money-lenders Act, 1940.
The Bengal Co-operative Societies Act, 1940.

INDEX